GOLDENEYE

GUIDEBOOKS

CORNWALL

WRITTEN AND PHOTOGRAPHED BY WILLIAM FRICKER

To my Mother and Father with love, who first introduced me to Cornwall.

Research & Text: William Fricker

Photography: William Fricker (unless as credited with an initial- see page 205)

Second Edition, 2008

First published in the United Kingdom, in 2006, by Goldeneye, Unit 10, Chivenor Business Park, Barnstaple, North Devon EX31 4AY
www.goldeneyeguides.co.uk

Text copyright © 2008, William Fricker

Photographs copyright © 2008, William Fricker

Maps copyright © Goldeneye, 2008

Cartographic Consultants: Cox Cartographic Ltd

Maps taken from Goldeneye's Digital Database

Book design and layout: Chris Dyer Design

A CIP catalogue record for this book is available from the British Library.

ISBN Number: 1-85965-183-6

EAN Number: 9 781859 651831

Printed in England

Abbreviations in Text

C14	14th Century
Mar-Oct	1 March to 31 October (inclusive)
NT	National Trust property
EH	English Heritage property
BHs	Bank Holidays
W/Es	Weekends
East	Easter
E/C	Early Closing
TIC	Tourist Information Centre
M	Monday
Tu	Tuesday
W	Wednesday
Th	Thursday
F	Friday
Sa	Saturday
Su	Sunday
SS	Supplied by Subject (reference illustrations)
WL	Wolsey Lodges

Correct Information

The contents of this publication were believed to be correct and accurate at the time of printing. However, Goldeneye accepts no responsibility for any errors, omissions or changes in the details given, or for the consequences arising thereto, from the use of this book. However, the publishers would greatly appreciate your time in notifying us of any changes or new attractions (or places to eat, drink and stay) that you consider merit inclusion in the next edition. Your comments are most welcome, for we value the views and suggestions of our readers. Please write to: The Editor, Goldeneye, 10 Chivenor Business Park, Barnstaple EX31 4AY, Great Britain.

Beach & Surfing Abbreviations

HT	High Tide
HZ	Hazardous/Dangerous
Ls	Lefts (left turns)
LG	Lifeguard
LT	Low Tide
N	North
P	Parking
Rs	Rights (right turns)
S	South
S-B	Surfboard
SW	Southwest
WC	Toilets

With special thanks to the guys at Atlantic Surfboards, and Surf South West, for checking our surfing details.

English Heritage Opening Times

The general rule is: Good F or 1Apr (whichever is earlier) to 30 Sept, daily 10-6, (from 9 in July/Aug). 1 Oct to Maundy Th or 31 Mar (whichever is earlier), Tu-Su 10-4, closed 24-26 Dec & 1 Jan.

The Smuggler's Song

On, through the ground-sea, shove!
Light on the larboard bow!
There's a nine-knot breeze above,
And a sucking tide below.

Hush! for the beacon fails,
The skulking gauger's by;
Down with your studding-sails,
Let jib and fore-sail fly!

Hurrah! for the light once more!
Point her for Shark's-nose Head;
Our friends can keep the shore;
Or the skulking gauger's dead!

On! through the ground-sea, shove!
Light on the Larboard bow!
There's a nine-knot breeze above
And a sucking tide below!

RS Hawker

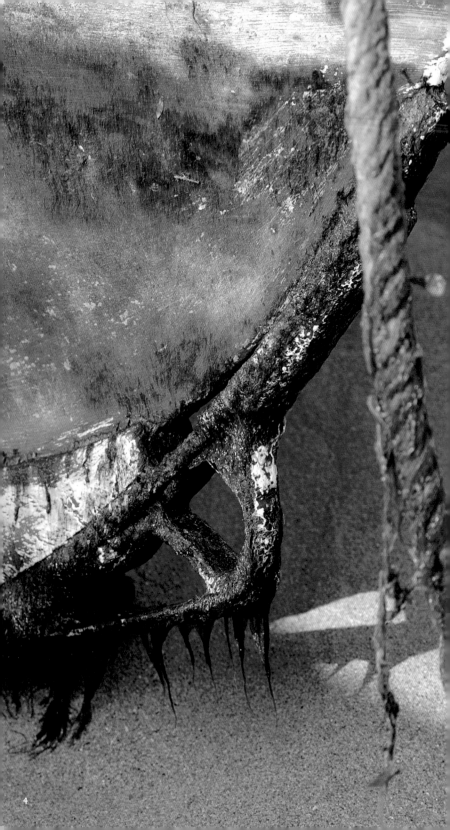

PREFACE

The first
s and is
new
vailable.

can be

ok's

or a
d a

n

CONTENTS

1   Title Page

2   Credits

3   Richard Stephen Hawker's Poem,
The Smuggler's Song

5   Preface

7   Contents

9   Introduction

11 Recommendations

12 Where to Stay

14 Where to Eat

16 Saxton's 1576 Map of Cornwall

18 Locator Map

20 The South East

22 Saltash, The Rame Peninsula Map

24 Saltash, The Rame Peninsula Guide

30 Coastal Fishing Boats

32 The East

34 Calstock, Launceston Map

36 Calstock, Launceston Guide

38 Altarnum, Blisland, Bodmin Moor,
Camelford Map

40 Altarnum, Blisland, Bodmin Moor,
Camelford Guide

44 Upper Tamar Image

45 Upper Tamar Map

46 The North Coast

48 Morwenstow, The Hartland Peninsula Map

50 Morwenstow Guide

53 Bude Shipwrecks

54 Boscastle, Bude Map

56 Boscastle, Bude Guide

62 Padstow, Port Isaac, Tintagel,
Wadebridge Map

64 Padstow, Port Isaac, Tintagel,
Wadebridge Guide

72 The Camel Trail Cycling Route Map

74 Padstow, Port Isaac, Tintagel,
Wadebridge Guide

78 Newquay, St Austell, St Columb Major Map

80 Newquay, St Austell, St Columb Major Guide

86 Surfing Images

88 Perranporth, St Agnes Map

89 Perranporth, St Agnes Guide

92 Camborne, Penryn, Redruth Map

94 Camborne, Penryn, Redruth Guide

100 The South Coast

102 Bodmin, Fowey, Liskeard, Looe,
Lostwithiel Map

104 Bodmin, Fowey, Liskeard, Looe,
Lostwithiel Guide

118 Contemporary Architecture

120 Falmouth, Mevagissey, St Mawes, Truro Map

122 Falmouth, Mevagissey, St Mawes, Truro Guide

136 The South West

138 The Lizard Peninsula Map

140 The Lizard Peninsula Guide

154 Geological Shapes

156 Beaches

158 The Penwith Peninsula Map

160 The Penwith Peninsula Guide

172 Deep Sea Trawlers

174 The Penwith Peninsula Guide

186 Contemporary Art

188 The Modernist Artists of St Ives

190 The Newlyn School of Painters

192 Celebrities

200 Tourist Information Centres

201 Calendar of Events

202 Acknowledgements

204 Index to towns, villages, places of interest
described in the book

208 Map Symbols Explained

Cornwall is a county of great diversity, of strange customs and superstitions, of romantic legends and Arthurian myths. A county with its own language, culture and outlook. Remote, and cut off from the rest of Britain by the River Tamar, the Cornish have developed a proud individuality and resilient independence. The close proximity to the Gulf Stream provides a warm and equable climate. The magnificent coastline, relentlessly shaped by the elements, with its contorted rocks, precipitous cliffs, deep estuaries, smugglers' coves, golden beaches and picturesque harbours, is unmatched elsewhere in England.

The landscape is haunted by countless landmarks of early man (and relics from the industrial past); Long Barrows (burial chambers), Quoits/Dolmens (stones from Megalithic-Neolithic tombs), Fogues (underground storage chambers), Hill Forts and Promontory Forts (strategic settlements or animal enclosures) and Stone Circles (ancient boundary/grave marks, or places of ritual). Only a small selection is described in this book - but many others are indicated on the maps. To put them into an historic context, the Neolithic Period gave place to the Bronze Age around 2000 BC, the Iron Age lasted from about 500 BC up to Roman times, the first 4 centuries AD.

The Cornish skyline has been shaped by the remains of chimneys and engine houses, and by ramshackle desolate buildings beside the road - the remains of a once prosperous tin and copper mining industry. Many examples are to be found in the Camborne - Redruth area, and on the Penwith Peninsula. A number of engine houses have been restored by the National Trust and other organisations. They often stand in spectacular positions and are worthy of a visit. The better known are Wheal Coates Engine House, Nr St Agnes and Wheal Prosper Copper Mine, Nr Porthleven. In areas of past mining activity it is vitally important to keep to the evident pathways. Walkers and their dogs have been known to disappear down hidden shafts!

With few exceptions, Cornwall has been noted for the setting of architecture rather than architecture itself. However, there are fine examples of medieval fortresses and elegant country houses surrounded by spacious gardens.

It is my purpose to present you with a comprehensive guide to all the 'must-see' attractions (natural and man-made) in an easy to digest format. The county is split up into regional or topographic areas, and is first illustrated in map form. Then each map is followed by its respective guide. This is made up of pages of text and illustrations. These have been colour coded to avoid confusion. The maps either overlap or juxtapose and have arrows indicating the adjoining map to allow easy navigation.

The accommodation listings and the places to eat and drink have not paid an advertising or inclusion fee to be part of this book (like so many other published guidebooks). They have been selected on merit alone. They offer a fine service, be it luxurious or that extra "something", perhaps a quirkiness of temperament, or an exceptional view. They may just be lovely people and fine hosts. Not all have interior design skills to please House & Garden, but, many do. For you to gauge your preferred style of accommodation I suggest you go to page 12-13, then visit the B & B's or hotels website. You may feel we have left out a favourite restaurant or inn. Please let us know. If you go to our sister website: www.goldeneyenet.co.uk we encourage you to send in details of your experiences, be they good, bad or indifferent. We have prizes for the best reviews, such as Week End Breaks in a luxurious B&B, or a Dinner For Two at a top restaurant. So please become an active participant with Goldeneye.

Botallack Engine Houses

Walk the causeway at low tide and explore St Michael's Mount.

Cycle the Camel Trail starting from Wadebridge.

Treat yourself to a surf lesson.

Evensong Truro Cathedral.

Port Eliot Literary Festival.

Descend the steps to the beach and wander among Bedruthan's steps.

Make a pilgrimage across the dunes to Sir John Betjaman's grave at St Enodoc.

Visit an engine house or tin mine preferably one overlooking the sea.

Admire the magnificent stained glass at St Neots.

Take a boat trip up the Fowey River to Lostwithiel.

Witness the magnificent camellias and magnolias in a Cornish spring garden.

Lunch in one of the stupendously sited cafes overlooking a golden beach.

Visit a RNLI station and make a lifetime's donation.

Listen to the Polperro fisherman's choir practice.

Walk a section of the coastal footpath. For drama, try the North Coast or Penwith Peninsula, for a flattish surface, the South Coast.

Bag five ancient monuments. Either from Bodmin Moor or Penwith.

Take home a piece of Cornish art.

Laze on a sandy beach, or while away the hours by picking up shells and coloured glass.

Play "Count the Windmill" on your journey through Cornwall. What percentage are actually working?

Fish 'n chips in Padstow. At Stein's of course. Where else?

Dance with Padstow's Obby Oss – fair maidens need only apply.

Mountain board or skate at Mount Hawke (SK8).

Visit the home of a former genius; Richard Trevithick or Barbara Hepworth.

Land's End - arrive by foot, preferably via the coastal footpath. Its more impressive and you will forego the parking charge.

Book a ticket at the Minack Theatre. Just being there is enough. It's the view, Darling.

Fly (via helicopter) to the Scilly Isles in March for the daffodils.

Ice Skate at Eden during the winter months.

Buy fresh fish from one of the Newlyn fish merchants for a beach barbeque.

Day out at the Royal Cornwall Show, Wadebridge.

Experience the contrast of colour and light. First wander the back streets of St Ives, then emerge into the open spaces and bathe in the brilliant, Mediterranean light.

Rame Head – for the views on either side. Imagine the ships who have passed this way, some for the last time, and for the sailors whose last glimpse of England this has been.

Join a sing-song with the Cadgwith Singers in the Cadgwith Cove Inn on a Friday night.

Old Quay House Hotel, Fowey ss

This is a selection to make choosing your B&B or hotel an easy and quick process. We suggest you view their websites to find one that suits your tastes, expectations and budget. It is often the unexpected that will surprise you with a luxurious bathroom, an exquisite view or a quirky temperament that will draw you back again and again.

Country House Hotel

Hotel Tresanton, St Mawes. 01326 270055   www.tresanton.com

Country House B & B

Collon Barton, Lerryn 01208 872908

Ennys, St Hilary. 01736 740262 www.ennys.co.uk

Hornacott, South Petherwin. 01566 782461
www.hornacott.co.uk

Jamies, Carbis Bay. 01736 794718 www.jamiesstives.co.uk

Levathan. 01208 850487 www.levathan.com

Merthen Manor. Constantine. 01326 340664
www.merthenmanor.co.uk

Molesworth Manor, Little Petherick 01841 540292
www.molesworthmanor.co.uk

Porteath Barn, St Minver 01208 863605

The Old Vicarage, Morwenstow 01288 331369
www.reshawker.co.uk

Tregoose, Grampound. 01726 882460 www.tregoose.co.uk

Trevilla House, Feock. 01872 862369 www.trevilla.com

Boutique Hotels

Driftwood Hotel, Portscatho. 01872 580644
www.driftwoodhotel.co.uk

Lugger Hotel, Portloe. 01872 501322   www.luggerhotel.co.uk

Marina Villa Hotel & Restaurant, Fowey. 01726 833315
www.themarinahotel.co.uk

Old Coastguard Hotel, Mousehole. 01736 731222
www.oldcoastguardhotel.co.uk

Primrose Valley Hotel, St Ives. 01736 794939
www.primroseonline.co.uk

Summer House, Penzance. 01736 363744
www.summerhouse-cornwall.com

Trevalsa Court Hotel, Mevagissey. 01726 842468
www.trevalsa-hotel.co.uk

Country Cottage B & B

Glendower B & B, Gunwalloe. 01326 561282
www.glendower-gunwalloe.co.uk

Organic Panda B & B, St Ives. 01736 793890
www.organicpanda.co.uk

Polrode Mill Cottage, Allen Valley 01208 850203
www.polrodemillcottage.co.uk

Tubbs Mill House, Caerhays. 01872 530715
www.tubbsmillhouse.com

Farm House B & B

Bodrugan Barton, Mevagissey. 01726 842094
www.bodrugan.co.uk

Buttervilla Farm, Polbathic. 01503 230315
www.buttervilla.com

Hartswell Farm, Lostwithiel. 01208 873419

Hay Barton, Tregony. 01872 530288 www.haybarton.com

Lantallack Farm, Landrake. 01752 851281
www.lantallack.co.uk

Sheviock Barton, Sheviock. 01503 230793
www.sheviockbarton.co.uk

Treglisson, Hayle. 01736 753141 www.treglisson.co.uk

Trevadlock Manor. 01566 782227 www.trevadlockmanor.co.uk

Family Hotels (Child Friendly)

Bedruthan Steps Hotel. 01637 872864
www.bedruthanstepshotel.co.uk

Fowey Hall Hotel. 01726 833866 www.foweyhallhotel.co.uk

Rosevine Hotel, Portscatho. 01872 580206 www.rosevine.co.uk

Sands Resort Hotel, Newquay 01637 872864
www.sandsresort.co.uk

Family-Run Hotels

Boscundle Manor, St Austell 01726 813557
www.boscundlemanor.co.uk

Boskerris Hotel, Carbis Bay. 01736 795295
www.boskerrishotel.co.uk

Meudon Hotel. 01326 250541 www.meudon.co.uk

Mount Haven Hotel, Marazion. 01736 710249
www.mounthaven.co.uk

Nare Hotel, Veryan. 01872 50111 www.thenare.com

Treglos Hotel, Constantine Bay 01841 520727
www.tregloshotel.com

Guest Accommodation

Anchorage House B & B, St Austell. 01726 814071
www.anchoragehouse.co.uk

Nanscawen Manor House. 01726 814488
www.nanscawen.co.uk

Treleaugue B & B, St Keverne. 01326 281500
www.treleaugue.co.uk

House Parties

Beachmodern No. 28, Bude 01288 275006
www.beachmodern.com/no28

Halzephron House, Gunwalloe 01326 240028
www.halzephronhouse.co.uk

Mesmear, St Minver 01208 869731 www.mesmear.co.uk

Pencalenick House, Lanteglos-By-Fowey 0207 7476858
www.pencalenickhouse.com

The Cove, Lamorna 01736 731411 www.thecovecornwall.com

The Vean, Caerhays. 01872 501310 www.thevean.co.uk

Inns With Rooms

Bay View Inn, Widemouth Bay. 01288 361271
www.bayviewinn.co.uk

Bush Inn, Morwenstow 01288 331242
www.bushinn-morwenstow.co.uk

Driftwood Spars Hotel, Trevaunance Cove 01872 552428
www.driftwoodspars.com

Gurnard's Head Hotel. 01736 796928
www.gurnardshead.co.uk

Halzephron Inn, Gunwalloe. 01326 240406
www.halzephron-inn.co.uk

Jamaica Inn, Bodmin Moor. 01566 86250
www.jamaicainn.co.uk

King of Prussia, Fowey www.kimngofprussiafowey.com

Napoleon Inn, Boscastle 01840 250204

Old Ferry Inn, Bodinnick. 01726 870237
www.oldferryinn.co.uk

Old Success Inn, Sennen Cove. 01736 871232
www.oldsuccess.com

Rising Sun, St Mawes. 01326 270233
www.risingsunstmawes.co.uk

Trengilly Wartha Inn, Constantine. 01326 340332
www.trengilly.co.uk

Luxurious B & B

Abbey Hotel, Penzance. 01736 366906
www.theabbeyonline.co.uk

Ednovean Farm, Perranuthnoe. 01736 711883
www.ednoveanfarm.co.uk

11 Sea View Terrace, St Ives. 01736 798440
www.11stives.co.uk

Landewednack House, Church Cove. 01326 290877
www.landewednackhouse.com

Warmington House, Camelford. 01840 214961
www.warmingtonhouse.co.uk

Wisteria Lodge, St Austell. 01726 810800
www.wisterialodgehotel.co.uk

Restaurant With Rooms

Cornish Range, Mousehole. 01736 731488
www.cornishrange.co.uk

Kota, Porthleven. 01326 562407 www.kotarestaurant.co.uk

Penzance Arts Club. 01736 363761
www.penzanceartsclub.co.uk

Prynns, St Merryn 01841 520976

Raval's, Camelford. 01840 213888 www.ravals.co.uk

Slipway Hotel & Restaurant, Port Isaac 01208 880264
www.theslipway.co.uk

St Petroc's Hotel, Padstow 01841 532700 www.rickstein.com

Zennor Backpackers & Café. 01736 798307
www.backpackers.co.uk/zennor

Room With A View

Blue Hayes Private Hotel, St Ives. 01736 797129
www.bluehayes.co.uk

Chydane B & B, Gunwalloe. 01326 241232 www.chydane.co.uk

Cliff House, Kingsand. 01752 823110
www.cliffhouse-kingsand.co.uk

Cormorant Hotel, Golant 01726 833426
www.cormoranthotels.co.uk

Greenbank Hotel, Falmouth. 01326 312440
www.greenbank-hotel.co.uk

Halftides B & B, Mullion. 01326 241935 www.halftides.co.uk

Mother Ivey Cottage B & B, Trevose Head 01841 520329

Old Quay House Hotel, Fowey. 01726 833302
www.theoldquayhouse.com

Pelyn B & B, Gerrans. 01872 580837 www.pelyncreek.com

Spa Style – The Works (gym, saunas, massage, sheer unadulterated hedonism)

Penmere Manor Hotel, Falmouth. 01326 312440
www.penmeremanorhotel.co.uk

Polurrian Hotel, Mullion 01326 240421
www.polurrianhotel.com

St Michael's Hotel & Spa, Falmouth. 01326 312707
www.stmichaelshotel.co.uk

St Moritz, Trebetherick 01208 862242
www.stmoritzhotel.co.uk

Restaurant Nathan Outlaw, Fowey ss

Primrose Valley Hotel, St Ives ss

Old Coastguard Hotel, Mousehole ss

Hotel Tresanton, St Mawes ss

Lugger Hotel, Portloe ss

Choosing the right café, restaurant or inn can make or break a romantic weekend. It may also determine where you decide to stay due to the recent phenomena of Cornwall as a destination for the gastronome. It does, however, have some of the most amazingly located places to eat and drink, either overlooking a golden beach or a rugged headland.

Many will choose a pub or café at the beginning or end of a circular or cliff top walk. I hope our selection below will make your life a little easier to plan. All establishments are described in the following guide but not all restaurants/eating places described in the guide are listed below. This is a judicious selection.

Beach Cafes/or Bars

Beach Hut, Watergate Bay. 01637 860877 www.watergatebay.co.uk

Beach Restaurant, Sennen Cove. 01736 871191 www.thebeachrestaurant.com

Blue Bar, Porthtowan. 01209 890329 www.blue-bar.co.uk

Fistral Blu, Fistral Beach, Newquay. (A5) 01637 878782 www.fistral-blu.co.uk

Godrevy Beach Café, Godrevy Towans. 01736 757999

Life's A Beach, Summerleaze Beach, Bude. www.dsibley.timart.co.uk

Porthminster Beach Café, St Ives. 01736 795352 www.porthminstercafe.co.uk

Sandsifter Bar & Restaurant, Gwithian Beach. 01736 758457 www.sandsiftergodrevy.co.uk

Saltwater, Polzeath. 01208 862333

Waterfront, Beach Road, Polzeath. 01208 869655 www.waterfrontcornwall.co.uk

Windswept Café, Fistral Beach (South side). 01637 850793 (E5) www.windsweptcafe.co.uk

Farm (Produce) Restaurants

Grange Fruit Farm. www.thegrangecornwall.com

Odds the Restaurant, Holywell Road, Cubert. 01637 830505 www.oddsthereataurant.co.uk

Roskilly's. www.roskillys.co.uk

Trevathan Farm, St Endellion. www.trevathanfarm.com

Rectory Tea Rooms, Morwenstow. 01288 331251 www.rectory-tearooms.co.uk

Foodie Pubs

Bush Inn, Morwenstow. 01288 331242 www.bushinn-morwenstow.co.uk

Cadgwith Cove Inn, Cadgwith.

Gurnard's Head Hotel. 01736 796928 www.gurnardshead.co.uk

Halzephron Inn, Gunwalloe. 01326 240406 www.halzephron-inn.co.uk

Rising Sun, St Mawes. 01326 270233 www.risingsunstmawes.co.uk

Roseland Inn. 01872 580254 www.roselandinn.co.uk

Ship Inn, Porthleven. 01326 564204

Trengilly Wartha Inn, Constantine. 01326 340332 www.trengilly.co.uk

Cafes/Restaurants With A View

Alba, Wharf Road. St Ives. 01736 797222 www.thealbarestaurant.com

Bay View Inn, Marine Drive. Widemouth Bay. 01288 361273 www.bayviewinn.co.uk

Driftwood Hotel, Portscatho. 01872 580644 www.driftwoodhotel.co.uk

Fifteen Cornwall, Watergate Bay. 01637 861000 www.fifteencornwall.co.uk

Miss Peapod's Kitchen Café, Jubilee Wharf, Penryn

Riverview Restaurant, Golant. 01726 833426 www.cormoranthotels.co.uk

The Cove Restaurant, Lamorna. (F9) 01736 731411 www.thecovecornwall.com

Old Coastguard Hotel & Restaurant, Mousehole. 01736 731222 www.oldcoastguardhotel.co.uk

Old Quay House Hotel, 28 Fore Street, Fowey. 01726 833302 www.theoldquayhouse.com

The Edge, 6 New Road, Port Isaac. 01208 880090 www.theedgecornwall.com

St Enodoc Bar, Hotel & Restaurant. 01208 863394 www.enodoc-hotel.co.uk

View Restaurant, Trenninow Cliff Road, Rame Peninsula. 01752 822345

Seafood Restaurants

Blue Fish, Norway Lane. St Ives. 01736 794204 www.bluefishrestaurant.co.uk

Cornish Range, 6 Chapel Street, Mousehole. 01736 731488 www.cornishrange.co.uk

Finns Restaurant, South Quay, Newquay. 01637 874062 www.finns2go.com

Kota, Porthleven. 01326 562407 www.kotarestaurant.co.uk

Lugger Hotel, Portloe. 01872 501322 www.luggerhotel.co.uk

Prynns, Shop Road, St Merryn. 01841 520976

Seafood Cafe, 45 Fore Street. St Ives. (K1) 01736 794004 www.seafoodcafe.co.uk

Seafood Restaurant. 01841 532700 www.rickstein.com

Seafood Bar, Lower Quay Street, Falmouth. 01326 315129

Three Mackerel, Swanpool, Falmouth. 01326 311886 www.thethreemackerel.com

2 ForeStreet, Mousehole. 01736 731164 www.2forestreet.co.uk

The Cove, Maenporth Beach. 01326 251136

Town Restaurants

Abbey Restaurant, Penzance. 01736 330680 www.theabbeyonline.com

Chapel St Bistro. Penzance. 01736 332555

Harris's, 46 New St. Penzance. 01736 364408 www.harrisrestaurant.co.uk

Hotel Tresanton, St Mawes. 01326 270055 www.tresanton.com

Hunkdory, 46 Arwenack Street, Falmouth. 01326 212997 www.hunkydoryfalmouth.co.uk

L'Estuaire, Rock Road, Rock. 01208 862622 www.l'estuairerestaurant.com

Nathan Outlaw, Marina Villa Hotel, Fowey. 01726 833315 www.themarinahotel.co.uk

No 6 Restaurant & Rooms, Padstow. 01841 532093 www.number6inpadstow.com

Raval's, Fore Street, Camelford. (E3) 01840 213888 www.ravals.co.uk

Restaurant Gaudi, 8 Edward Street, Truro. 01872 227380 www.gaudis.co.uk

Tabb's Restaurant, 85 Kenwyn Street, Truro. 01872 262110 www.tabbs.co.uk

Trewithen Restaurant, Fore Street, Lostwithiel. 01208 872373

SEPTENT[RIO]

DIEV ET MON DROIT

PROMONTORIVM HOC
IN MARE PROIECTVM
CORNVBIA DICITVR

OCCIDENS

OC   E   A[NGLIA]

MERID[IES]

Scala Miliarium

1 2 3 4 5 6 7 8 9 10

16

LOCATOR MAP

- The South East
- The East
- The North Coast
- The South Coast
- The South West

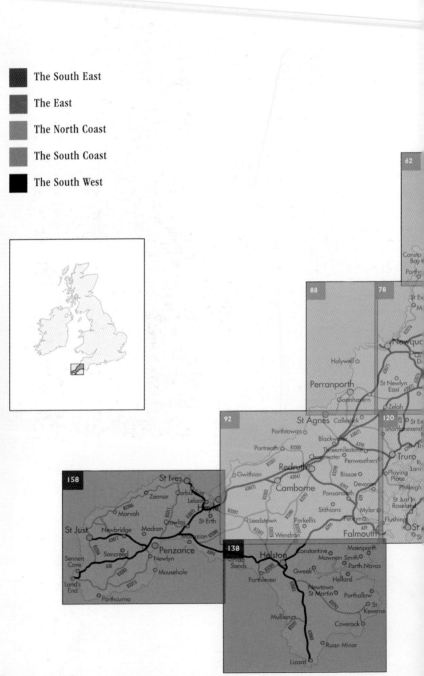

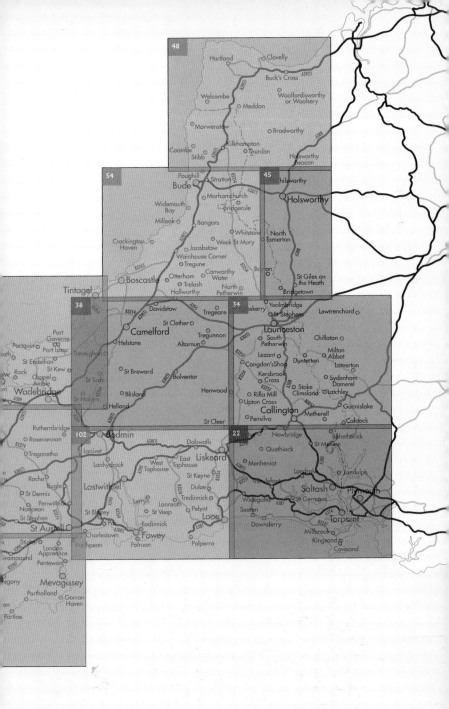

For Peace & Tranquility, Smugglers' Haunts, the Cry of the Curlew and Sub-Tropical Gardens.

As you enter Cornwall over the River Tamar on the A38, stop and admire Isambard Kingdom Brunel's last great masterpiece of engineering, the Prince Albert Bridge. Looking south down river, you may be able to spy the Rame Peninsula, the "Forgotten Corner". Here you will discover the former smugglers' villages of Kingsand and Cawsand. Their narrow streets snake between colour washed cottages, pubs and art galleries. There are fine views over Plymouth Sound, and if feeling energetic you may wish to tackle the coastal path through Mount Edgcumbe, or walk south to Rame Head, where you will counter more stunning views. All about you is peace and calm, an oasis of tranquillity, the antidote to a stressful life.

Travelling west you must make a special journey to St Germanus Church to admire the stained glass window designed by Edward Burne-Jones, and made up by the William Morris Co. The St Germans or Lynher River passes by, to rise up and down with the tides. You will hear the baleful cry of the curlew and the screech of the oyster-catcher, both reminders of the calming effects of estuary life.

But, if you choose to cross the Tamar further upstream via the A390 you must tackle the densely wooded lanes through St Dominick to Cotehele Quay with fine views over the Tamar. This is an area rich in industrial heritage. You may wish to think back an age and imagine the bargees working the riverbank between Cotehele and Morwellham, as they shipped the iron ore down to Plymouth. '

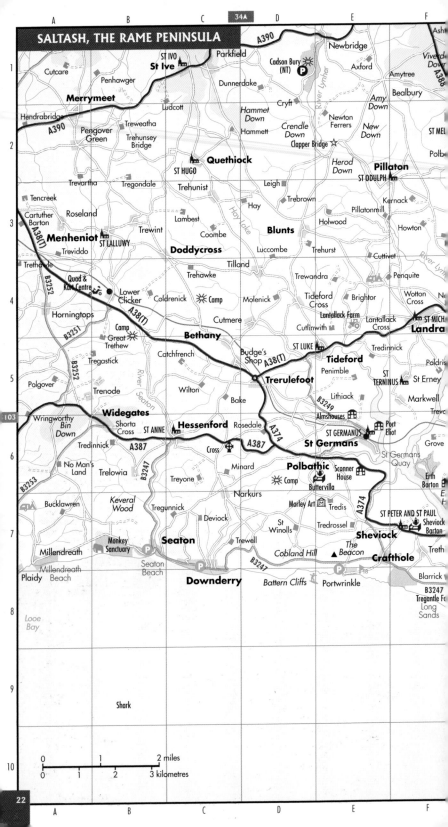

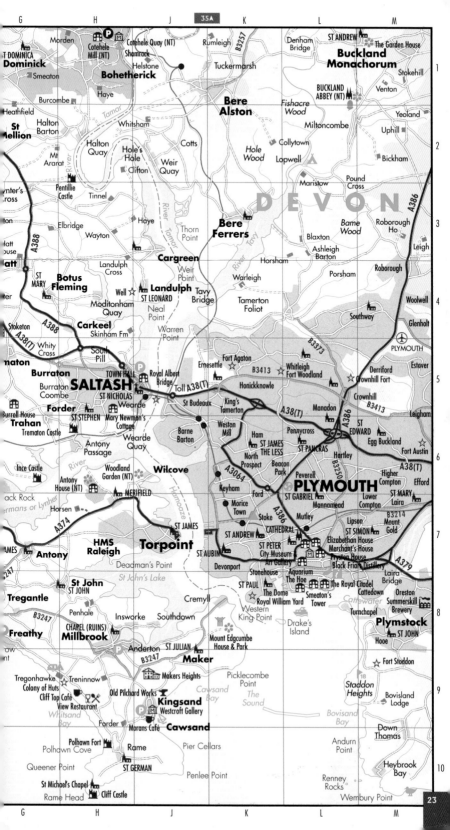

CAWSAND & KINGSAND

Twin villages and former C18 smuggling centres with narrow streets and colourful houses, and an historic anchorage for Plymouth. Park in Kingsand and walk through to Cawsand, the prettier of the two. A stroll across the bay to the ancient pilchard works is worthwhile. If pub crawls are your hobby you will have found a true home. Fine walks along the coast to Cremyll Ferry. (J9)

The Library, Antony House   ab/nt

Freathy Colony of Huts

Special Places of Interest to Visit and to Eat, Drink & Be Merry...

Antony Woodland Gardens. Privately owned by the Carew Pole Garden Trust have 100 acres of woodland, 300 types of camellias bordering the River Lynher. Open daily except M & F Mar-Oct 11-5.30. (H6)

Antony House & Gardens (NT). Built for Sir William Carew from 1711-1721 and considered the most distinguished example of early C18

Where to Stay...

Buttervilla Farm, Polbathic. Recently transformed into an eco-friendly, organic farm of 15 acres. The décor is contemporary and comfortable, the showers are solar heated. Dinner is by arrangement. Most vegetables are home grown. Wi-Fi access. (E6) 01503 230315 www.buttervilla.com

Cliff House, Kingsand. Grade 11 listed house with three bedrooms and bath. First floor Living Room overlooking Plymouth Sound and coastal path. Whole food cuisine from local suppliers. Self-catering cottages. (J9) 01752 823110 www.cliffhouse-kingsand.co.uk

Lantallack Farm, Landrake. Grade II Georgian farmhouse provides large, comfy bedrooms and organic breakfasts. Your hostess Nicky is an artist and will teach you printmaking, painting and sculpture. (E4) 01752 851281 www.lantallack.co.uk www.nickywalker.org.uk

Cawsand

Sheviock Barton. Spacious old farmhouse epitomises the good life, symbolised by the oak beams and flagstone floors of the kitchen. You can relax in your bedroom, the sitting room, games room or large gardens. (F7) 01503 230793 www.sheviockbarton.co.uk

architecture in Cornwall. Colonades, panelled rooms and family portraits. Open 24 Mar-30 Oct Tu, W, Th & BH M's 1.30-5.30 (also Su June-Aug). (H6) 01752 812191 www.nationaltrust.org.uk

Freathy Colony of Huts. To avoid the Plymouth Blitz during World War II many set up camp on the cliffs of Freathy. Their tents and shelters grew into cabins and a community was born. The location is dramatic and properties sell for large sums. The Cliff Top Café (01752 822069) is open throughout the year. (G8)

Landulph Church. Woodland setting beside the River Tamar. Rood screen. Bench Ends. Fine wagon roof in north aisle. (J4)

Open East-Sept Su-Th 11-4.30. (B7) 01503 262532 www.monkeysanctuary.org

Mount Edgcumbe House & Park. Sensitively restored Tudor mansion in beautiful landscaped parkland. Formal English, French and Italian Gardens. National Camellia Collection. Park and gardens open daily all year. House and Earl's Garden open Apr-Sept W-Su & BH's 11-4.30. (K8) 01752 822236 www.mountedgcumbe.gov.uk

Rame Chapel, Rame Head

Rame Church. C11-15. Rough stone with spire. No electricity; hand-pumped organ. Nearby, simple chapel on Rame Head built by monks who directed ships with fire beacons into Plymouth Sound. A place for contemplation and solitude; the last sighting of an English shore for many sailors buried at sea, and beyond these shores. (H10)

Tregantle Fort. In imposing position overlooking Whitesands Bay. Built to guard the sea approaches to Devonport Dockyard. During World War I various Worcestershire Battalions were stationed here, and injured soldiers were sent here to convalesce from their wounds. In use today by the MOD. For the rare "Open Days" see local advertising. (F8)

Morley Contemporary Art

Makers Heights. Belongs to the Rame Conservation Trust; the woodland is being tended and there are plans to finance it all by operating a campsite, studio and as a venue for music festivals. From 1926-1985, thousands of inner-city children holidayed here, inspired by Nancy Astor in 1925, the first female MP (Sutton, Plymouth). (J9) www.makerheights.org.uk

Monkey Sanctuary (Trust). The first protected breeding colony of Amazon Woolly Monkeys in the world. It's also a rescue centre for ex-pet capuchin monkeys. Refreshments.

Morans Café & Deli, Garret Street Cawsand. Coffee, hot choc, paninis and sandwiches galore. (J9)

Morley Contemporary Art, Tredis Barn, Polbathic. Exhibits works by Cornish artists and beyond. Open daily 10-4 during exhibs, or every Th 7.30-9.30pm. (E7) 01503 230995 www.morleyart.co.uk

Quad & Kart Centre. Zip karts, quads, scorpions, kiddies electric cars in disused quarry. Open daily East-Oct 10-5.30. Paintball parties open daily, all year. (A4) 01579 340678

Monkey Sanctuary ss

Brunel's Royal Albert Bridge, Saltash

View Restaurant, Trenninow Cliff Road. Fabulous position. Food is classic French with English ingredients. Can't better that. Child and Veggie friendly, and a cool place to relax and admire the view. Open W-Su 12-1.45, 7-9. (H9) 01752 822345

Westcroft Gallery, Market Street, Kingsand. Set up to promote artists living on the Rame Peninsula, and to publicise this enchanting corner of the West Country. (J9) 01752 822151 www.westcroftgallery.co.uk

SALTASH

An attractive river port with steep streets running down to the Tamar Estuary. C18 Guildhall. Royal Albert Bridge. May Fair - 1st week. Regatta - June 3rd week. (H5) www.saltash.gov.uk www.thisissaltash.co.uk

Mary Newman's Cottage, 48 Culver St. C15 Cottage of Mary Newman, first wife of Sir Francis Drake. Furniture supplied by the Victoria and Albert Museum. Open May-Sept Th 12-4 and BH M's 11-4. (H5)

Royal Albert Bridge. This "Bowstring Suspension Bridge" is an iron, single-track railway bridge, built by I.K. Brunel in 1859, his last great feat of engineering. The design comprises a wrought iron tubular arch or bow, in the form of a parabola, in a combination with sets of suspension chains hanging on each side of the tube in a catenary curve. (J5) www.royalalbertbridge.co.uk

ST GERMANS

Cornwall's great Cathedral City until 1043. An attractive village with almshouses (six houses with six gables and miniature ground and upper floors), and the magnificent church. Port Eliot, the ancient seat of the Eliot family, holds an annual Literary and Music Festival. (E6) www.porteliotlitfest.com

St Germanus Church. Founded as an Augustinian priory, and later a cathedral in the Anglo-Saxon period. Only the south aisle and nave remain. Magnificent Norman doorway and East Window stained glass by E. Burne-Jones executed by William Morris's company. (E6)

Cornish Owl Centre. One of the largest collections, from all corners of the world. Open daily 10-6. (E6) 01503 230079

Cotehele ab/nt

Trevor Price, Cotehele Gallery ss

600 BC   Iron Age settlement at Trevelgue Head

325 BC   The Greek traveller Pytheas records seeing the people of Land's End preparing metal by beating it on leather, and then trading it at St Michael's Mount.

27

Crab & Lobster Pots

Salmon fishing, Cotehele Quay nt

COTEHELE

Cotehele Gallery (National Trust Cotehele). Showcasing professional artists and makers from the South West in seven exhibitions annually. Open daily Feb to Christmas - Summer 11.30-5, Winter 11.30-4.30. (DH) www.nationaltrust.org.uk.

Cotehele House (NT). Medieval house of grey granite built from 1485-1627 set in a romantic position overlooking the River Tamar, and Devon beyond. For centuries, the Edgcumbe family home containing their original furniture, C17 tapestries, armour and needlework. The gardens lie on several levels. Medieval dovecote. Ancient clock in chapel. Refreshments and shop. Open daily except F (house closed), 15 Mar-2 Nov 11-4.30 (4 in Oct). Gardens open all year 10-dusk. (H1)

Cotehele Quay (NT). Picturesque C18 and C19 buildings beside the River Tamar. A small outstation of the National Maritime Museum and berth for the restored Tamar sailing barge 'Shamrock'. Museum, Art and craft gallery and tea room. Open daily Apr-Oct. (H1)

Coastal Footpath...

Looe to Cremyll Point: Approx 26 miles. The path crosses National Trust land and soon descends into Seaton to be followed by a stiff climb up to Battern Cliffs (450ft), the highest cliffs in South Cornwall, and a reminder of the gruelling ascents and descents of the North Coast, all now a distant memory. A quick descent to the little harbour of Portwrinkle. The path now hugs the cliff edge and you can walk through

the M.O.D. ranges at Tregantle, except during firing when you will be re-routed inland. Around the great sweep of Whitsand Bay to Rame Head with splendid views of Plymouth Sound, and beyond. Along to the twin villages of Kingsand and Cawsand, passing Mount Edgcumbe, and to Cremyll Ferry which has carried passengers across the Tamar since the C13.

Beaches and Surfing...

Mildendreath Beach.
Sands with patches of rock, bathing pool for children. P/WC/Café. (A7)

Seaton. Fine bathing, safe beach with pebbles and grey sand. P/W. Surfing - Sheltered position. (K8)

Downderry. Grey sands and rocks, palm trees. P/WC/Inn. (L8)

Portwrinkle.
Surfing - Good following big swells. At HT rocks are invisible so take care with your fins. (M8)

Whitsand Bay. 4 miles of sand is glorious on a sunny day. But BEWARE, this bay has a history of fatal bathing accidents, and is also a graveyard of many ships. The strong currents make bathing very HZ and is not recommended for the casual swimmer. Difficult access. Surfing - Warm up with the 10 minute walk to (H9)

Tregantle. Good breaks at HT. Rips are powerful. Popular location for Plymouth surfers. (F8)

Tregantle Longsands.
Access near M.O.D. range. Prohibited when red flag flies. P/WC. (F8)

Freathy / Tregonhawke.
Smooth white sands, strong currents, surfing. P/LG. (G9)

Cawsand / Kingsand.
Easy access to shelving, pebbled beach - sand at LT. Good bathing, well protected from Sou'westerlies. Glorious views of ships sailing up to Plymouth Sound. P/WC/cafe. (J9)

Kingsand

For Ancient Sites, Castles, Country Lanes, Stone Circles, Steam Railways and Wilderness.

Between the County Town of Bodmin and the walled town of Launceston lies the mysterious Bodmin Moor. A compact area of open moorland, a mere ten miles by ten in size. And yet it appears far more expansive given its wildness and isolation. But beware of sudden mists and descending clouds for they foster disorientation amidst bog and Tor.

All about you is ancient history. Early Man settled here to escape the wild beasts of forest and plain. Stone Age Man left Stone Circles and burial chambers. The Moor's appearance of bareness was hastened by the clearance of granite boulders for building stonewalls, farms and villages. In the centre, isolated and bruised by the elements, stands Jamaica Inn, the legendary smugglers' haunt, widely known through Daphne du Maurier's novel. Imagine arriving on foot, or cart, lonely, tired and drenched, to be greeted by rough-tongued smugglers and highwaymen.

Not to be overlooked is the fertile countryside on the eastern side of the Moor drained by the rivers Tamar and Lynher. A blissful, pastoral landscape reminiscent of old England. Small farmsteads and hamlets with beautiful churches such as Linkinhorne, South Hill and Lezant, and often to be found, surprisingly good inns, for example the Springer Spaniel at Treburley. These villages are linked by narrow lanes and steep banks.

Launceston is dominated by its Norman castle and is the only walled town in Cornwall. It is a town of hills that calls for exploration. The exterior walls of the church of St Mary Magdalene are quite exceptional with images of foliage and shields carved out of the granite.

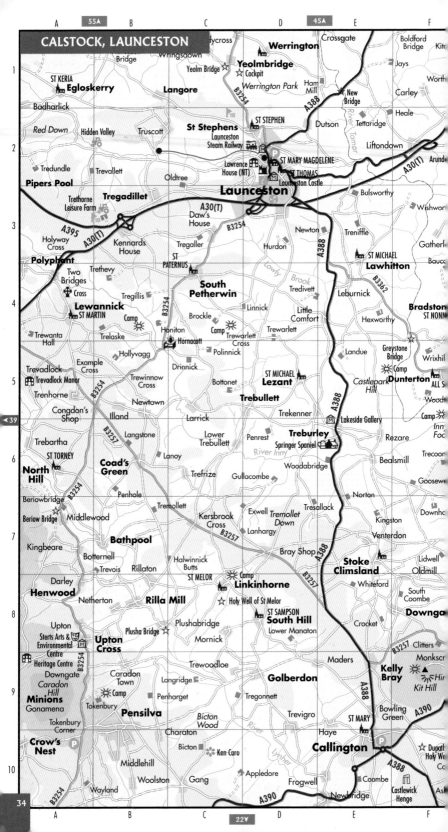

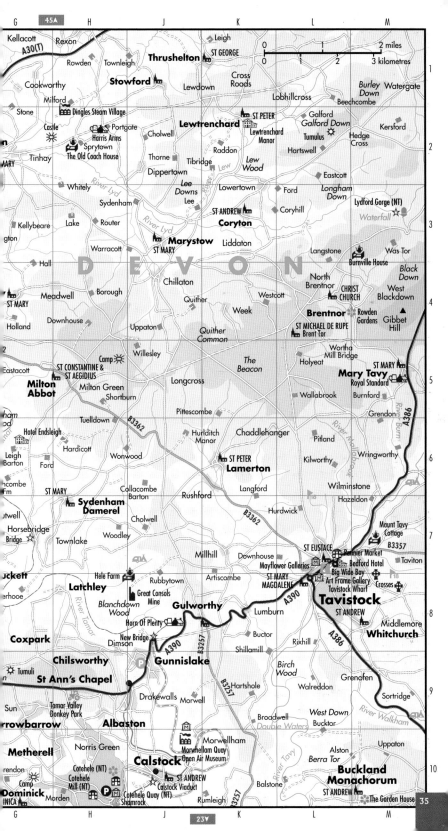

Launceston Castle

LAUNCESTON

A town of hills dominated by the commanding position of the Castle, and the only walled town in Cornwall. Splendid collection of Georgian houses in Castle Street. C16 packhorse bridge. Agricultural show - Aug (2/3 weeks). E/C Th. (D2)

Special Places to Visit...

St Mary Magdalene.
Noted for the famous exterior; panels of foliage and shields carved in granite cover most of the walls. C14 tower and a rare painted pulpit. (D2)

Launceston Castle (EH). Norman castle built in c.1070 in timber. It was the main seat of Robert de Mortain, brother of William the Conqueror. Rebuilt C12-13. Good example of a motte and bailey structure. Open as English Heritage times. (D2)

Launceston Steam Railway.
Two-foot gauge steam railway using Victorian Locomotives along a beautiful country line. After 2 1/2 miles, Newmills Station, access to farm park. Transport and Industrial Museum with working exhibits. Cafe, shop and bookshop. Open East week, Spring BH & Oct 1/2 term, July-Sept Su-F, also June Su-W, 10.30-4.30. (D2) www.launcestonsr.co.uk

Lawrence House Museum. NT property used as a local history museum. Many objects of interest including the Feudal dues. Open 31 Mar-26 Sept M-F 1030-.30. (D2) 01566 773277 www.nationaltrust.org.uk

Special Places to Visit Outside Launceston...

Hidden Valley. Adventure park and garden railway centre. Treasure hunts based around a shipwreck. Play area. Farm animals. Cafe. Open daily mid-Apr to Sept Su-F 10.30-5.30. (B2) www.hiddenvalleydiscoverypark.co.uk

AD43 · Dumnoni Tribe overcome the South West　　500-600　The Age of the Saints' as Arthur, Doniert and Celtic Kings invade

Ken-Caro Gardens. Five acre connoisseur's garden full of unusual plants and shrubs, making it a garden of interest all year. Panoramic views. Open late Feb - Sept 29 Su-F 10-5.30. (C10) 01579 362446

Lakeside Gallery, Nr Treburley. Permanent Tolkien Collection. Original paintings, drawings and prints by Linda, Seth and Roger Garland. Open daily 10-5. (E5) 01579 370760 www.lakeside-gallery.com

St Mary Magdalene, Launceston

Lakeside Gallery, Treburley ss

Sterts Arts & Environment Centre. Lively programme of music, amphitheatre(canopied) and dance. Open daily (theatre June-Sept) except Su. (A8) 01579 362382 www.sterts.co.uk

Trethorne Leisure Farm. Undercover family entertainment; milk a cow, bottle feed lambs, see chicks hatch. Ten pin bowling (open

10am-11pm), gladiator duels, dropslide, astraslide, restaurant, bar and shop. Open all year M-Sa 10-6. (B3) 01566 86324 www.trethorneleisure.com

Where to Stay...

Hornacott, South Petherwin. (C5) 01566 782461 www.hornacott.co.uk

Churches of Interest...

Calstock Church. Grand position above Tamar Valley. Two C17 monuments to the Edgcumbe family. (J10)

North Hill Church. Large, ambitious church with C15 granite

tower, elaborate and endearing C17 monuments. Set in unspoilt village. A pilgrimage to be undertaken by all church enthusiasts. (A6)

CALSTOCK

Attractive old river port on the Tamar. Steep wooded riverbank and the abundance of fruit trees provide a splendour in spring. 12 arch viaduct. Numerous disused mining chimneys and engine houses haunt the landscape. (J10)

Calstock Viaduct. 12 arch viaduct built to carry railway wagons from local mines to Calstock Quay. Whence the wagons were raised and lowered in a lift. (J10)

Launceston

705   The Saxons advance into Cornwall. Battle between the Dumnoni tribe and the Saxons; Ide of Essex defeats Geraint of the Dumnoni and advances across the Tamar

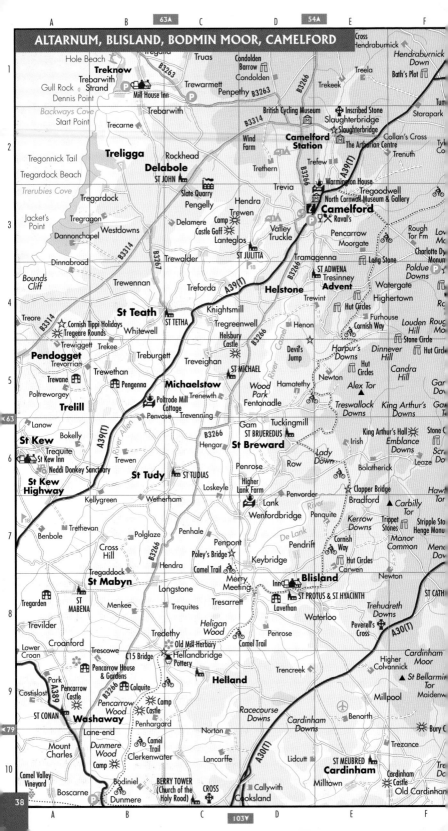

ALTARNUM, BLISLAND, BODMIN MOOR, CAMELFORD

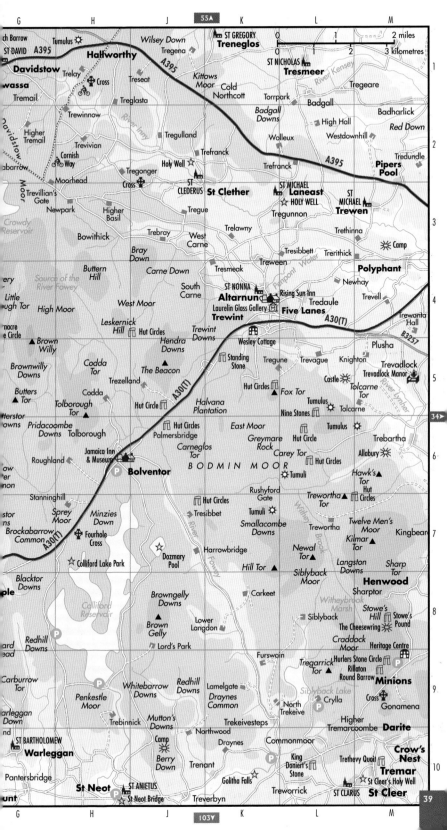

BODMIN MOOR

A wild and remote landscape of sudden mists and mysterious legend. A vegetation of boggy moorland, open heathland, granite tors and hidden valleys. The highest point is Brown Willy (1377ft). This remote wilderness, far from the dangerous beasts of the forest and plain, attracted prehistoric man. Hut circles, burial grounds and stone circles litter the landscape. An exhilarating place for pony trekking and walking, but beware of sudden mists. (K6) www.bodminmoor.co.uk

Minions, Bodmin Moor

The Cheesewring, Bodmin Moor

Special Places of Interest...

Colliford Lake Park. Multiple attraction: alternative technology and education area, nature conservation, indigenous species and undercover play area, café and crafts (The Best of Bodmin Moor's Arts & Crafts), and gift shop. Open East-Sept 10.30-5, & winter W/Es 11-5. (H8)

Doniert's Stone. Possibly remains of Durngarth's grave d.875, King of Cornwall. Interlaced with Hibernia-Saxon inscription. (L10)

Dozmary Pool. Remote, uninspiring pool where 'Excalibur was thrown into these waters'. (J7)

Fernacre Stone Circle. 64 stones, 150ft in diameter. Numerous hut circles. (G4)

Hurlers Stone Circle. Three stone circles 110ft, 135ft and 105ft in diameter. According to legend, men turned to stone for playing the old Cornish game of hurling on a Sunday. Similar game to Australian Rules. Access via 1/4-mile path from road. (M8)

King Arthur's Hall. Neolithic enclosure 159ft x 60ft with large facing stones. (F6)

Rillaton Round Barrow. A bronze dagger, and the Rillaton Cup were unearthed here in 1818. A gold cup, of ribbed and handled design (in British Museum) suggests it may have originated in Mycenae, Greece. (M9)

The Cheesewring. Extraordinary formation of granite slabs weathered by wind and rain. Bronze Age cup (now residing in the British Museum) found in grave on Stowe's Hill. It's a good fifteen minute walk from the car park. Follow the old quarry track. (M8)

Trethevy Quoit. Impressive Neolithic dolmen; 6 uprights support a massive capstone pierced by a circular hole. Park opposite. (M10)

ALTARNUM

A charming linear village with a superb C16 church, 'Cathedral of the Moors'. Packhorse bridge. (K4)

Rising Sun Inn. Popular pub on the edge of Bodmin Moor providing a full range of ales. Delabole slate flagtone floors. Coal fires. Uncomplicated food. (K4)

Laurelin Glass Gallery & Studio. Handmade glass blown on the premises, from wine glasses to chandeliers. Open Tu-Sa 10-5. (K4) 01566 880122

St Nonna. Superb C16 church; tall perpendicular tower rises to 109 ft. Norman font with bearded faces at corner. C16 carved bench ends including man with bagpipes. Rood Screen. Known locally as 'The Cathedral of the Moors'. Overlooks an attractive linear village. (K4)

St Nonna ac

787   Vikings invade and make a pact with the Cornish to repel the Saxons

814   The Saxon king Ecgberht of Wessex conquers Cornwall destroying all in his path.

Trevethy Quoit

Wesley Cottage. John Wesley, the founder of Methodism, preached and rested during his preaching tours of Cornwall. Furnished in C18 style, collection of Wesleyana. Open daily 9-dusk. (K4) 01566 86158 www.wesleycottage.ukonline.co.uk

North Cornwall Museum, Camelford

Camelford Tower

CAMELFORD

Attractive main square with some fine building; note the splendid clock. Worth stopping here if you've been held up on the A39. Free parking. Leisure Centre. (E3) www.camelford.org

British Cycling Museum, The Old Station. Cycling from 1818 with over 400 machines. Open all year Su-Th 10-5. (D2)

North Cornwall Museum & Gallery, The Clease. Award winning museum of rural life depicting life of 50 to 100 years ago. The owner is a mine of local knowledge and worth seeking out should you require a lengthy guided chat. She holds regular exhibitions of contemporary art. TIC. Open Apr-Sept 10-5 M-Sa. (E3) 01840 212954

Where to Stay, Eat, Drink & Be Merry...

Raval's, Fore Street. Family-run café-bar and restaurant serving modern English food. Gets very busy in season so book early. Children's menu. Accommodation. (E3) 01840 213888 www.ravals.co.uk

Warmington House, 32 Market Place. A welcome addition to North Cornwall's accommodation. This is a beautiful Queen Anne house with six luxurious bed and bathrooms with all the mod-cons; LCD flat screen TVs, crisp bed linen…and enormous breakfasts. (E3) 01840 214961 www.warmingtonhouse.co.uk

Churches of Interest...

Advent Church.
Rare 8 pinnacle tower in lonely moorland setting. (E4)

St Protus & St Hyacinth, Blisland. Wonderfully restored church (a favourite of John Betjeman) in village with attractive village green and fine inn. C15 granite tower and Norman font. C15 brasses. (D8)

Paul Jackson, Helland Bridge Pottery ss

Cardinham Church. C15 buttressed and pinnacle tower with Celtic cross. (E10)

Laneast Church. Originally a C13 Norman church with fine C16 pulpit, granite south porch and wagon roofing. Notable restored benches, the bench ends are interlaced knots, coats of arms and stars. Remarkable 9ft high Rood Screen. C15 stained glass. (L3)

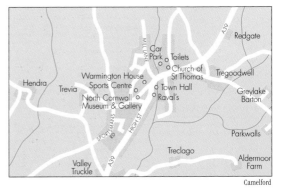

Redgate
MILLNE
Car Park ○ Toilets
○ Church of
Hendra   Warmington House   St Thomas   Tregoodwell
Trevia   Sports Centre ○
North Cornwall ○ ○ Town Hall   Greylake
Museum & Gallery   ○ Raval's   Barton
SPORMANS
KINSMANS   HIGH ST   Parkwalls
Treclago
Treclago   Aldermoor
Valley   A39   Farm
Truckle   Camelford

Wesley Cottage ss

825 The Cornish rise against Ecgberht but are defeated at Galford

838 The Cornish-Viking alliance is defeated at Hingston Down near Callington

Lanteglos-By-Camelford Church. In picturesque valley, much restored, C10 Saxon pillars and 4 Celtic crosses. Evidence of Norman construction. Attractive C19 monument. (D3)

Linkinhorne Church. Tall C16 granite tower - the second highest in county at 120ft with wagon roof, stained glass, wall paintings in remote village. (C8)

Michaelstow Church. Original wagon roof. Font, bench ends and interesting C17 monument. (C6)

accommodation & gift shops. Attractions include the Daphne du Maurier Room, 'The Smugglers at Jamaica Inn'. Inn open all year. (H6) 01566 86250 www.jamaicainn.co.uk

Minions Heritage Centre, South Phoenix Mine. Explores the history of the local landscape. Open daily from 10-dusk. (M9) 01579 362350 www.caradon.gov.uk

Old Mill Herbary. 5 acre semi-wild garden by the River Camel. C14 Helland Bridge, mature woodland, island walks, 1.75 acre Arboretum,

Slaughter Bridge. Possible burial place of King Arthur. A granite slab marks the grave. (E2)

Where to Stay...

Higher Lank Farm, Nr Wenfordbridge.
This is unique. No question about it. A working farm specialising in the needs of parents, and pre-school children (toddlers). Self-catering and guest house accommodation available. (D7) 01208 850716 www.higherlankfarm.co.uk

Old Mill Herbary ss

Special Places to Visit...

Arthurian Centre. Site of Arthurian legend and folk lore. Exhibition centre, woodland and river walks, tea room and gift/bookshop. Play area. Open daily. (E2) www.arthur-online.co.uk

Helland Bridge Pottery. Riverside home and studio of Paul and Rosie Jackson. A wide range of stunningly decorated hand-made pottery and garden sculpture. Fabulous water gardens. Open any time, but advised to 'phone first. (C9) 01208 75240 www.paul-jackson.co.uk

Jamaica Inn. Former old coaching inn and inspiration for Daphne du Maurier's novel. Bars, restaurants,

mill leat, bog garden, camomile seat around unabashed fertility theme. Unique botanical and historical interest. A tranquil oasis (now Site of Special Scientific Interest & Special Area of Conservation status). Open daily Apr-Sept except W, 10-5. (C8) 01208 841206 www.oldmillherbary.co.uk

Pencarrow House. Busy Georgian home of the Molesworth-St Aubyn's set in extensive grounds. A fine collection of pictures, furniture and porcelain. Cafe, craft centre, plant shop and children's play area. Open daily from Apr-Oct except F & Sa 1.30-5.30, BH M's and June-Aug from 11am. (A9) 01208 841369 www.pencarrow.co.uk

Lavethan, Blisland.
A Grade II manor house set in its own secret river valley of 30 acres. Recorded in the Domesday Book. Spacious rooms with open fires. Heated swimming pool in walled garden. Dinner an option. WL. (D8) 01208 850487 www.lavethan.com

Trevadlock Manor, Lewannick. Overlooks the upper reaches of the beautiful Lynher Valley. A substantial L-shaped manor built in 1530. You have the choice of farmhouse style B&B or self-catering cottages on the estate. (M5) 01566 782227 www.trevadlockmanor.co.uk

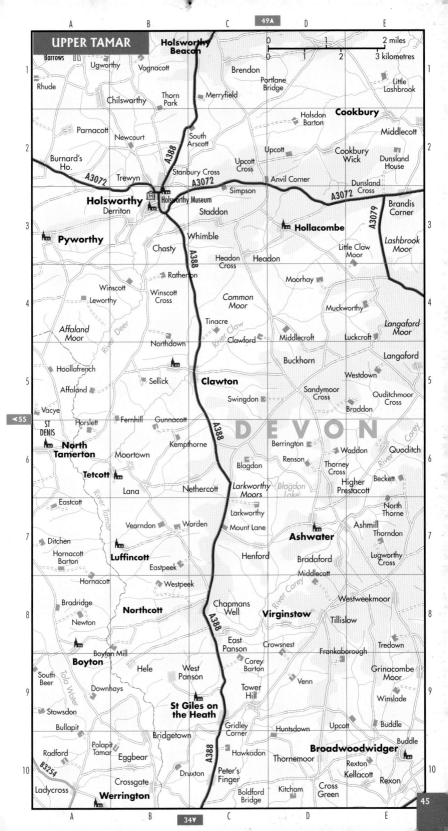

For Dramatic Scenery, Family Holidays, Gastronomic Delights, Safe Beaches and Surfing.

The coastal footpath that runs along the North Coast must be one of the natural wonders of Britain. At times, wild and remote, and hard going in places, it affords spectacular views and rewards you with sheltered harbours where you can sample local fayre and fine ales. When the Equinoxes arrive you can, in places, walk the golden sands and admire the Atlantic waves that have rolled in untouched for 3,000 miles.

The North Coast is a fabulous playground for family holidays. Accommodation is available in many forms: camp sites, holiday cottages, farmhouses, gastronomic B&Bs and hotels. The style of your holiday may lean to the surfing camaraderie of Bude or the quieter villages of the far north, the gastronomic pleasures and indulgences of Padstow, or the frenetic pace of Newquay to the more soulful, arty atmosphere of St Agnes. Cornwall now has a wealth of sophisticated hostelries offering superb food and luxury accommodation. It still has surf hostels although their numbers are dwindling for many on the road leading to Fistral Beach have been torn down and are being replaced by luxurious apartments.

Inland are small farms and hamlets, with the villages increasing in size as you move south nearer to the towns of Bodmin, Truro and Falmouth. In the Camborne-Redruth area there is much to interest the industrial archaeologist, and perhaps the most spectacularly located engine house is to be found at Wheal Coates, north of Chapel Porth.

This stretch of Cornwall has long held a special hold on many families who return year after year for their annual holiday. It is not uncommon to see three generations of the same family enjoying the calm waters of Daymer Bay or Trevone, that is, until their offspring progress to the surf schools of Polzeath, and the rips of Booby and Constantine Bays.

In recent years extreme sports such as surfing and kite-boarding have exploded onto the scene. Surfing is no longer a niche activity. It is now an everyday sport available to all through the many surf and life-saving schools, and because of the access to protective wet suits and learner boards. This guide will direct you to the best beaches. The locals have a saying in Newquay: "Arrive with a bucket and spade....and leave with a surfboard!" So go and search for the Perfect Wave.

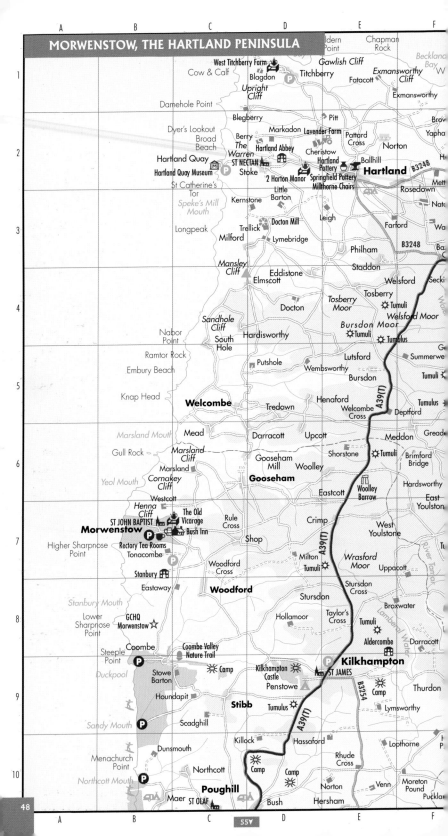

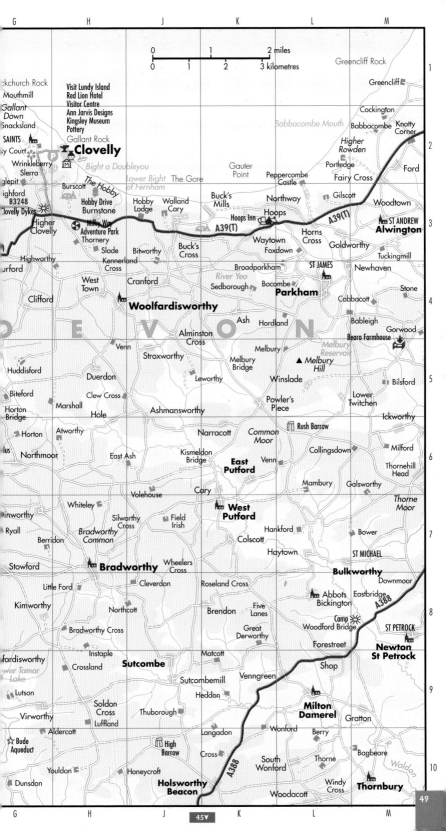

MORWENSTOW

Famous for Richard Stephen Hawker (1803-75), the eccentric and original vicar-poet, and originator of harvest festivals. A compassionate man, he would stalk the wild coast in beaver hat, fishermen's long boots and yellow cloak in search of shipwrecked sailors. Many are buried in his churchyard. And to stir his congregation he would dress as a mermaid. Hawker's Hut, made up of driftwood, stands on the edge of the cliffs. The Rectory Tea Rooms are opposite the church entrance. (B7)

Where to Stay, Eat, Drink & Be Merry...

Bush Inn. Historic C13 Freehouse with log fires and flag stone floors offers fine ales and is developing a growing reputation as fine, dining pub with its new, bright restaurant. Country B & B and self-catering accommodation. (C7) 01288 331242 www.bushinn-morwenstow.co.uk

Rectory Tea Rooms.
Savour old England at its very best: Cornish cream teas and farmhouse hospitality. Overlooks RS Hawker's famous church in the dip below the parking area, the Old Vicarage. Open daily Apr-Oct 11-5. (B7) 01288 331251 www.rectory-tearooms.co.uk

The Old Vicarage. To gauge the RS Hawker Experience you must stay here in his former home. Your hosts are a mine of information. Comfortable B & B with mounds of home cooking. Carrow's Stable to let. (B7) 01288 331369 www.rshawker.co.uk

What to See & Visit...

Church of St John The Baptist.
Impressive Norman doorway with vulgar heads of men and beast on the porch, original wagon roof and wall painting remains. C16 Rood Screen. Bench ends. In superb, lonely location overlooking the Atlantic. (B7)

Combe Valley Nature Trail.
The route starts at Combe Cottages and takes you through a green and peaceful wooded valley, rich in oak woods, honeysuckle and birdlife - buzzards, woodpeckers, dippers... Nearby Stowe Barton (National Trust property), home of Sir Richard Grenville (see Celebrities), County Sheriff of Cornwall in 1577 who was immortalised in Tennyson's poem 'The Revenge'. (C8)

St John the Baptist, Morwenstow

St Christopher Wallpainting, Poughill

Bush Inn

Kilkhampton Church (St James). Norman South doorway. Perpendicular church of late C15 with superb collection of carved bench ends. Grenville family tombs. Fine East window. Jacobean pulpit. (E9)

927   King Athelstan decrees the Tamar to be the boundary between Anglo-Saxon Wessex and Celtic Cornwall

981   Padstow Monastery destroyed by a "host of Danes"

Poughill Church.
Carved bench ends with large wall painting of St Christopher repainted by Frank Salisbury RA in pretty village. (C10)

Tamar Lake Wildlife Refuge.
Fisherman's paradise, trout and coarse; boats for hire. (F8)

Coastal Footpath...

Marsland Mouth to Northcott Mouth
Approx. 14 miles. A remote and wild coastline; the rocks, razor sharp and contorted, the pathway hard going, yet exhilarating and rewarding. Rest at Morwenstow and visit the church and tearoom or Inn. Onwards to pass beside RS Hawker's Hut. Two miles on, the white dish aerials of GCHQ, then into Duckpool where a path leads up to the Coombe Valley Nature Trail. At low tide one can follow the sands to Bude, or take the cliff top path.

Beaches and Surfing...

Welcombe Mouth.
Haunt of cruel Coppinger, an C18 smuggler. Pebbles, rocks and sandy beaches at LT. (C5)

Stanbury Mouth.
15 minute walk from P to isolated beach, sand, swift currents, HZ at LT. (B8)

Duckpool.
Rocky with strong currents. Footpath leads to Coombe Valley Nature Trail. P. Surfing - LT R breaks off the rocks. (B9)

Sandy Mouth.
Expansive beach, rocky at HT, swift currents, superb rock formations at top of beach. HZ at LT. Bass fishing, P/cafe. Surfing - Clean with good beach breaks. Fine, small swell, off banks. Beware rip tides. (B9)

Northcott Mouth.
Extensive sand, pebbles and some fascinating rock formations. Bathing HZ two hours either side of LT. P. Surfing - Banks at LT create heavy hollow waves backing off at HT except on big swells. Good R hander on N side. Beware rip tides. (B10)

Duckpool

Sandy Mouth

059   Bishop's Seat of Devon and Cornwall appointed to Exeter (until 1876)

1066   Battle of Hastings starts Norman rule

These images were discovered in the Archives of The Castle (Museum), Bude

0   1   2 miles
0 1   2   3 kilometres

Wider
Sar
Wanson M
Foxhole Point
Millook Haven
Outdoor Adventure
Cancleave Strand   Mi
Dizzard Point   *Millook
Common*
Chipman Strand   Trebarfoot
Cornish
Way
Dizzard
Tresmorn   Trengayor
Pencannow   Camp   Trewint
Point
ST GENESIUS   Treworgie
St Gennys   Coxford   Trenc
Bray's Point
Cambeak   **Crackington
Haven**   Rosecare

Little Strand
The Strangles   Hallagather   **Wainhouse
Trevigue   **Crackington**   Corner**   Be
Voter Run   Baypark
Trevigue Wildlife Conservation   Rosecur
Rusey Beach   *High   Pengold   Pencuke   Villa
Cliff*   Round
Buckator   Camp   Hayes
Tumuli
Gull Rock   Newton   Tresparrett   Trengur
Beeny Sisters   Posts   B3263   Collamoor
Fire Deacon Point   Camp   Cansford   Head
Beeny Cliff   Tresparrett   Trevillian
Pentargon   Beeny   Trebyla B3263 Downs   Marshgate Cocksport
Cornish
Way
Penally Point (NT)   Museum of Witchcraft   Cardew
Wilapark (NT)   Rocky Valley   **Tresparrett**   Mill
Short   Gallery   ST JULIOT'S   Hennett
Island   **Boscastle** Napoleon Inn Valency   ST DENIS
Long   ST SYMPHORIAN'S Bottreaux Valley (NT) Trevilla   **Otterham** Roose
Island   Castle   Treworld   Trelash
Trevalga   MINSTER   **Lesnewth**   *Trevilla* *Otterham*
Cross   ST PETROCK   ST MICHAEL   Helset   *Down*   *Down*
Polrunny   Tredorne   Tregrylls   Hallgarden
Trethevey   Otterham
St Nectan's Glen   Copplestone   Station   Tregray
Halgabron   Waterfall & Chapel   Vendown   Hallwell Tumuli
St Nectan's   *Waterpit*   Hendra   Tumuli
Kieve   *Down*   **Hallwo**
Trenale   Cross Hendraburnick   Tich Barrow   Tumulus

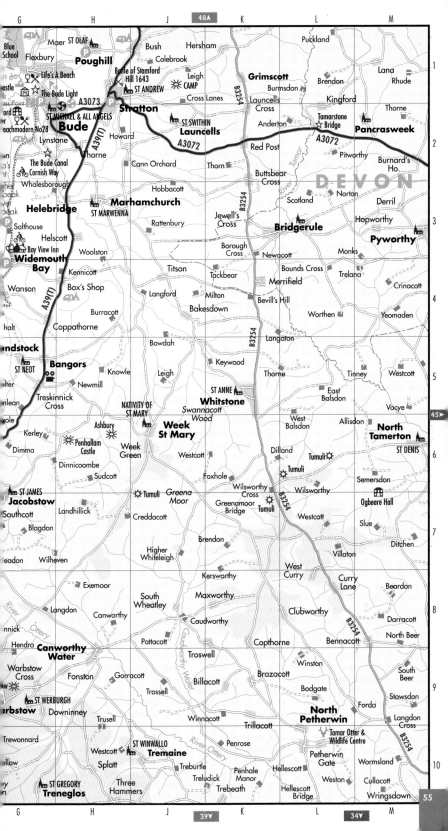

BUDE

A seaside resort first developed by the Victorians that has witnessed, of late, much resurgence, in no small part due to the popularity of surfing and beach activities. The long, extensive beaches, just a short walk from the town centre, and those to the south and north of the town, are breathtaking. The coastline has been the sad scene of many shipwrecks - 80 ships were foundered or wrecked between 1824-74. The town abounds with surf shops and surf hostels, and when the Low Pressure is in force the beaches are populated with black shadows in summer and winter. It is the most accessible of Cornish surf resorts. Canal, carnival and fete - August (third week). 'Blessing of the Sea' - Aug. E/C Th. (H2) www.bude.co.uk www.visitbude.info www.budewebcam.co.uk

What to See & Visit...

Old Canal. Built in 1819-26 at a length of 43 miles (61km). For 60 years used to transport coal and lime inland, and to export grain and slate. Killed off by the railways. Best sections are at Marhamchurch, Hobbacott Down and Werrington. (G1) www.bude-canal.co.uk

The Castle Bude. Newly restored museum celebrates the heritage of Bude and Stratton with a tableaux of interactive displays and exhibits: Canal, shipwrecks, lifeboats and railways. New "Gurney" exhibition of Bude's Forgotten Genius, Sir Goldsworth Gurney Restaurant. Open daily, all year from 10. (G1) www.bude-stratton.gov.uk

Life's a Beach, Bude

Where to Stay...

Beachmodern No. 28.
This is 5-star stylish self-catering accommodation. Perfect for families as there are eight bedrooms, three bathrooms and a classy chef on hand. 01288 275006 www.beachmodern.com

STRATTON

A pretty village with a long and fascinating history. Now very much a suburb of Bude. C15 church. Battle of Stamford Hill, 1643. (H2)

Churches to Visit...

Crackington Haven Church. Dedicated to Celtic missionary St Gennys. Norman origins. C12 font of Purbeck stone. Bench ends. Headstone inscribed by Eric Gill. (D6)

Launcells Church. Fortunate to be the only Cornish church not tampered with by the Victorians. Wall painting and 60 carved bench ends shown off in the light interior. Monument. Fine wagon roof.

A haven of solitude beside the little stream in a wooded valley. (J2)

Tintagel Church. Norman origins in isolated cliff-top position. Sailors' graves. Rood Screen, bench ends and monument. (L2)

Where to Eat, Drink & Be Merry...

Life's A Beach, Summerleaze Beach. Bistro restaurant offers all types of food from locally caught bass to burgers and pizzas. A great place to watch the sunset, and to relax after a day's surf. Open daily in season. (G1) www.dsibley.timart.co.uk

The Bay View Inn, Marine Drive. Surfers' hangout overlooking the roaring Atlantic. Currently being refurbished with chic, modern bedrooms. Wholesome menu uses local farms for hungry surfers. (G3) 01288 361273 www.bayviewinn.co.uk

Aerial View of Bude

Xtreme Sports...

Big Blue Surf School, Summerleaze Beach. Learn, improve, excel at one of Europe's top schools with National Team coach, Jon Price. Open Apr-Oct. (G1) 01288 331764 www.bigbluesurfschool.co.uk

Outdoor Adventure, Atlantic Court. Activity centre for the ultimate coastal experience: coasteering, surfing, coastal traversing, sea cliff abseils, rock climbing, sea kayaking. Activity Weekends. Accommodation. Tuition. (F5) 01288 362900 www.outdooradventure.co.uk

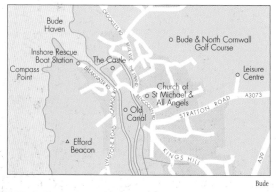
Bude

1066 Robert de Mortain becomes the Earl of Cornwall and builds Launceston Castle

1067 William I grants Cornwall to Count Brian of Brittany

Blue Rock, Porthcoth

STRATTON

A pretty village with a long and fascinating history. Now very much a suburb of Bude. C15 church. Battle of Stamford Hill, 1643. (H2)

Churches to Visit...

Crackington Haven Church.
Dedicated to Celtic missionary St Gennys. Norman origins. C12 font of Purbeck stone. Bench ends. Headstone inscribed by Eric Gill. (D6)

Launcells Church. Fortunate to be the only Cornish church not tampered with by the Victorians. Wall painting and 60 carved bench ends shown off in the light interior. Monument. Fine wagon roof. A haven of solitude beside the little stream in a wooded valley. (J2)

Tintagel Church. Norman origins in isolated cliff-top position. Sailors' graves. Rood Screen, bench ends and monument. (L2)

Where to Eat, Drink & Be Merry...

Life's A Beach, Summerleaze Beach. Bistro restaurant offers all types of food from locally caught bass to burgers and pizzas. A great place to watch the sunset, and to relax after a day's surf. Open daily in season. (G1)
www.dsibley.timart.co.uk

The Bay View Inn, Marine Drive. Surfers' hangout overlooking the roaring Atlantic. Currently being refurbished with chic, modern bedrooms. Wholesome menu uses local farms for hungry surfers. (G3) 01288 361273
www.bayviewinn.co.uk

Outdoor Adventure ss

Launcells Church

Xtreme Sports...

Big Blue Surf School, Summerleaze Beach. Learn, improve, excel at one of Europe's top schools with National Team coach, Jon Price. Open Apr-Oct. (G1) 01288 331764
www.bigbluesurfschool.co.uk

Outdoor Adventure, Atlantic Court. Activity centre for the ultimate coastal experience: coasteering, surfing, coastal traversing, sea cliff abseils, rock climbing, sea kayaking. Activity Weekends. Accommodation. Tuition. (F5) 01288 362900
www.outdooradventure.co.uk

BOSCASTLE

Attractive village within steep valley leads down to a sinuous and dramatic harbour. A safe haven on a treacherous coastline, but despite this it remains an extremely difficult destination to navigate into (especially on a stormy night). More recently, featured in the national news following the horrific flooding on the 16th August 2004. Cars and caravans were swept into the sea. Houses and shops were destroyed. The Royal Naval helicopter squadron from Chivenor was magnificent in its efforts to save life and limb. (B9)
www.boscastlecornwall.org.uk
www.visitboscastleandtintagel.com

Entrance to Boscastle

What to See & Visit...

Museum Of Witchcraft.
Long established Museum holds
the world's largest collection of
genuine witchcraft related artefacts.
Open daily East to Halloween,
10.30-6, 11.30-6 on Sun. (B8)
www.witchcraft.co.uk/boscastle

Where to Eat, Drink & Be Merry...

Napoleon, High Street.
A full range of beers feeds three beer
gardens and two bars - public and
officers. Boney's Bistro provides fresh
fish, homemade soups and puddings.
Children (restaurant) and dogs
welcome. B&B. (B9) 01840 250204

Tamar Otter & Wildlife Centre.
Set in 20 acres of mature woodlands
where you will see Asian and British
otters in semi-natural enclosures, as
well as deer, owls, wallabies and
waterfowl. Tearoom with homemade
food. Gift shop. Open daily Apr-Oct
10.30-6. (L10) 01566 785646
www.tamarotters.co.uk

Coastal Footpath...

Ascend to Compass Point for
extensive views northwards. The
path overlooks reefs, buttresses and

Tamar Otter & Wildlife Centre ss

pinnacles. Easy going to Widemouth
Sands. Through car park, up Penhalt
Cliff and on to Millook Haven with
cliffs of contorted slate. Rough ascent
to Dizzard Point (500ft), prone to
landsliding, so beware, on to the
veined and contorted rock forms of
Pencannow Point. What follows is an
easy descent to the fine sands of
Crackington Haven. It's a hard slog
up to Cambeak - but your efforts are
rewarded with views across from
Hartland Point to Trevose Head.
Climbing beside further land slipped
sections, passing jagged cliffs and
The Strangles (beach), scene of many
shipwrecks, to High Cliff, at 731ft the
highest cliff in Cornwall (although

slumping has created a massive
sloping undercliff so it lacks the
drama of a precipice) and supposedly
a favourite courting and riding spot
for Thomas Hardy and his first wife
Emma Gifford. Then to Beeny Cliff,
the only headland carved from Chert,
a tough black flint-like rock, and
often below, basking seals. Along to
Pentaragon Waterfall which falls
100ft down a deep chasm. And
then to Boscastle Harbour for
refreshments, via Penally Point,
and below a fine views of the
tortuous, harbour entrance.

Beaches and Surfing...

Bude - Crooklets Beach. Spacious
firm sands at LT, bathing HZ at LT.
S-B hire, cafe, LG. Surfing - Fine,
short breaks for body boarders. With
hollow sandbanks waves flow at all
stages of tide. At HT Tower Rock
produces a good shallow wave. Try
Wrangles Rocks to N at LT. (G1)

Bude - Summerleaze Beach.
Popular surfing beach, roomy firm
sands and bathing pool at LT. S-B
hire. Access. Surfing - HT sheltered
from SW wind. R breaks into harbour.
Take care, can be steep. Beware
strong rips. Ls at LT. Hollow fast wave
off The Barrels. (G1)

1086   The Domesday Book records that Robert controls
277 Cornish manors

1086   The Domesday Book records there are 340
manors in the county; 5,500 working males and
a population of 27,000

Widemouth Sand

Bude - Middle Beach.
Surfing - Good Ls and Rs with swells up to 6ft. Popular with locals. (G1)

Bude - Upton. Surfing - Good Rs and Ls on the N and S side. Difficult access down cliff. (G1)

Widemouth Sand. Large sandy beach, rock pools, HZ at LT. Tent and S-B hire/WC/P/cafe. Surfing - A popular break for all abilities, at all stages of the tide. Best up to 6ft. (G4)

Millook Haven. Secluded cove, shelves steeply - HZ bathing. (F4)

Crackington Haven.
Popular bathing beach, sands and rocks. HZ at LT. S-B hire/WC/cafes. Surfing - Sheltered from N winds. Holds big swells. Good waves break off at HT. (D6)

The Strangles. Steep descent down 700ft cliffs. Rocks, sand at LT, swift currents; bathing very HZ. (C7)

Rusey Beach.
P near Newton Farm, steep descent, sand at LT, very HZ bathing. (C7)

Bossinney Haven.
P in village, steep 1/2 mile descent to little coves below huge cliffs. Popular surfing. (B8)

Bude Sunset

1090   Robert de Mortain dies and his lands pass to William de Mortain

1106   William dispossessed of his lands following a baronial struggle against Henry I

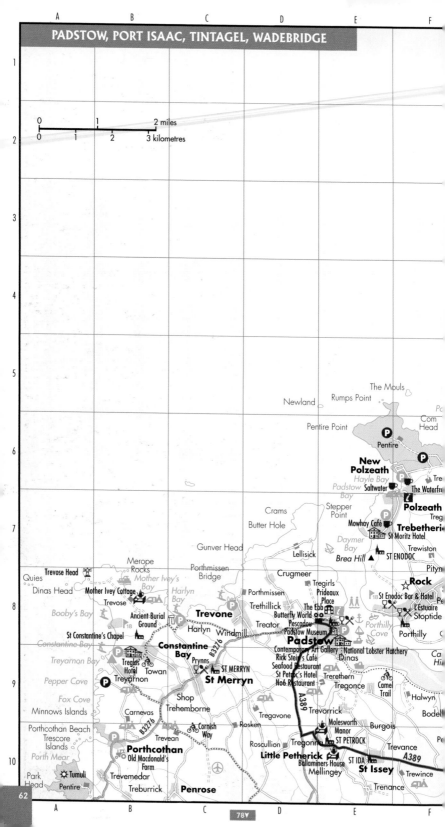

0   1   2 miles

0   1   2   3 kilometres

The Mouls

Newland   Rumps Point

Pentire Point

Com Head

Pentire

New Polzeath

Hayle Bay

Padstow Bay   Saltwater   The Waterfr

Crams   Stepper Point   **Polzeath**   Treg

Butter Hole   Mowhay Café   **Trebetheri**

St Moritz Hotel

Gunver Head   Lellisick   Daymer Bay   Trewiston

Merope Rocks   Brea Hill   ST ENODOC   Pity

Trevose Head   Mother Ivey's Bay   Porthmissen Bridge   Crugmeer   **Rock**

Quies   Dinas Head   Mother Ivey Cottage   Tregirls   Prideaux   St Enodoc Bar & Hotel   Pe

Trevose   Harlyn Bay   Porthmissen   Place   L'Estuaire

Booby's Bay   **Trevone**   Trethillick   The Ebb   Stoptide

Ancient Burial Ground   Butterfly World   Pescadou   Porthilly   Porthilly   Cove

St Constantine's Chapel   Harlyn   Treator   **Padstow**   Ca

Constantine Bay   Windmill   Contemporary Art Gallery   National Lobster Hatchery   Hi

Treyarnon Bay   **Constantine Bay**   Prynns   Rick Stein's Café   Dinas

Treglos Hotel   Towan   Seafood Restaurant   Trerethern   Camel

Pepper Cove   Treyarnon   **ST MERRYN**   St Petroc's Hotel   Trereance   Trail

Fox Cove   **St Merryn**   No6 Restaurant   Tregonce

Minnows Islands   Shop   Camel   Halwyn

Carnevas   Trehemborne   Tregavone   Trevorrick   Bode

Porthcothan Beach   Rosken   Burgois

Trescore Islands   Cornish Way   Molesworth Manor   Trevance

Porth Mear   Trevean   Roscullion   **ST PETROCK**

Park Head   **Porthcothan**   Tregonna   A389

Pentire   Old Macdonald's Farm   **Little Petherick**   ST IDA   Trewince

Tumuli   Ballaminers House   **St Issey**   Trenance

Trevemedar   Mellingey

Treburrick   **Penrose**

Padstow Harbour

PADSTOW

A labyrinth of narrow alleyways and picturesque houses, and a safe haven on the treacherous North Coast. May Day heralds the arrival of the Padstow Hobby Horse ('Obby 'Oss) who prances and dances the streets taunting young, and not so young, maidens. A celebration of spring fever and the coming of summer. C16 Raleigh's Court House on South Quay. C15 church. Boat trips. Centre of fine cuisine with many restaurants, most notably Rick Stein's various enterprises. Some have labelled the town Padstein. Understandable, but a little unfair. True, he may have dominated our TV screens for an age but his success has rippled out across Cornwall and made this old county a destination for lovers of sea food and local produce. It is worth walking away from the crowded harbour front and exploring the side streets or heading out for the coastal footpath to the nearby beaches. The Camel Trail starts here and you can hire a bike from one of the hire centres located beside the car park at the bottom of the hill. (E8)
www.padstow-cornwall.co.uk
www.padstow.com
www.padstowlive.com

Padstow

The Great Hall, Prideaux Place ss

1120   Cornwall chronicled as a separate country by Ingulf the Scribe

1130   Truro granted a Charter

May Day Carnival, Padstow

Where to Eat, Drink & Be Merry in Padstow...

Rick Stein's Cafe, 10 Middle St. Light lunches, coffees, pastries and a reasonably priced three-course dinner each evening. B&B. (E8) www.rickstein.com

Stein's Seafood Delicatessen, Riverside. Treat yourself to hot takeaway seafood dishes and stir fries. A great destination to head to after a night under canvas, a rip tide surf or a head-butting sou'westerly on the coastal footpath. (E8) 01841 532700

Stein's Fish & Chips, South Quay. Cod is sourced from well-managed Icelandic stock, haddock is line caught, plus plenty of locally caught fish. (E8)

St Petroc's Hotel & Bistro. Stein's smaller hotel has been renovated to provide a light and airy feel. As you'd expect, there's plenty of seafood, and meat and veggie dishes. (E8) 01841 532700

No 6 Restaurant & Rooms. Smart, chic dining establishment no doubt taking advantage of the Stein-Effect. Private dining rooms available for parties etc. (E8) 01841 532093 www.number6inpadstow.com

What to See & Do...

National Lobster Hatchery, South Quay. The fascinating world of lobsters and their environment. Open daily from 10. (E8)

Padstow Contemporary Art Gallery, 3a Parnell Court. Displays local artists and craft persons work: sculpture, ceramics, furniture and paintings. Open Apr-Oct M-Sa 11-4. (E8)

Padstow Museum, Market Place. Maritime and local interest - 'Obby' Oss. Open East to Oct M-F 10.30-4.30, Sa 10.30-1. (E8) www.padstowmuseum.co.uk

Prideaux Place. Home of the Prideaux-Brune family. Filled with treasures, pictures, portraits, porcelain and exquisite furniture. Open Easter week, then 14 May-6 Oct Su-Th 1.30-5. (E8) 01841 532411 www.prideauxplace.co.uk

'Obby' Oss, Padstow

The Seafood Restaurant ss

The Seafood Restaurant.
Needs no introduction. Rick Stein's restaurant has established a reputation since opening 30 years ago. The fish comes literally straight off the boats in the harbour (via a judicious by-your-leave in the kitchen) and onto your plate. Essential to book. (E8) 01841 532700

Pescadou, South Quay.
Modern, friendly restaurant providing value for money in foodie Padstow. Serves fish dishes, too. (E8) 01841 532359
www.staustellbrewery.co.uk/hotels

The Ebb. 1a The Strand.
Minimalism and artworks in tandem with international cuisines provide tasty fayre. Dinner. (E8) 01841 532565

Outside Padstow…

Prynns, Shop Road, St Merryn.
Fresh fish shop, deli and seafood restaurant. This family know their trade having been at it for 16 years.

The mother and daughters cook, the son plays professional Rugby, and looks great on home cooking. Sandwiches and veggie meals. Open 10-3, 7-10pm. B&B. (C9) 01841 520976

Trevathan Farm.
Strawberry farm with shop and restaurant. Fruit in season. Pets corner. Open daily. (J7)
www.trevathanfarm.com

Where to Stay…

Mother Ivey Cottage, Trevose Head.
Former "Fish Cellar" used for processing the day's catch stands on the cliff edge in an enviable position overlooking an emerald-turquoise sea. The interior style reminds me of a Victorian shooting/fishing lodge. Hunting prints adorn the walls. Two simple guest rooms. Evening meals an option. Next door, a self-catering cottage for 8. (B8) 01841 520329

PORT ISAAC
A charming north coast fishing inlet and old port. A steep street runs down to beach and harbour, hazardous when a northerly wind blows. Lobster fishing centre. Trips for mackerel, pleasant inns and parking on beach at LT. Fresh fish for sale. Restaurants. St Endellion Music Festival - Aug. (H5) www.portisac-online.co.uk

Port Isaac Pottery. Individual one-off stoneware pots influenced by the sea and Cornish landscape. Seascape paintings by Barbara Hawkins. Open daily East-Oct 10-4. (H6) www.portisaacpottery.co.uk

Where to Stay, Eat, Drink & Be Merry…

The Edge, 6 New Road.
Smart bar and restaurant overlooks the sea. Contemporary art covers the walls. Specialises in local fish and meat dishes. Lunches and cream teas. (J6) 01208 880090
www.theedgecornwall.com

The Old School Hotel & Restaurant.
Set half way down the steep hill, the position invites grand views across the pretty harbour. A hotel of character, for each bedroom is different. No better place to relax and enjoy the slow tempo of a Cornish fishing village. Attractive restaurant with bright works of art, and a fair portion of fish dishes. (J6) 01208 880271
www.theoldschoolhotel.co.uk

Port Isaac

The Estuary at Dawn, Rock

The Slipway Hotel & Restaurant. Set in the middle of the village opposite the harbour and the local fish merchant who supplies the restaurant. Comfortable bedrooms, a bar and al fresco dining area will relax and endear you to t his enchanting old fishing village. (J6) 01208 880264 www.portisaachotel.com

Harbours of Interest...

Port Quin.
A hamlet with few cottages on an inlet, pebble beach and C19 folly, Doyden Castle (NT). Invigorating clifftop walks. (G6)

Portgaverne.
C19 pilchard fishing centre and exporter of Delabole slate. Remains of large pilchard cellars. Small hotel ideal for afternoon tea. (J6))

ROCK

Why, Oh Why do the chattering classes continue to come here in droves? It is an unspectacular village with one building of note - the Sailing Club. Yet, despite some fine domestic houses there are surely more beautiful spots in Cornwall? Its popularity may be because of the close proximity to the surf breaks of Polzeath and the gastronomic excesses of Padstow. The Hooray Henries who take over in late June when schools are out have had a bad press of late. Their unruly behaviour has woken the local, sleepy police force to be on their mettle. One day the rich and famous will tire of this place, move on and the families who have had second homes here for four or five generations (like Betjeman) will be left in peace. I wonder. So many have taken advantage of the crazy land prices that they have sold off the bottom of their gardens for development of yet more over-priced properties. Will it never end?

Daymer Bay

1259 Walter de Bronescombe, Bishop of Exeter dedicates 19 parish churches

1256 Glasney College is made the centre of ecclesiastical scholarship.

67

Follow the road through the village with the sea on your left and park at the end of the lane. Walking back, you have a couple of eateries to choose from. Art Galleries in village. L'Estuaire Restaurant is recommended. At nearby Trebetherick the new swish development, St Moritz Hotel. (F8)

TINTAGEL

One long street peopled with gift shops and tearooms. The village remains a popular destination still associated with Arthurian legend, as

The Old Post Office, Tintagel jh/nt

Tintagel

inspired by Geoffrey of Monmouth in the C12, and later by Tennyson's 'The Idylls of the King'. Enhanced by the castle ruins and the wild and rugged coast, King Arthur's mythological past lives on. Summer Carnival. (M2) www.tintagelweb.co.uk

Special Places to Visit in Tintagel...

King Arthur's Great Hall & Hall of Chivalry. A magnificent hall built in memory of King Arthur and his Knights, using 50 types of Cornish stone and 70 stained glass windows. The Arthurian Experience tells the story of Arthur and his Knights. Dogs welcomed. Open daily, summer 10-5, winter 11-dusk. (M2) www.kingarthursgreathalls.com

The Old Post Office (NT). A miniature C14 manor house used in the C19 as a Post Office. Open daily mid Mar to Oct 11-5.30 (4 in Oct). (M2) 01840 770024 www.nationaltrust.org.uk

Stone Circle Sculpture Studio, Fore St. Working studio and gallery of Sonjia Tremain whose work reflects archaeology and shamanism. Open daily 10-5. (M2) www.stonecirclessculpture.co.uk

Tintagel Castle (EH). An early Celtic settlement 350-800 AD, later developed into an island fortress by the Earls of Cornwall in C12 and C13s. Fragments of the great hall c.1250, and the gate and walls survive. The wild and windswept coast married with the romantic legends of King Arthur and encouraged by Geoffrey of Monmouth and Tennyson's Idyll (although doubted by scholars) provide an atmosphere of mystery and wonder. Open as English Heritage times. (L2) www.english-heritage.org.uk/tintagel

Tintagel Church. Norman origins in isolated cliff-top position. Sailors' graves. Rood Screen, bench ends and monument. (L2)

Toy Museum, Fore St. Step back in time through three generations of toys. Over 1,000 exhibits. Collectors' shop. Open daily 10-5. (M2) www.tintageltoymuseum.co.uk

Trebarwith Strand

1280 The Mappa Mundi depicts Cornwall as one of the 4 constituent parts of Britain

1305 The Stannary Charter decrees that Cornish tin must be administered

Special Places to Visit outside Tintagel...

Slate Quarry. 1 1/2 mile circumference at depth of 500ft, 375 million years of geological history. Worked continuously since the C16, and possibly by the Romans. Viewing platform and showroom open M-F 8-4.30. (M4) www.delaboleslate.co.uk

Where to Stay...

Mill House Inn, Trebarwith Strand. A welcome retreat tucked away in a secluded coastal valley, a short distance from one of Cornwall's finest beaches. A working mill until the 1930s, the hotel is a charming building made cosy with comfy bedrooms, wood fires and flagstone floors. (L3) 01840 770200 www.themillhouseinn.co.uk

Ancient Cornwall...

Tregeare Rounds. 500ft diameter banks and ditches used as cattle enclosure. Strategically unsound. (F9)

WADEBRIDGE

A busy and good-feel market town that has seen much recent development; new shops, eateries and galleries have brought a buzz and liveliness to this old, sleepy town, and venue for the Royal Cornwall Show in June. Magnificent C15 bridge with 17 arches. Superb views from the New Bridge on the A39. Mid-point for cycling the Camel Trail. Cinema. E/C W. (H10) www.visitwadebridge.com www.royalcornwallshow.org

Poley Bridge, Camel Trail

Camel Trail. Eleven-mile trail from Bodmin to Padstow; suitable for jogging, walking, cycling and birdwatching. Cycle hire in Padstow and Wadebridge. (E9)

Arts & Crafts in Wadebridge...

Chase Art Gallery, The Platt. Two galleries (in town, and by Camel Trail) display original paintings, pottery, sculpture and jewellery. Open M-Sa 9.30-5.30. (H10) www.chaseart.fsnet.co.uk

Tristan's Gallery, 49 Molesworth St. Fine Art photographic galler: Nudes, Landscapes, Seascapes and Still Life. Open M-Sa 10-4. (H10) www.tristansgallery.com

Outside Wadebridge...

Eglos Pottery, Egloshayle. Handmade stoneware and porcelain pieces by Penny McBreen with images of fish, lizards and flowers. Studio and showroom open daily. (J10)

Yvonne Arlott Studio. Unique traditional and contemporary artwork created from a mixture of turning and carving techniques. Open daily. (J10) 01208 832315

Wave 7 Studio Gallery. Enthusiastic new gallery displaying a fine mix of arts and crafts. Open daily Tu-Su from 10.30. (H7) www.wave7gallery.co.uk

Wood Design. Stephen Roberts makes made-to-order custom pieces of contemporary furniture. Showroom open daily from 10. (J10)

Where to Stay...

Cornish Tippi Holidays, Tregeare. Something different. Hire a traditional North American tent amidst a haven of birdsong, wild flowers, buzzards and rabbits. No cars on site. Warden on hand. (L6) 01208 880781 www.cornish-tipi-holidays.co.uk

Longcross Hotel & Victorian Garden. 2 1/2 acres: lake, maze-walkway, herbaceous plants, cream teas. Plant sales. Disabled facilities. Large decking area for al fresco dining. Open daily 11-dusk. (H6) www.longcrosshotel.co.uk

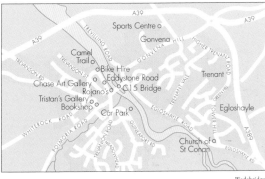

Wadebridge

Ancient Cornwall...

Harlyn Bay - Ancient Burial Ground. Iron Age cemetery discovered in 1900. Well preserved cists and skeletons unearthed. (C8)

Pawton Quoit. Massive damaged megalithic chamber 7.5ft X 3.5ft. (J1)

Rumps Point. Ramparts and ditches visible. Huts discovered. (E5)

Tregeare Rounds. 500ft diameter banks and ditches used as cattle enclosure. Strategically unsound. (K6)

Churches of Interest...

Little Petherick Church. Quaint C14 church in wooded valley. Developed by the Tractarian, Molesworth family into an Anglo-Catholic centre of worship. (D10)

Minster Church. The mother church of Boscastle overlooks a wooded valley and the sea. Several monuments. (B9)

St Endellion Church. In excellent condition in solitary hill-top position which thankfully enabled it to avoid the Reformation. Norman font. Famous music festival. Exquisite detail on monument. (H7)

St Kew Church. Fine C15 interior with wagon roofing and a collection of magnificent stained glass windows that tell the story of Christ's Passion. (K8)

St Mawgan-In-Pydar Church. Large with C13 nave and Arundell arms within the tall Rood Screen and family brasses. C15 Bench Ends. (D3)

St Enodoc Church. C13 origins with a crooked spire. It's recently hosted the grave of Sir John Betjeman, poet and lover of North Cornwall. This church lay hidden beneath the dunes until it was dug out in 1863. (E7)

St Enodoc Church

Special Family Places to Visit...

Neddi Donkey Sanctuary. Feed and groom the animals. Coffee shop. Bouncy castle. Open daily Apr-Oct 10-5. (K8)

Old Macdonalds Farm. Small farm park, especially for young children. Pet the animals, bottle feed lambs, pony rides, train rides, trampolines, crazy golf, cafe, camping. Open daily East-Sept 10-6. (B10) 01841 540829. www.oldmacdonalds.co.uk

Porteath Bee Centre. Living honeybee exhibition behind glass. Honey products for sale and cream teas. Pooh Corner for kids. Shop open daily all year 10.30-4.30. Exhibition East-Oct M-Sa. (G6) www.porteathbeecentre.co.uk

Gardens to Visit...

Japanese Garden & Bonsai Nursery. Set in a sheltered valley. Features Water, Stroll and Zen gardens. Woodland garden. Open daily from 10-6. (D3) www.thebonsainursery.com

St Kew Church

1322   Edward III appoints Piers Gaveston to be the Earl of Cornwall which drives the Cornish gentry to support the Earl of Lancaster to rebel against the king

1338   Edward III, the Black Prince creates the first Duke of Cornwall, a title bestowed on the first-born son of the Monarch

St Enodoc Bar & Restaurant ss

Where to Stay...

Mesmear, St Minver. Three chic, boutique-style barns are available to rent for holidays and short breaks. Ideal for parties of up to 10, 4 and 4. Swimming pool. Private cook. (G7) 01208 869731 www.mesmear.co.uk

Molesworth Manor, Little Petherick. Former Rectory close to Padstow offers spacious B & B accommodation. Three Living Rooms. Continental breakfast (no fatty fry-ups). No dogs. (E10) 01841 540292 www.molesworthmanor.co.uk

Polrode Mill Cottage, Allen Valley. Rustic charm exudes throughout this C17 cottage set amidst the beautiful Allen Valley with low ceilings, beams, flagstone floors and open fires, plus luxurious bathrooms. An added bonus is that your host is a mad keen chef and serves up delicious suppers. (M7) 01208 850203 www.polrodemillcottage.co.uk

Porteath Barn, St Minver. This is a quite delightful conversion of two barns into an H-shaped dwelling. Add your hosts' impeccable taste, a sprinkling of light and humorous conversation, and a garden-valley with endless views and private path to the beach, and you have elegant, old-style luxury B&B. (G6) 01208 863605

St Moritz Hotel, Trebetherick. Spanking new hotel, apartment and spa complex provides all the amenities you would expect from such a venture: gym, indoor pool, saunas etc., bar, games room and more. (E7) 01208 862242 www.stmoritzhotel.co.uk

Special Places to Eat, Drink & Be Merry...

Saltwater, Polzeath. Overlooks the beach in enviable position. Opens for late breakfast/brunch at 10. Al fresco lunches and evening meals. Style more bistro than restaurant. Proudly serves local produce where possible. Open daily in season. (E6) 01208 862333

Maltsters Arms. Pretty pub overlooking village green. Customised Sharps beers. Log fires. Restaurant serves fresh fish, local ice creams. (H8) 01208 812473

Mowhay Café & Restaurant, Trebetherick. Great place to stop for coffee, lunch or evening meal. Always interesting arts and crafts for sale. Open daily in season. (E7) 01208 863660

Rojano's, Eddystone Rd, Wadebridge. Spacious and light with cool ambience. Pizzas and pasta (takeaway). Also in Padstow. (H10)

St Enodoc Bar & Restaurant. Family-friendly hotel noted for its great location and superb cuisine. Look out for the Special Breaks. (E8) 01208 863394 www.enodoc-hotel.co.uk

St Kew Inn. Hidden away down narrow lanes. Dine in the RH rooms if you can. Large garden. Specials board - try the fish or steaks. (K8)

L'Estuaire, Rock Road. French chef blends the subtlety and nuance of French flavours with the wonders of local produce to near culinary perfection. Great art covers the white walls. Open all year; Lunch 12.30-2, Dinner 7-9.30 W-Su. (F8) 01208 862622 www.l'estuairerestaurant.com

The Waterfront, Beach Road, Polzeath. First floor bar and café has an extended decking area and overlooks the beach. Gets very busy so arrive early. Full range of lagers. Bar food. Open for breakfast from 9 am. (E6) 01208 869655 www.waterfrontconrwall.co.uk

L'Estuaire ss

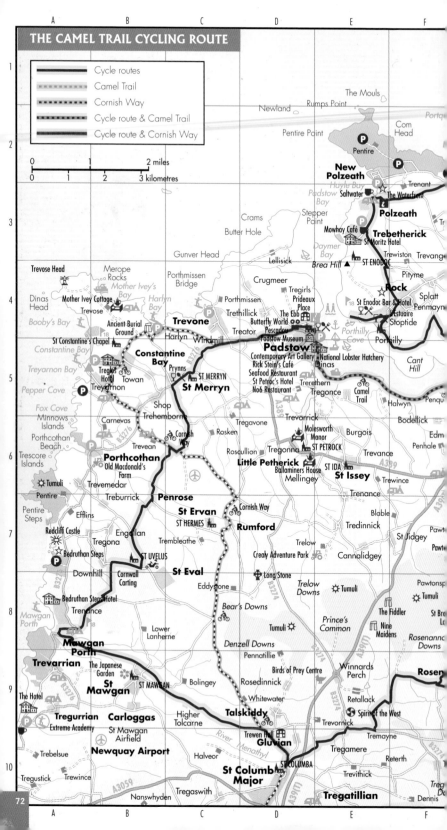

THE CAMEL TRAIL CYCLING ROUTE

Cycle routes
Camel Trail
Cornish Way
Cycle route & Camel Trail
Cycle route & Cornish Way

0   1   2 miles
0   1   2   3 kilometres

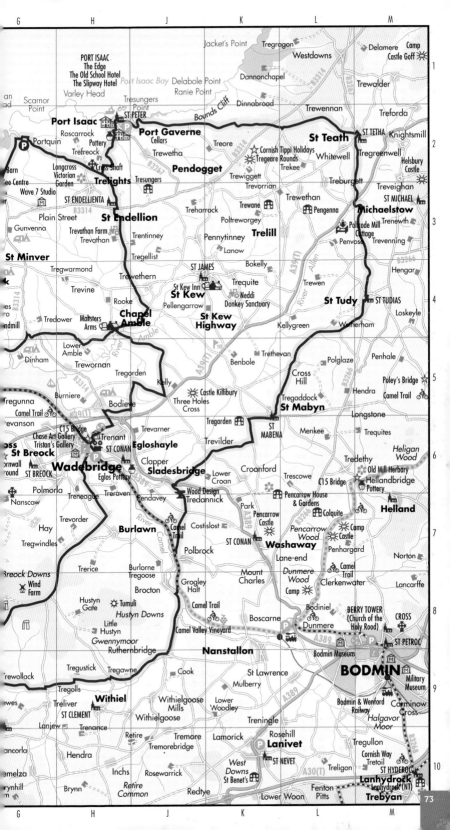

RNLI Lifeboat Station, Trevose Head

to Port Isaac. Choice of strenuous coastal or gentler inland route as far as Port Quin. For inland route: from Pine Haven follow the path for a half mile, then it turns westwards, passing Roscarrock Farm, south of Reedy Cliff to Port Quin, a tiny hamlet, mostly owned by the National Trust. On the headland beyond stands Doyden Castle, a Gothic folly built as a pleasure house and drinking den in C19. Below are black fearsome rocks stained with green. The path west passes rocky-sandy surfing coves of Epphaven and Lundy, and the dramatic collapsed sea cave of Lundy Hole, before heading out to the headlands of The Rumps (with remains of Iron Age cliff castle) and Pentire. Now the path follows the Camel estuary, past Polzeath and Daymer Bay and across the dunes to ferry at Rock for crossing the Camel to Padstow. What follows is a coastline dotted with superb sandy beaches and pounded by mighty Atlantic rollers but best appreciated out of season. Splendid views at Stepper Point, then on past caves and sheer cliffs at Butter Hole and Pepper Hole. Passing by the surf beaches of Trevone and Harlyn Bay, then to overlook the turquoise waters of Mothey Ivey's Bay, passing the new Lifeboat Station. The path continues to hugs the coastline past camping sites and beaches ideal for a quick dip, or if you have a board to hand, a surf. The coastline is peppered with stacks and islands and none more spectacular than at Bedruthan Steps just below Park Head.

Coastal Footpath...

Boscastle to Park Head Approx. 46 miles. The cliff walk to Tintagel along springy turf with spectacular views seaward to jagged rocks is quite superb. Worth a diversion inland to visit Rocky Valley, and St Nectan's Kieve, a 60 ft waterfall, and ancient hermitage. Return to the coast path; offshore Lye Rock was renowned as a puffin colony; now the cliffs are nesting sites for fulmars, guillemots, razorbills and shags. The landscape is wild and remote, a place of legends, and the romantic setting for the C13 Tintagel Castle and the mass of older remains on Tintagel Island. On leaving the castle ruins, the path climbs sharply to the cliff top church of St Materiana, guardian of many shipwrecked sailors. Along Glebe Cliff

past numerous old slate quarries to Trebarwith Strand, a lovely beach to freshen up before the switchback path

Bedruthan Steps

1346   Cornish archers distinguish themselves with their Long Bows at the Battle of Crecy

1347   The "Gallants of Fowey", all 777 of them, fight at the siege of Calais

Treyarnon Bay

Beaches and Surfing...

Hayle Bay, New Polzeath.
Wonderfully spacious family beach, S-B hire/P/WC/cafe/access. Surfing - Crowded and popular beach break. Picks up most swell. RH wave off Pentire Point produces big swells. (E6)

Daymer Bay. Sheltered with firm golden sands, dunes and bathing safest at HT. WC/P. (E7)

Porthilly Cove, Rock.
Spacious sands, ferry to Padstow, access/WC/cafe. (E8)

Padstow, St Georges Cove.
Sheltered inlet, 10 minute walk from town. (E7)

Padstow, Harbour Cove.
Spacious sandy cove 20 minutes walk from town. (E7)

Trevone Bay. Sands, rock pools, Round Hole - collapsed cave. WC/LG/cafe. (C8)

Harlyn Bay.
Firm sands sheltered from south westerlies. WC/P/LG/Inn/café. Surfing - Popular beach with strong SW winds and big swells. Can be fast and hollow at all stages of tide. Best with incoming tide. (C8)

Mother Ivey's Bay.
Private beach with access from the caravan park. Effervescent, turquoise sea. Spacious sands at LT. (B8)

Booby's Bay.
Spacious sands, swirling currents, HZ bathing, rock pools at LT,

access/P/LG. Surfing - Good R reef break from low to mid tide. Strong rips, for the experienced only. (B8)

Constantine Bay. Spacious sands, swirling currents, HZ bathing, rock

pools at LT, access/P/LG. Surfing - One of the best swell magnets. In the middle are good Rs and Ls. At S end break L off the reef. (B9)

Treyarnon Bay. Sheltered, popular family beach, bathing is HZ near rocks/access/WC/LG/P. Surfing - Popular beach. Good at mid to HT. Various peaks. LH wave for experienced with breaks off reef at LT. (B9)

Trethias, Pepper Cover & Fox Cove. Access by foot to small inlet with sandy patches. (A9)

Porthcothan.
Sandy bay, bathing HZ at LT. P/WC. Surfing - L & R beach breaks. (A10)

Bedruthan Steps. One of Cornwall's most dramatic and spectacular beaches. Firm golden sands and massive rocks, and caves. Steep staircase descends to beach. Solar panelled café above beach. NT Info Centre/cafe//WC at P. (C1)

Harlyn Bay

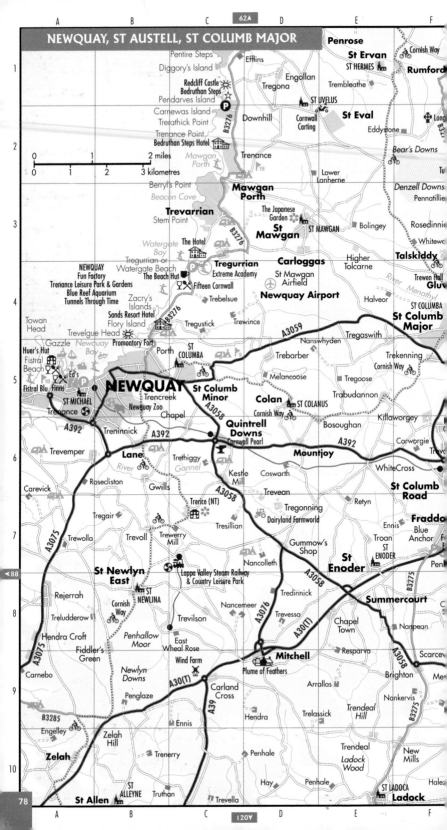

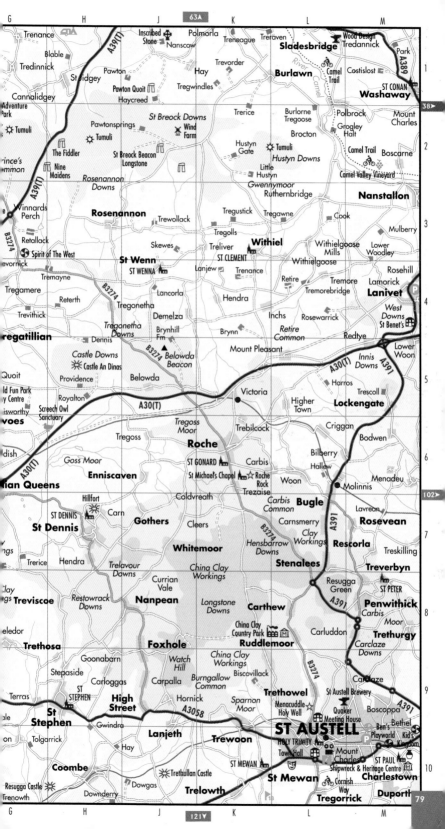

NEWQUAY

Popular seaside resort; the superb beaches give it the edge as Cornwall's foremost surfing centre. Has all the facilities of a modern resort: indoor and outdoor pools, cinema, 2 theatres, fishing/boat trips from Quay. Huer's Hut on headland (an ancient Lookout for pilchards). The recent, mainstream popularity of surfing has encouraged billions of pounds worth of property development. Tacky, old hotels and guesthouses are being pulled down to make way for luxurious apartments. The area continues to be surrounded by countless campsites, some very good ones. The town still gets its fare share of stag weekenders but it is slowly dawning on those with the clout that the only way forward is to go up-market, and to provide a professional and dedicated service. Carnival week - End May/early June. (B5) www.newquayguide.co.uk www.newquay.com www.visitnewquaycornwall.co.uk www.surfnewquay.co.uk

Where to Eat, Drink & Be Merry...

Ed's, The Edwardian Hotel, 3-7 Island Crescent. Laid back unpretentious restaurant offering well prepared food for catholic tastes. Great puds. (B5) 01637 874087

Finns Restaurant, South Quay Hill. Overlooks the harbour. Fish is the speciality (and possibly supplied by local fisherman, just off the boats). Open from 10.30 am. (B5) 01637 874062 www.finns2go.com

Fistral Blu, Fistral Beach. In superb position overlooking the beach. Two restaurants (bistro and formal) produce ever-changing menus using local produce. (A5) 01637 878782 www.fistral-blu.co.uk

Where to Stay & Relax (with kids)...

Bedruthan Steps Hotel. One of Cornwall's great family hotels set high on the cliff's edge overlooking Mawgan Porth beach. Awarded a Green Tourism Gold Award. It uses solar panels and light sensors, helps clean the local beach and uses local

Fistral Blu

suppliers. (C2) 01637 860555 www.bedruthanstepshotel.co.uk

Sands Resort Hotel. Family/spa hotel offering modern facilities with many sporting options, spacious suites, health and beauty centre and children's clubs. (B4) 01637 872864 www.sandsresort.co.uk

The Hotel, Watergate Bay. Family-style hotel overlooking the beach with separate restaurant. The Brasserie is yet another destination for foodies to unleash their waistlines. (C3) 01637 860543 www.watergatebay.co.uk

What to Visit in Newquay...

Blue Reef Aquarium. Overlooking one of England's most popular surfing beaches - houses the creatures which live beneath those crashing waves! Journey through the wonderful underwater worlds from the Cornish coastline to the undersea gardens of the Mediterranean. Café/gift shop. Open daily, 10-5. (B5) www.bluereefaquarium.co.uk

Newquay Fun Factory, 1 St Georges Road. Adventure play centre for children, 2 to 12 years old. Coffee shop. Open daily Jul-Aug 10-9, Sept-Jul 10-6. (B5)

Newquay Zoo. Experience the wildlife amongst the exotic lakeside gardens live 100s of animals from around the world. Highlights are feeding times and animal encounters. Cafe. Open daily Apr-Sept 9.30-6, Oct-Mar 10-5. (B5) 01637 8733342 www.newquayzoo.co.uk

Newquay Zoo ss

Trerice nt

1351 Tin production drops by 80% due to bubonic plague · 1400-1500 Intense church building programme across the county

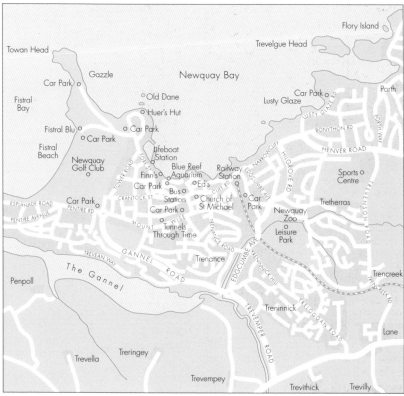

Flory Island

Trevelgue Head

Towan Head

Gazzle

Newquay Bay

Car Park

Old Dane

Car Park

Porth

Lusty Glaze

Fistral
Bay

Huer's Hut

LUSTY GLAZE RD

BONYTHON RD

NORTH WAY

Fistral Blu

Car Park

Car Park

HENVER ROAD

Fistral
Beach

Newquay
Golf Club

Lifeboat
Station

Sports
Centre

TOWER ROAD

Finn's

Blue Reef
Aquarium

Railway
Station

NARROWCLIFF

EDGCUMBE AVE

HILGROVE RD

TREVENSON ROAD

Car Park

Ed's

Car Park
Station

Bus
Station

CLIFF RD

Car
Park

Tretherras

CRANTOCK ST

Church of
St Michael

ESPLANADE ROAD

Car Park

PENTIRE RD

Car Park

Newquay
Zoo

PENTIRE AVENUE

MOUNT WISE

Tunnels
Through Time

Leisure
Park

TRENANCE ROAD

TREVEAN WAY

Trenance

GANNEL ROAD

EDGCUMBE AVE

TRENINNICK HILL

Trencreek

TRELOGGAN ROAD

TRENCREEK RD

Penpoll

The Gannel

Treninnick

TREVEMPER ROAD

Lane

Trevella

Treringey

Trevempey

Trevithick

Trevilly

Newquay

Trenance Leisure Park & Gardens. Multi-leisure park with Zoo, Waterworld, mini railway, tennis courts, crazy golf and boating lake, all set in lakeside gardens. Open daily. (B5) www.restormel.gov.uk

Tunnels Through Time. Life-size figures and scenes capture Cornwall's exciting and legendary past:

smugglers, giants, sea creatures, highwaymen, mermaids. Open East-Oct Su-F & BHs 10-dusk. (B5) www.tunnelsthroughtime.co.uk

Family Fun Places to Visit Outside Newquay...

Cornish Birds Of Prey Centre. Falcons, hawks and owls. Waterfowl

lake. Flights twice daily at 12 & 2.30. Open daily 10-5. (G3) www.cornishbirdsofprey.co.uk

Cornwall Pearl. Exhibition centre/workshop/gemstore selling a complete range of jewellery. Tea house. Champagne & Oyster Bar. Open daily 9.30-5.30. (C6) www.cornwallpearl.co.uk

Crealy Adventure Park. Megaslides, twisters, water slides. Shire horses, farm museum, 120 acres to wander. Restaurant. Open daily East-Oct 10-5. (G1) www.crealy.co.uk

NO.1

Lappa Valley Railway ss

Dairyland Farmworld ss

Extreme Academy, Watergate Bay ss

Dairyland Farmworld.
Britain's Leading Farm Park: Milking Parlour, Cornish Countrylife Museum, 12,000sq.ft indoor play area, Nature Trail & Playground and the county's friendliest farm animals to pat, feed & pet. Open Apr-Oct 10-5. (D7) www.dairylandfarmworld.co.uk

Lappa Valley Railway & Leisure Park.
Steam railway giving a two-mile return trip along a 15" gauge line to a pleasure area with boating lake, crazy golf, maze, two miniature railways, walks and film show. Cafe and gift shop. Open daily East-Oct & 1/2 term 10.30-5.30. (H7)(C7) www.lappavalley.co.uk.

Screech Owl Sanctuary.
Rescue and rehabilitation centre for sick and injured owls. Guided tours. Open daily Apr-Oct 10-6, winter 10-4. (G6)

Spirit Of The West.
American theme park with cowboy museum, gun fights and 'Silver City' ghost tours. Adventure Soft Air (pre-booked only) Open daily East-Sept 10.30-dusk. (G3)

Springfields Fun Park & Pony Centre.
Pets corner, bottle feeding, tractor rides and play areas.

Cafe. Open daily mid-Apr to Sept 10-6, Oct-Nov 10-4. (G5) www.springfieldsponycentre.co.uk

Houses & Vineyards to Visit Outside Newquay...

Trerice (NT). A delightful, small secluded Elizabethan manor house rebuilt in 1571, containing magnificent fireplaces, plaster ceilings, oak and walnut furniture. Small lawn mower museum. Refreshments. Open daily except Sa, 9 Mar-2 Nov 11-5. (C7) 01637 875404 www.nationaltrust.org.uk

Camel Valley Vineyards.
Award-winning wines from 8,000 vines growing on the south-facing valley. Tastings, shop and pre-booked tours at 2.30 and 5 pm W. Open East-Sept M-F 2-5, some W/Es. (M2) 01208 77959 www.camelvalley.com

Special Places to Visit outside St Austell...

China Clay Country Park.
Mining and Heritage Centre. New exhibitions, open air displays, historic nature trails with spectacular views of modern clay pit. Children's challenge trail, licensed cafe and shop. Open daily Mar-Oct 10-5. (K8) 01726 850362 www.chinaclaycountry.co.uk

The Background to the China Clay Industry...

William Cookworthy.
The Plymouth chemist discovered kaolin at Tregonning Hill in 1768, a substance to form the basis of England's porcelain industry. Later, extensive finds were discovered around Hensbarrow Downs close to St Austell which became the centre of the industry. Kaolin is a product of changed granite; the rock is extracted from enormous pits, 300ft deep and 1/2 mile across. Only a portion is used, the rest is piled in great white heaps, hundreds of feet high, like towering snow mountains, the 'Cornish Alps' on which vegetation scarcely grows (unless the Alp is part of the Eden Project).

China Clay Country Park

1437   Fowey's importance as a port attracts emigrants from Brittany, Holland, Ireland and Flanders making up one-third of the population

1470   Edward VI initiates a Royal Commission to stop the piratical seafarers of Fowey, Polruan and Bodinnick from going to sea

ST COLUMB MAJOR

Isolated town of slate-hung houses noted for its superb C14 church. Hurling competition every Shrove Tuesday and Saturday of following week. Also a venue for Cornish wrestling. (F4)

Church of St Columba.

One of Cornwall's major churches that is visible from a great distance. C14 font, bench ends and brasses of the Arundell family. (F4)

Fraddon Pottery. Stoneware pots of Celtic design made from local materials. Tuition on hand. Open Tu-Sa 10-4. (F7)

The Beach Hut

Pub to Visit...

Plume Of Feathers.

Simple, wholesome fare. Cream teas. Large garden. Dogs and children welcome. B & B. (D9) 01872 510387 www.theplume.info

Ancient Cornwall...

Castle An Dinas.

Four massive concentric rings, crowned by 'Roger's Tower', an C18 folly. Iron Age pottery found. (H5)

Roche Rock. C15 St Michael's chapel/hermitage is a granite construction perched on top of jagged rocks affording fine views. (K6)

WATERGATE BAY

Extreme Academy.

It's all beach action: kitesurfing, traction-kiting, buggying and kite-boarding, waveski, mountain boarding, and of course surfing. Tuition and kit hire. Beach Hut Bistro. Annual events. (C3) 01637 860840 www.watergatebay.co.uk

Fifteen Cornwall.

Launched with the "Jamie Oliver' branding - they call it modern, Italian influenced food. Whatever that means. Profits go to the Cornwall Foundation of Promise - assisting young people from difficult backgrounds. Open daily for breakfast, lunch and dinner from 8.30 am. (C3) 01637 861000 www.fifteencornwall.co.uk

The Beach Hut.

Fresh, simply cooked food in a sensational location. What more could you ask for? Fish and burgers feature strongly. Daily Specials. Open from 10.30 (C3) 01637 860877 www.watergatebay.co.uk

Fistral Beach

Watergate Bay

Beaches and Surfing...

Mawgan Porth.
Popular family beach, fine bathing and access/S-B hire/LG/WC/café. Surfing - Good beach break favouring Ls into River Menathyl. Beacon Cove less crowded. (C2)

Watergate Bay. Two miles of glorious sands and access to hotel, surf-canoeing. S-B hire/WC/P/café. Surfing - Good beach break. Popular with Newquay locals. (C3)

The Cribber. Big wave spot for the experienced big wave surfers only. Very dangerous rips. Beware! (B4)

Newquay - Porth Beach.
Flat spacious golden sands. Fine surfing and bathing (avoid river). Blow Hole at Trevelgue Head. P/LG/WC/cafe. (B4)

Newquay - Lusty Glaze.
Sands sheltered by cliffs, access via steps from cliff top, surfing S-B/LG/WC. (A5)

Newquay - Tolcarne Sands.
Suntrap below Narrowcliff Promenade, surfing. (A5)

Newquay - Great Western Beach. Sheltered suntrap, access via path beside Great Western Hotel, surfing S-B hire/LG. (A5)

Newquay - Towan Beach.
Ideal family beach; golden sands, good bathing. Near harbour and town centre. S-B hire/LG/WC. (A5)

Newquay - Fistral Beach.
Surfing Venue for European Championships. Consistent swell across beach with peaky barrelling Ls and Rs. South Fistral breaks L, better at HT. North and Little Fistral break L and R. North breaks at HT. The LT barrels have made the waves at N end a crowd puller. (A5)

Coastal Footpath...

Park Head to Newquay.
Approx 12 miles. Southwards, the tremendous view of the Bedruthan Steps where legend so claims the stacks (or rocks) were used as stepping stones by the Cornish giant, Bedruthan. In summer, you can walk the cliff tops beside carpets of wild flowers for the air is bursting with the scent of burnet rose and gorse. Reaching Stem Point it's possible to walk the sands to Newquay at low tide, alternatively the headland path is easy going.

Huer's Hut, Newquay

Learning to Surf, Fistral Beach

Watergate Bay

Portreath

Chapel Idne, Sennen Cove

Walking the dog

Father and Son   Harlyn Bay

Watergate Bay

Lifeguards   Porth Towan

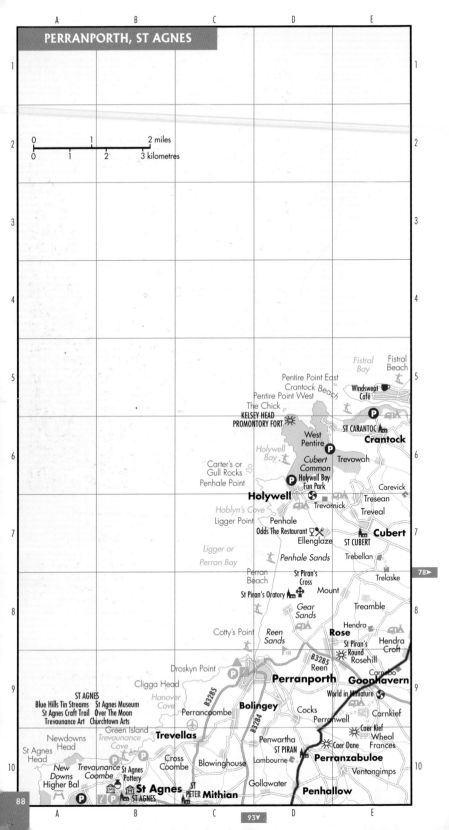

0 1 2 miles
0 1 2 3 kilometres

Fistral Bay
Fistral Beach
Pentire Point East
Crantock Beach
Pentire Point West
The Chick
Windswept Café
KELSEY HEAD PROMONTORY FORT
ST CARANTOC
Crantock
West Pentire
Cubert Common
Trevowah
Carter's or Gull Rocks
Penhale Point
Holywell Bay
Holywell Bay Fun Park
Carevick
Tresean
Treveal
Holywell
Trevornick
Hoblyn's Cove
Ligger Point
Penhale
Odds The Restaurant
Ellenglaze
ST CUBERT
Cubert
Trebellan
Ligger or Perran Bay
Penhale Sands
Trelaske

78►

Perran Beach
St Piran's Cross
Mount
St Piran's Oratory
Gear Sands
Treamble
Cotty's Point
Reen Sands
Rose
Hendra
St Piran's Round
Hendra Croft
Droskyn Point
Rosehill
Reen
Carnebo
B3285
Perranporth
Goonhavern
Cligga Head
Hanover Cove
World in Miniature

ST AGNES
Blue Hills Tin Streams   St Agnes Museum
St Agnes Craft Trail   Over The Moon
Trevaunance Art   Churchtown Arts

Bolingey
Perrancoombe
Cocks
Perranwell
Carnkief
B3285
Green Island
Trevaunance Cove
Trevellas
Penwartha
ST PIRAN
Caer Kief Wheal Frances
Caer Dane
Perranzabuloe
Newdowns Head
St Agnes Head
Cross Coombe
Blowinghouse
Lambourne
Ventongimps
New Downs
Higher Bal
Trevaunance Coombe
St Agnes Pottery
ST AGNES
Gollawater
St Agnes
ST PETER
Mithian
Penhallow

PERRANPORTH

The glorious 3 miles of sand has made this beach into a popular holiday and surfing centre. Now buried beneath the dunes, the St Piran's Oratory, a site reached by a 30-minute walk. The main street is festooned with surf shops and tacky gift shops. The cliffs on the southern edge of the beach have restricted access, are dangerous and must not be climbed due to constant erosion. (D9) www.perraninfo.co.uk

Specal Family Places to Visit...

Holywell Bay Fun Park. All action outdoor fun park - go karts, battle and bumper boats, laser day pigeon shooting, cafe. Open daily East-Oct 10-5. (D6) www.holywellbay.co.uk

World In Miniature. Miniatures of the Taj Mahal to the Great Sphinx. Children's entertainment centre and cafe. Open daily Mar-Oct from 10. (E9) www.miniaturapark.co.uk

Historic Interest...

St Piran's Round.
The ancient amphitheatre where plays were performed in the C17. (E9) www.st-piran.com

ST AGNES

Former mining community, hence the skyline is jagged with disued engine houses. There is an arty ambience to this corner of Cornwall, quite different from other parts, perhaps more akin to Penwith. The birthplace of John Opie in 1761, Cornwall's most famous painter who became a Fellow of the Royal

Perranporth

Academy at 26 and who is buried in St Paul's Cathedral. Family resort and centre for dramatic coastal walks. Museum. Arts and Crafts Trail. (H1) www.stagnes.info www.st-agnes.com

Where to Eat, Drink & Be Merry...

Driftwood Spars Hotel.
C17 Inn built of massive granite blocks and timbers, a stone's throw from the beach, hosts three bars (real ales), mixed menus, a family room, brewery and a carvery. Accommodation. (B10) 01872 552428 www.driftwoodspars.com

Galleries & Museums to Visit...

Blue Hills Tin Streams. The skills of the ancient tinner, from rock to metal. Giftware. Open Apr-Oct M-Sa 10.30-5. (B10) www.bluehillstin.com

Churchtown Arts, 5 Churchtown. C15 building houses arts and crafts gallery. Workshops and studios to view. Open 9.30-5.30, Su 10-5. (B10)

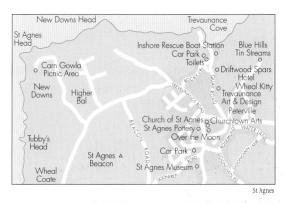

St Agnes

Over The Moon, 6a Churchtown Square. Display of 30 artists' work; large sculpturals and ceramic pieces. Open M-sa 9.30-5.30. (B10)

St Agnes Museum. Tin mining to turtles, fishing to folklore. Open daily East to Sept 10.30-5. (B10)

St Agnes Pottery. Wide range of hand-thrown stoneware, earthenware and porcelain. Open M-Sa 9.30-5. (B10)

Trevaunance Art & Design, Trevaunance Cove. Eight workshops produce work on their premises: paintings, jewellery, shoe making, needlework. Open daily 10.30-5. (B10)

Churches to Visit...

Crantock Church. Religious community established in C5, Norman font, C14 chancel and village stocks. C15 sculpture inside south wall. (E6)

Cubert Church. C14 tower, pulpit made of old bench ends. Original wagon roofs. Attractive slate monuments. (E7)

St Piran's Oratory. Ruins of C7 church and burial place of St Piran the early Celtic missionary. Now buried beneath sand for protection. (D8)

CRANTOCK

Early religious centre and busy port until the Gannel estuary silted up. Village stocks in churchyard, superb beach. (E6)

Special Places to Eat, Drink & Be Merry...

Odds the Restaurant, Holywell Road, Cubert. Grew out of the farmer's (owner) passion for food, wine and organic produce. His beef and lamb are reared here on Ellenglaze. Coastal views. (D7) 01637 830505 www.oddsthereataurant.co.uk

Windswept Café, Fistral Beach (South side). Building a reputation for imaginative cuisine and a location for superb views of the surf. 01637 850793 (E5) www.windsweptcafe.co.uk

Trevaunance Cove

Beaches and Surfing...

Crantock Beach. Spacious golden sands sheltered by Pentire Point. Bathers must avoid The Gannel, and take the pedestrian ferry to Newquay. S-B hire/LG/WC/P. Surfing - long hollow Rs at S end over the sand bank. Protected from N and NE winds. Good Ls when S end has big swell. (E5)

Porth Joke (Polly Joke). 15 minutes walk from P to a suntrap of yellow sand, nestling between low cliffs. Seals laze opposite on the Chick. (D6)

Holywell Bay. Popular family beach, dunes, bathing HZ at LT. Access P/WC/LG/cafe. Surfing - Average beach break. Protected at S end. 10 minute walk from P. (D6)

Penhale / Perran Beach, Perranporth. The ideal family beach, a vast 3 mile stretch of sand with dunes behind, bathing HZ at LT and near Chapel Rock. S-B hire/WC/LG/cafe at southern end. (D7)

Penhale. Surfing - Rs peel off at N end. (D7)

Perranporth. Surfing - Good at mid-tide with long rides. Watch your position with strong tidal flow. Ls break off the headland. (D8)

Trevaunance Cove (St Agnes). Smallish sandy beach, effervescent blue sea and strong currents on ebbing tide. S-B hire/WC/P/LG/café. Surfing - SAS HQ. Yet water quality still poor. Mid-tide produces powerful surf. SW wind unusually creates waves. Can be crowded. (B10)

St Piran

1534   Parliament passes the Act of Succession, sanctioning the annulment of the King's marriage to Catherine of Aragon

1535   Cornwall is considered a separate state in Polydore Vergill's Anglia Historia

Wheal Coates Engine House ab/nt

Coastal footpath...

Newquay To Chapel Porth.
This section is a very busy holiday area with many camping sites and seductive beaches. First cross the Gannel by the tidal bridge or ferry (in summer). Out of season, follow the road to Trevemper (or cross the Trethellan tidal bridge at low water). Worth a detour to visit pretty Crantock. Then easy going around Penhale Point; alternatively, a route via Holywell Bay, Ellenglaze, Mount and Gear. At Penhale Sands one sees the first sign of Cornish tin mining, desolate engine houses and chimneys on hill tops, silhouettes which appear increasingly frequently as one walks westwards. Climbing out of Perranporth the path is relatively easy-going and follows the cliff edge to Trevaunance Cove. From Perranporth the coast is quite magnificent. Around St Agnes Head, a profusion of heather, gorse and sea pinks, and much evidence of tin workings with the ruins of many old mine shafts. Rounding the headlands the views are distant and dramatic, bare cliffs and rolling heathland stretching westwards, the sea below all sparkling blues and turquoise. Scramble up St Agnes Beacon (630ft) for spectacular views west down the coast and inland to Bodmin Moor, and across the peninsula to Falmouth and St Michael's Mount.

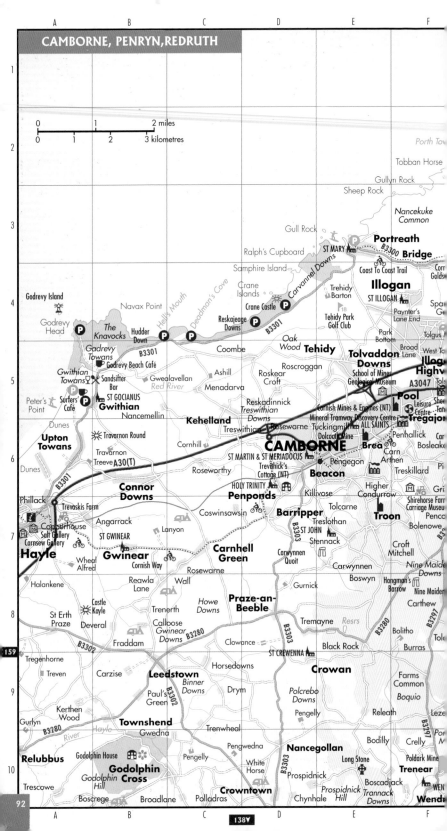

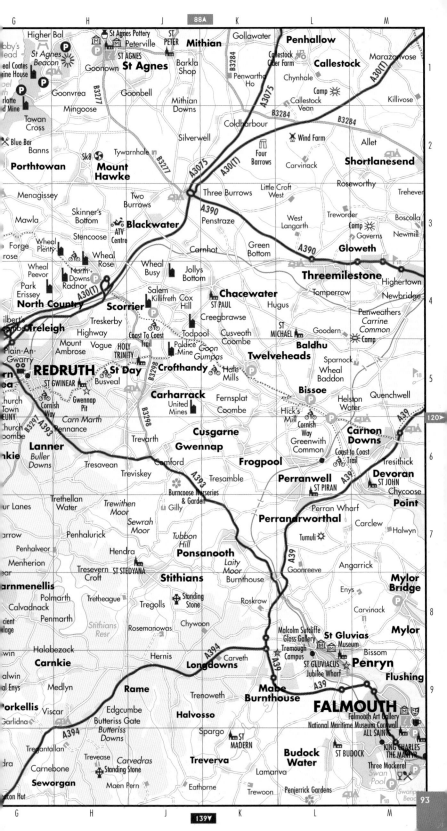

CAMBORNE & REDRUTH

These two towns appear as one. Formerly a mining centre, and the hive of great industry and skill. The birthplace of Richard Trevithick, 1771 - 1833 designer of the high-pressure steam pump which revolutionised mining, enabling water to be pumped out at great depths. Tin mining halted in the 1930s due to imports of cheap Malaysian tin. There are some handsome buildings to be seen and many pretty rows of terraced houses, which if up country, would be in great demand. Cinema. (E6 & H5) www.camborneonline.co.uk

Cornwall's Industrial Heritage - What to See & Visit...

Cornish Mines & Engines (NT). These two great beam engines built in 1892 were used for pumping water and winding men and ore up and down from depths of over 550 metres. Site includes the Industrial Discovery Centre at East Pool. Open daily except Tu & Sa 19 Mar-2 Nov 11-5. (F5) 01209 315027 www.nationaltrust.org.uk

Dolcoath Mine. At 3,500 ft below the surface, Cornwall's deepest mine. Shut down in 1921 following the tin slump after WWI. (E6)

Mineral Tramways Discovery Centre, Penhallick. Cornwall's industrial past revealed by following the Portreath Tramroad, the 11km and the Great Flat Lode trail of 10km. Interpretation Centre. The King Edward Mine. Open all year Tu-Su 10-4, Sa 1-4. (F6)

Poldark Mine. Underground exploration with easy and difficult routes. Suitable for elderly and the fit and fearless. Poldark museum and film. Surface fun for the family. Open East, then all year 10-6. (F10) www.poldark-mine.co.uk

School Of Mines Geological Museum & Art Gallery. Pool. World-wide collection of minerals. Exhibition of local artists. Open daily. (F5)

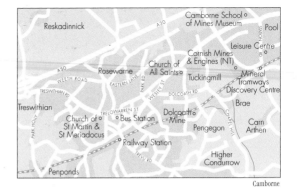

Camborne

South Crofty Mine, Dudnance Lane, Pool. The former tin and copper mine are open for underground trips, so wear old clothes and gum boots. Hard hats provided. Open M-Sa. Pre-book on: 01209 715777. (F5) www.southcrofty.co.uk

Trevithick's Cottage (NT). Richard Trevithick, the Cornish engineer and inventor of the high-pressure steam engine, lived here between 1810-1815. Open Apr-Oct W 2-5, donations welcome. (D6) www.nationaltrust.org.uk

Cylinder Cover and Valve Chest, Taylor's Shaft, Cornish Mines & Engines nt

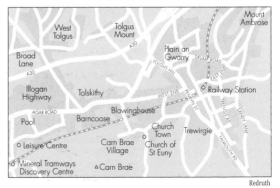

Redruth

1542   Andrew Boorde's First Boke records there are two speeches in Cornwall: naughty Englysshe, and Cornysshe Speche

1549   Edward VI's Act of Uniformity whereby church services are to be held in English, as opposed to Latin, starts the Prayer Book Rebellion

Engine House, Troon

beautiful Victorian and Georgian gardens with splendid Fountain Garden Conservatory, unique range of craft workshops and Museum. Open daily, all year 10.30-4.30. (D1) www.trevarno.co.uk

Mount Hawke - Sk8.
Skateboarding park undercover. Youth Group charity status. Open daily. (H2) 01209 890705 www.sk8m8.com

Shire Horse Farm & Carriage Museum.
Shire and Suffolk Punches. Horse-drawn, agricultural and private vehicles. Open East-Sept M-F, Tu & Th in Oct, 10-6. (F6) 01209 713606

GWENNAP

A district with an abundance of disused mines, engine houses, and old engine tracks from former copper and tin mines.

Gwennap Pit.
Amphitheatre caused by mining subsidence. Landscaped in 1803. Has excellent acoustics, and is known as the Methodist 'Cathedral'. Open all year. John Wesley first preached here in 1762, and in 1773, to a congregation of 32,000. How on earth did they fit in? Annual Methodist Meeting - Spring BHM. Visitor Centre open June-Sept M-F 10-4.30, Sa 10-12.30. (H5)

Special Places to Visit...

Burncoose Nurseries & Garden.
30 acre woodland garden. Also nursery with 3,000 varieties of trees, shrubs and unusual plants. Light refreshments. Open daily 8.30-5 (Su 11-5). (J6) www.burncoose.co.uk

Callestock Cider Farm. 40 varieties of fruit products made, from scrumpies to chutneys. Open all year M-F 9-5, except 25 Dec to mid-Jan. (L1) www.thecornishcyderfarm.co.uk

Godolphin House. Romantic Tudor and Stuart mansion, c.1475. The Godolphin family's courtly ambitions and taste are expressed in the evolving design of the house. Tin mining provided wealth for this family of entrepreneurs, soldiers,

poets and officials. C16 and C17 English furniture. Estate open daily. Conservation work is being undertaken so the house's opening times will be advertised locally. (B10) www.godolphinhouse.com www.nationaltrust.org.uk

Penjerrick Gardens.
Essentially a spring flowering garden of 16 acres: camellias, azaleas, rhododendrons and tree ferns. Magnificent trees, pond gardens, bamboo. Woodland walk. Open Mar-Sept W, F & Su 1.30-4.30. (L10) www.penjerrickgarden.c.uk

Trevarno Estate Gardens & National Museum Of Gardening. An unforgettable gardening experience combining

Where to Stay...

Treglisson, Wheal Alfred Road.
For all lovers of industrial archaeology, why not stay in the former mine owner's house which is a comfortable and relaxed farmhouse B&B. Swimming pool. Adjacent, a small caravan and camping site. (A7) 01736 753141 www.treglisson.co.uk

PORTREATH

Harbour built by Francis Bassett to serve local mines. In 1809 the terminus for one of the country's first railway lines. Many interesting industrial remains. (E3) www.portreathslsc.co.uk

Godrevy Island

Portreath

Gwennap Pit

Jubilee Wharf, Penryn

PENRYN

An attractive granite town at the head of Penryn Creek. Picturesque steep main street and handsome restored Georgian houses. Granted Charter in 1236, and hence a much older town than its more famous neighbour, Falmouth. In the C17, England's busiest port after London. The granite from Penryn's quarries helped to build New Scotland Yard, four London Bridges and the Fastnet Lighthouse. The home of the Tremough Campus, the new University and Art College buildings. Town Fair - Aug BH W/E. (L9)

Places to Visit...

Jubilee Wharf. A triumphant design by Bill Dunster Architects. This is where Cornwall leads the field: a carbon neutral building that is sustainable, holistic, green, and built for the community at large. It incorporates art and craft workshops, flats, a toddler group and Miss Peapod's kitchen café (open Tu-Su from 10) overlooking the estuary. (L9) 01326 374424 www.jubileewharf.co.uk

Malcolm Sutcliffe Glass Gallery, 2 West St. Blown studio glass made on the premises by Malcolm Sutcliffe, plus jewellery, paintings and cards. Open W-F 11-5, Sa 10-1. (L9) 01326 377020 www.malcolm-sutcliffe.co.uk

Penryn Museum.
History of ancient town established in the C13: Neolithic, Medieval Glasney College, trade and victualling, piracy and smuggling, copper and tin mining. Open M-F 10-3.30. (L9) 01326 372158

Where to Eat, Drink & Be Merry...

Blue Bar, Porthtowan.
Surfers' bar attracts all ages. Live bands and discos at weekends. (G2) 01209 890329 www.blue-bar.co.uk

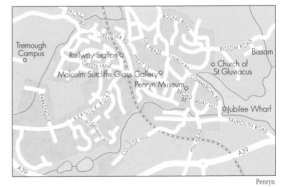

Penryn

1582 The Cornish fleet has grown to 88 ships

1584 The war with Spain determines 5,000 troops to be stationed at St Michael's Mount

First year students' sculptures, Falmouth Art College, Gwithian Beach

Godrevy Beach Café, Godrevy Towans.
Serves breakfast, lunch, dinner. Choose from organic cakes, take-aways and barbeques. Great views of sunsets from the decking area. Open from 10, seven days a week. (A5) 01736 757999

Sandsifter Bar & Restaurant, Gwithian Beach.
Apres-surf fun, pizzas, tapas and live music. (A5) 01736 758457 www.sandsiftergodrevy.co.uk

Trevaskis Farm. PYO fruit. Farm shop. Restaurant. Open daily 10-5. (A7) www.trevaskisfarm.co.uk

Ancient Cornwall...

Carwynen Quoit. Fine specimen, three legs and large capstone. (E7)

Carn Brea. Traces of neolithic settlers. Focus of legends and giants. Site of C15 castle. A 90ft Obelisk built in c.1836 in memory of Lord de Dunstanville, at 783ft, a superb viewpoint. (F6)

Beaches and Surfing...

Chapel Porth.
Spacious sands at LT, but beware of fast-flowing incoming tides along this coast and strong currents, bathing can be HZ. Bass fishing/caves, S-B hire/LG/P/WC. Surfing - Submerged at HT. Powerful surf. (G1)

Porthtowan. Surfing - Fine beach break. HT protected from SW winds. Crowded in summer. (G2)

Portreath. Popular family beach with golden sands, fast HZ incoming tides, caves, S-B hire/LG/P/WC/cafe. Surfing - On beach beginners keep L and surf the beach break. Can be crowded. The harbour's N end produces good breaks in a fair swell. (E3)

Godrevy Towans.
Sand, rocks and dunes. Enter beside Red River. WC/LG/Cafés. (A5)

Gwithian Towans. Surf, dunes and P/WC/LG/cafe. Surfing - Peaks suitable for novices. At HT cut off by rocks. (A5)

Coastal Footpath...

Trevaunance Cove (St Agnes) to Hayle (& St Ives): Approx 30 miles. From Perranporth to Godrevy Point the coast is quite magnificent. Around St Agnes Head, a profusion of heather, gorse and sea pinks, and much evidence of tin workings with the ruins of many old mine shafts. Rounding the headlands the views are distant and dramatic, bare cliffs and rolling heathland stretching westwards, the sea below all sparkling blues and turquoise. Scramble up St Agnes Beacon (630ft) for spectacular views west down the coast inland to Bodmin Moor, and across the peninsula to Falmouth and St Michael's Mount.

From Chapel Porth to Porthtowan The path climbs up over Mulgram Hill past Great Wheal Charlotte. On to Portreath and for much of the way a barbed wire fence on your left marks the perimeter of Nancekuke airfield.

From Portreath to Godrevy Point Along North Cliffs there's superb cliff scenery and invigorating walking. The lonely stretch from Bassett's Cove to the savage Hell's Mouth has been a graveyard of many ships over the centuries; a place of drama, and melancholy, and fierce crashing seas. The path passes inland to Gwithian then returns seaward to follow the edge of the towans (sand dunes) to Hayle. Thereafter it follows the road round the Hayle estuary and returns to the coast for the last stretch into St Ives.

Malcolm Sutcliffe Glass Gallery ss

For Chic Hotels, Culture, Glorious Gardens, Harbours, Shopping, Stylish Living, Watersports, Waterside Pubs & Cafes

This is the affluent heart of Cornwall. The great harbour of Falmouth visited by the Romans and Phoenicians is today a centre of maritime excellence. The magnificent Fal Estuary, home to thousands of sailing craft, is a playground for water sports. Connected by water, Truro lies twelve miles up river and is Cornwall's only Cathedral city. It's busy and attractive with designer shops, flea markets, restaurants and art galleries, and host to a food and drink festival on Lemon Quay in late September.

Across the estuary from Falmouth lies the sedate village of St Mawes and the exquisitely beautiful Roseland Peninsula. Not to be missed is the church at St Just. The coastal footpath is now tamer and the landscape gentler. It passes some fine chic hotels and pretty harbours on its journey towards St Austell and Charlestown. Hereabouts is Eden, visited by many hundreds of thousands. This project has brought prosperity to this area, and has reminded many (who may have forgotten in their search for Mediterranean or Caribbean sun) of the hidden delights of Cornwall. Fowey has benefited too, and here the gastronome is spoilt for choice, for the many sophisticated eating and drinking holes on offer. It is also a fine place to stay. Take a trip up the Rivey Fowey and you will reach Lostwithiel, a small, charming town often overlooked by the traveller in a hurry. Or you may continue eastward along the coast; the delightful fishing harbours of Polperro and Looe await you. Not far away are many great gardens to visit: Caerhays Castle, Heligan, Trelissick and more. Spring is the best time, for on display are the camellias, azaleas, magnolias and rhododendrons.

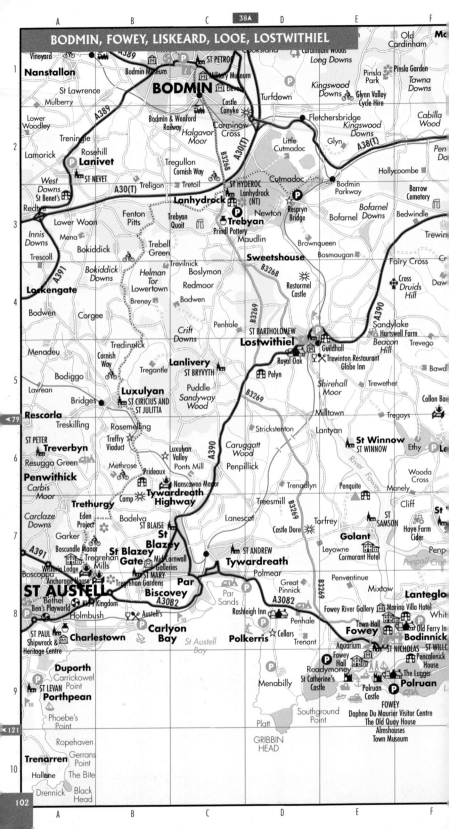

39A

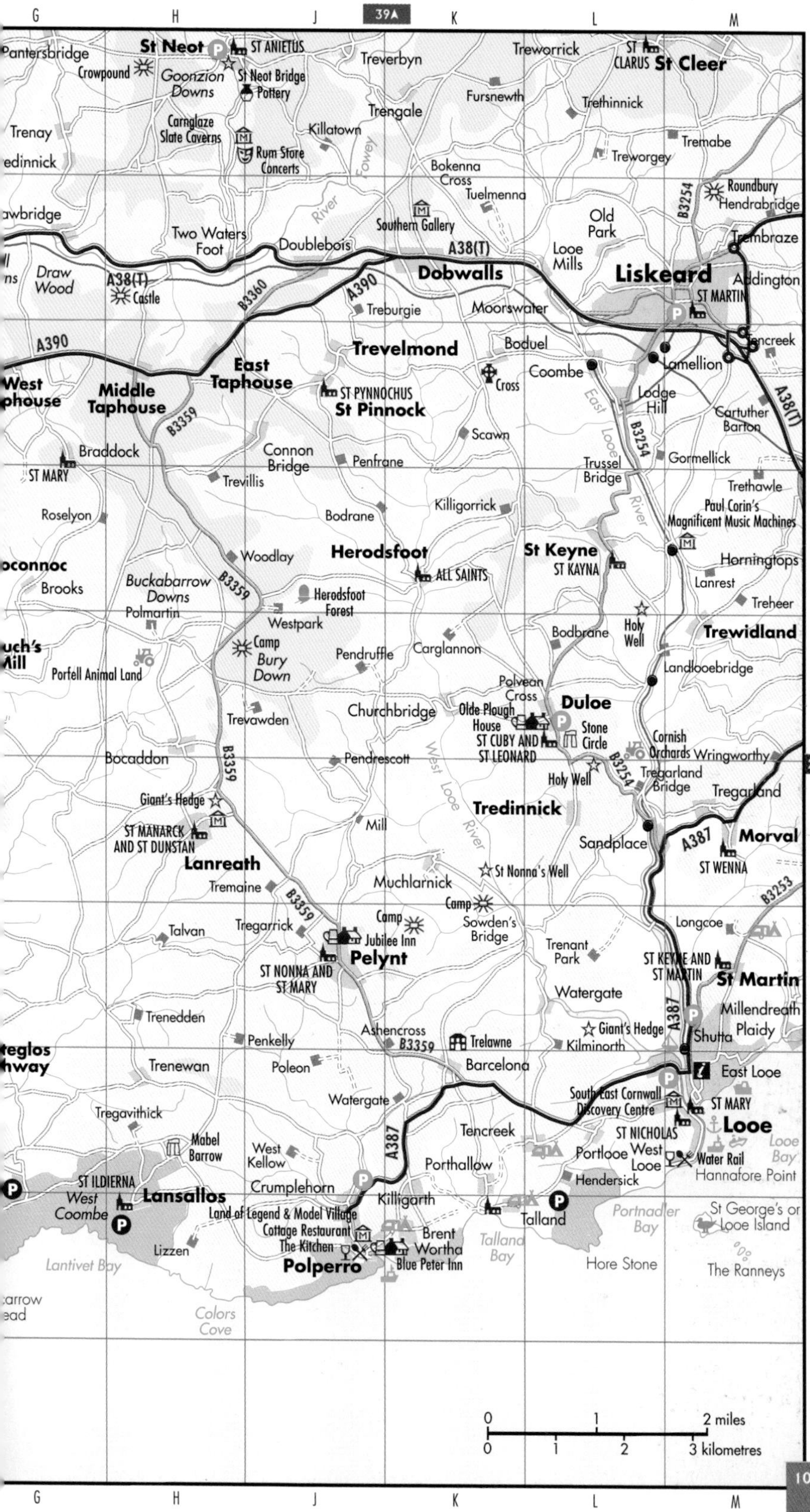
G
H
J
K
L
M
1
2
3
4
5
6
7
8
9
10
Pantersbridge
Crowpound
St Neot
ST ANIETUS
Goonzion Downs
St Neot Bridge Pottery
Carnglaze Slate Caverns
Rum Store Concerts
Trenay
edinnick
awbridge
Treverbyn
Trengale
Killatown
Fowey
River
Southern Gallery
Bokenna Cross
Tuelmenna
Fursnewth
Treworrick
ST CLARUS
St Cleer
Trethinnick
Tremabe
Treworgey
Roundbury
Hendrabridge
B3254
Old Park
Looe Mills
Trembraze
Liskeard
Addington
ST MARTIN
Two Waters Foot
Doublebois
A38(T)
Dobwalls
Draw Wood
Castle
B3360
A390
Treburgie
Moorswater
Tencreek
Lamellion
A390
Trevelmond
Boduel
Coombe
Cross
West Taphouse
Middle Taphouse
East Taphouse
ST PYNNOCHUS
St Pinnock
East Looe
Lodge Hill
Carduther Barton
A38(T)
B3359
Braddock
ST MARY
Connon Bridge
Penfrane
Scawn
Trussel Bridge
B3254
Gormellick
Trethawle
Trevillis
Roselyon
Bodrane
Killigorrick
Paul Corin's Magnificent Music Machines
Woodlay
Herodsfoot
ALL SAINTS
St Keyne
ST KAYNA
River
Horningtops
oconnoc
Brooks
Buckabarrow Downs
B3359
Polmartin
Herodsfoot Forest
Westpark
Lanrest
Treheer
uch's Mill
Porfell Animal Land
Camp
Bury Down
Pendruffle
Carglannon
Bodbrane
Holy Well
Trewidland
Landlooebridge
Polvean Cross
Duloe
Olde Plough House
ST CUBY AND ST LEONARD
Stone Circle
Trevawden
Churchbridge
Cornish Orchards
Wringworthy
Bocaddon
B3359
Pendrescott
West Looe River
Holy Well
B3254
Tregarland Bridge
Tregarland
Giant's Hedge
ST MANARCK AND ST DUNSTAN
Mill
Tredinnick
Sandplace
A387
Morval
ST WENNA
Lanreath
St Nonna's Well
Tremaine
Muchlarnick
B3253
Camp
Sowden's Bridge
Camp
B3359
Talvan
Tregarrick
Jubilee Inn
Pelynt
ST NONNA AND ST MARY
Trenant Park
Longcoe
ST KEYNE AND ST MARTIN
St Martin
Watergate
Millendreath
Trenedden
Penkelly
Ashencross
B3359
Trelawne
Giant's Hedge
A387
Shutta
Plaidy
Kilminorth
teglos hway
Trenewan
Poleon
Barcelona
East Looe
Watergate
South East Cornwall Discovery Centre
ST MARY
Tregavithick
Mabel Barrow
Tencreek
ST NICHOLAS
Looe
Looe Bay
West Kellow
A387
Porthallow
Portlooe
West Looe
Water Rail
Hannafore Point
ST ILDIERNA
West Coombe
Lansallos
Crumplehorn
Killigarth
Hendersick
Talland
Portnadler Bay
St George's or Looe Island
Land of Legend & Model Village
Cottage Restaurant
The Kitchen
Brent
Wortha
Blue Peter Inn
Lizzen
Lantivet Bay
Polperro
Talland Bay
Hore Stone
The Ranneys
arrow ead
Colors Cove
0
1
2 miles
0
1
2
3 kilometres

22

The High Garden, Lanhydrock ejs/nt

BODMIN

The County town of Cornwall is positioned right in the centre of the county just off the busy A30. It is worth a stop-over to explore the interesting museums and the C15 St Petroc, the largest Parish Church in the County. It does not have the chic shops of Truro or the dramatic locations of Falmouth and Penzance. It is a quiet, country town full of history. Witness the historic prison, scene of public executions until 1862, and keeper of the Crown Jewels in WWI. The Information Centre is set in the old Court House where the ghosts and spirits of unlucky souls foundered. A good start-off point for the Camel Trail. Indoor swimming pool. E/C W. (C1)
www.bodminlive.com
www.bodmin.gov.uk

Special Places to Visit...

Bodmin & Wenford Railway, Bodmin General Station.
Standard gauge steam railway. Café at Bodmin and a buffet car on most trains. Open East, Spring BHs and Su & W to end May, then daily June-Sept. Su Tu & W in Oct & Dec Specials. (C2) 01208 73666
www.bodminandwenfordrailway.co.uk

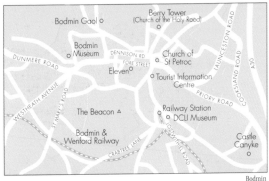

Bodmin

Bodmin & Wenford Railway ss

1588   Spaniards attack and invade Mousehole, Newlyn and Penzance   1588   The Spanish Armada

Bodmin Museum, Mount Folly.
Exhibits of local history, Victorian
kitchen. 'Echoes of Bodmin Moor!'.
Open East-Sept 10.30-4.30,
Oct 11-3. (B1)

Camel Trail. Eleven-mile
trail from Bodmin to Padstow,
suitable for jogging, walking, cycling
and bird watching. Cycle hire in
Padstow and Wadebridge. (A1)
www.sustrans.org.uk

**Duke of Cornwall's Light
Infantry Museum, The Keep.**
Three hundred years of military
history, including weapons, medals,
uniforms, memorabilia and extensive
archive/research facilities. Open
M-F 10-5. (C1) 01208 72810
www.lightinfantry.org.uk/regiments/d
cli/duke_museum.htm

**Eleven, Market House
Arcade, Fore St.** The gallery
exhibits modern, classical and
contemporary paintings, sculpture
and ceramics. Monthly exhibitions.
(C1) 01208 78444

Lanhydrock House (NT).
Cornwall's grandest house was built
in the C17 but following a fire in
1881 was largely rebuilt. It has
superb Victorian kitchens and some
magnificent plaster ceilings depicting
scenes from the Old Testament, and a
Long Gallery 116 feet long. C17
Gatehouse. Fine shrub and formal
gardens. Woodland walks.
Restaurants. Shop. Open daily 15
Mar-2 Nov except M when House
only closed, but open BH Ms 11-5.30
(-5 in Oct), Gardens open all year
10-6. (C3) 01208 265950
www.nationaltrust.org.uk

Prindl Pottery. Japanese inspired
pots; some are of enormous size
and originality, others are simply
shaped in stoneware or porcelain.
Open M-F 10-5, W/Es by appoint.
(C3) 01208 269493
www.prindlpottery.co.uk

St Petroc's Church, Bodmin. In
C6 Cornwall's patron saint, St Petroc,
founded a priory here. Later, in the
C9, a monastery was established, and
in the Middle Ages the town became
an important religious centre. The
present large church was built
mainly in the C15. Norman font,
monuments and Wagon roof. (C1

Charlestown Harbour

CHARLESTOWN

There's a nostalgic atmosphere about
this C18 china clay harbour built by
Charles Rashleigh for the export of
coal, tin and china clay. Home port
for famous tall ships of the Square
Sail Shipyard Company. Diving
centre. Location for many TV/Films,
notably Jane Austen's Persuasion, The
Three Musketeers, The Onedin Line,
Poldark and The Voyage of Charles
Darwin. Pottery. Café/bistro overlooks
the harbour. (A8)

Shipwreck and Heritage Centre.
The largest shipwreck artefact
collection in the UK. Titanic display.
Hands-on rescue equipment and lots
more. Open daily Mar-Oct 10-5. (A8)
www.shipwreckcharlestown.com

FOWEY

Narrow streets and brightly coloured
houses overlook the superb natural
harbour. Fowey is today a chic and
fashionable town populated with
many restaurants and art galleries.

Look out Padstow, you have serious
competition. One of England's
busiest towns in the Middle Ages,
and home of the 'Fowey Gallants',
a bunch of reckless and invincible
pirates who raided French and
Spanish shipping. Still a busy
exporter of China Clay. Fishing
trips and passenger ferry to
Polruan. Royal Regatta & Carnival
week - Aug (2/3 week). (E8)
www.fowey.co.uk
www.foweyharbour.co.uk
www.fowey.com
www.foweyroyalregatta.co.uk

Special Places to Visit...

**Daphne Du Maurier Literary
Centre, 5 South St.**
Explores Foweys literary connections.
Houses the Information Centre. Open
daily, all year. (E8) 01726 833616
www.dumaurier.org

Fowey Aquarium.
Wide collection of marine life
taken from our in-shore waters.
Open daily East-Sept. (E8)

Bodinnick Ferry, Fowey

View of Polruan from Nathan Outlaw's Restaurant

Cormorant Hotel, Golant ss

Fowey River Expeditions. Travel the river upstream by kayak, canoe or motorboat. Stopping off at Golant or Lerryn for lunch. Accompanied by staff and safety boat. Runs from May to early Sept. (E8) 01726 833627 www.foweyriverexpeditions.co.uk

Fowey River Gallery, 38 Fore St. Cornish contemporary art for serious buyers, and plenty of crafts: ceramics, glass, jewellery. Open M-Sa 10-5 (& summer Su). (E8) www.foweyrivergallery.co.uk

Fowey River. Rises on Bodmin Moor, especially beautiful between Lostwithiel and Doublebois - richly wooded riverbanks. Trout and Sea Trout fishing. (E6) www.ukriversguidebook.co.uk/fowey www.foweyriversailing.com

Luxulyan Valley. Wooded ravine overgrown with flowers and fauna. Watered by nearby clay pit. (B6)

Town Museum, Trafalgar Square. Local history and bygones. Open May-Sept M-F 10-5. (E8)

Where to Stay, Eat, Drink & Be Merry...

Cormorant Hotel & Riverview Restaurant, Golant. Just the place to unwind after fretful days in the City or days stuck in traffic jams. The gentle sway of the tidal Fowey River (which this hotel so spectacularly overlooks) will calm and rebuild your nerves. Small, comfortable bedrooms, a restaurant (lunch & dinner) with an award-wining wine list and al fresco seating. Relax, admire the view, Mary Tozer will look after your every need. (E7) 01726 833426 www.cormoranthotels.co.uk

Fowey Hall Hotel & Restaurant. This is a luxurious (Von Essen) hotel very much designed for families with large pockets. Set in a quite superb

Fowey & Polruan

hilltop location overlooking Fowey. It's thus child-friendly and has masses of attractions (and suggestions) on offer. It could be described as an expensive nursery. I loved the children's bright paintings adorning the walls. Dogs (and mothers-in-law) welcome, too. A pity there aren't just 'cheaper' hotels like this one. (E9) 01726 833866 www.foweyhallhotel.co.uk

Marina Villa Hotel & Restaurant Nathan Outlaw. Former summer residence of the Bishops of Truro. Bedrooms with balconies. Now has a mouth-watering restaurant with chef,Nathan Outlaw, of increasing fame. Fish a delight! (E8) 01726 833315 www.themarinahotel.co.uk

Restaurant Nathan Outlaw ss

1601   Richard Carew's survey of Cornwall   1602   On Queen Elizabeth I 's death, the Venetian Ambassador comments that she ruled over five peoples: the English, Cornish, Irish, Scottish and Welsh

107

The King of Prussia, Town Quay.
Excellent pub grub: local fish, burgers with a view to match. Open daily, (E8)
www.kingofprussiafowey.com

Old Ferry Inn, Bodinnick.
Its position overlooking the Fowey River brings in a lot of trade, especially in summer. Three cosy rooms with nautical objects and old photos. Accommodation. Free house. (F8) 01726 870237
www.oldferryinn.co.uk

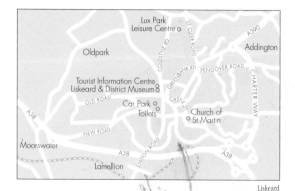

Liskeard

Luxulyan Valley ac

Pencalenick House, Lanteglos-By-Fowey.
Perfect for that one-off, once-in-a-lifetime house party. This is luxury, par excellence - for you get 5 Star treatment: luxurious bedrooms, your own chef and full time house manager. Sleeps up to 16. Minimum stay: three nights. (F8) 0207 74 76858
www.pencalenickhouse.com

The Old Quay House Hotel, 28 Fore St.
Set in one of the most beautiful estuaries in Cornwall with a resplendent waterside location offering stylish accommodation which is chic, welcoming and relaxed. Award-winning restaurant (2AA Rosettes and a Remy Award). Open all year. (E8) 01726 833302
www.theoldquayhouse.com

LISKEARD

Once an important Stannary Town surrounded by prosperous copper mines. Today, it's a busy market town for the agricultural community with attractive Georgian and Victorian cottages. Impressive large C15 Church, carnival - June (3rd week). Fat stock show - Nov (2nd week). (M2) www.liskeard.gov.uk

Where to Eat, Drink & Be Merry...

Olde Plough House, Duloe.
A warm welcome awaits you in this neat and well laid out hostelry. Interesting mixture of seating. Food from local suppliers - delicious sausages and hams. Fine ales. Dogs welcome (Jack Russells rejoice). (L5)

The Old Quay House Hotel ss

1608   The death of Sir Francis Godolphin, the man who did so much for Cornish mining and who added £1,000 per year to the Queen's coffers

1620   Sir Richard Robartes, Truro tin and wool merchant buys Lanhydrock Estate

109

Bass, Pengellys Fishmongers, East Looe

LOOE

An active Cornish fishing village. The busy quay, tidal harbour and the web of narrow streets provide an unforgettable tableaux of Cornish life. Today, a popular embarkation point for deep-sea fishing. It is worth wandering through the narrow streets on the East side. Perhaps, too many gift shops selling unnecessary junk. You can forget all this and walk the Looe Valley Line, where a number of way-marked trails lead off along 8 miles of railway track from Looe to Liskeard - leaflets available from the local Information Centres. Fish Market on East Looe Quay, Sub-Aqua club, boat trips. (M8) www.looe.org www.looedirectory.co.uk

South East Cornwall Discovery Centre. The gateway to exploring the beauty, culture and wildlife of South East Cornwall. Open Mar-Dec; East, then May-Sept daily 10-6. Other times M-F 10-4, Su 11-3. (L8) www.caradon.gov.uk

Where to Eat, Drink & Be Merry...

Water Rail, Lower Market St. Retro-style dining rooms offering seafood with rich sauces. Try the Specials. (M8) 01503 262314

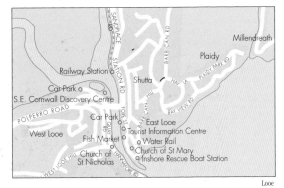

Looe

1642-46   English Civil War

1643   Cornish hero Sir Bevil Grenville is killed at the Battle of Lansdown, near Bath fighting for the Royalists

LOSTWITHIEL

A charming town, and a great favourite of mine, often overlooked because travellers fail to drive off the main road into the side streets. It became the C13 capital of Cornwall and as the Stannary Court oversaw the administration of the medieval tin industry. The town has many beautiful buildings - the C13 Duchy Palace on Quay Street, C13 Parish Church with splendid spire, C17 and C18 Georgian houses on Fore Street and the C18 Guildhall. Also, not to be missed, the important early C20 corrugated iron, army drill hall. C13 bridge. Boat trips to and from Fowey along the beautiful Fowey Valley. May Making ceremony, 'Beating the Bounds' - May (1st Monday) Carnival week - late July. E/C W. (D5)
www.lostwithiel.org.uk
www.lostwithieltic.org.uk

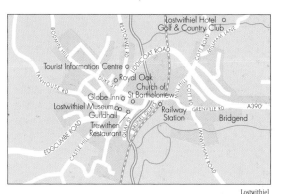
Lostwithiel

Where to Eat, Drink & Be Merry...

Trewithen Restaurant, Fore Street. Intimate restaurant building a reputation. Roast peppers glazed with Cornish Brie, or King Scallops drizzled with black pudding, and that's just for Starters. Open M-Sa 7-9.30 (last orders), and Tu-Sa for lunch 12-2pm. (D5) 01208 872373

Try the Globe Inn or the Royal Oak, two pubs offering good pub grub and a wide selection of ales.

Where to Stay...

Collon Barton, Lerryn. Fortress-like country house, high on a hill (like a lonely goatsherd, lahee-ho, lay-hee-ho lay he he...) overlooks a pastoral landscape of pastures green and emerald. Family portraits of the Grenville Fortescues adorn the walls, the furnishings and bedrooms are comfortable and understated. Ideal centre for circular walks, canoeing and biking (from the village). (F5) 01208 872908

Hartswell Farm, Lostwithiel. Conveniently situated just outside the ancient capital of Cornwall. This C17 farmhouse has witnessed Civil War battles and much more. Today, a Twitcher's delight with farm trail, birds (feathered variety) galore and rare breeds. (E4) 01208 873419

Special Places to Visit...

Golitha Falls. Trail starts at Redgate Bridge. Follows riverbank and profusion of wild flowers to tranquil resting place. (K1) 01872 265710 www.english-nature.org.uk

Lostwithiel Church. Unusual octagonal spire and tower. Norman, octagonal font. C15 monuments. Clerestory windows. (D5)

Lostwithiel Church

Restormel Castle (EH). A model of military architecture, classically symmetrical with circular moat, and strategically positioned allowing breathtaking views across the River Fowey. Built c.1100 with C13 additions. Owned by Simon de Montfort and Richard, Earl of Cornwall. Open daily Apr-Oct 10-6 (5 in Oct). (D4)

Restormel Castle

Lostwithiel

Polperro Reflections

POLPERRO

Exquisitely picturesque in a dramatically steep valley where a timeless ambience pervades the narrow streets, pastel-shaded cottages and busy fishing harbour. Tea/gift shops aplenty. Fishing trips. Regatta - mid July. Park above the village. (J9) www.polpero.org

Special Places to Visit...

Ebenezer Gallery, The Coombes. East Cornwall Society of Artists members exhibit here, plus two floors of paintings and ceramics. Open May-Oct. (J9)

Land of Legend and Model Village. Replica of Polperro built locally with animated display of Cornwall's history and legends. Open daily East-Oct 10.30-6 (9 high season). (J9)

Where to Eat, Drink & Be Merry...

Blue Peter Inn. You can't miss it, and you won't want to. It overlooks the harbour and is an ideal spot to succour fine ales, tasty sandwiches and a most pleasing view. Music nights: jazz to rock. (K9) 01503 272743

Cottage Restaurant. Cosy and snug white-washed cottage, locally caught fish in a picture-perfect village. No dogs. (J9) 01503 272217

The Kitchen, The Coombes. Park at top of village and walk down to this snug fisherman's cottage for spicy Goan and Thai cuisine. Dinner 7-9.30. (J9) 01503 272780

POLKERRIS

Former pilchard fishing port. Harbour breakwater built by the Rashleighs of Menabilly. Remains of huge pilchard 'palace', possibly Elizabethan. (D8)

Polperro

POLRUAN

Attractive village with busy boatyard. The main street plunges almost vertically to the small quay on Fowey estuary. Cars not encouraged. Superb views from hill-top car park and walks east to Lantic Bay. Pedestrian ferry to Fowey. (F9)

The Lugger. Famous Inn noted for its high quality pub grub and fine ales. Worth the ferry trip. (E9

south porch has interesting openwork tracery. Original wagon roof. Carvings of Cornish saints. (A8)

Eden Project. Major multi-million pound project to turn old china clay pits into vast steel-framed domes (biomes) housing a tropical rain forest and a Mediterranean climate. This project of enormous vision, and ambition, has been an outstanding success, and has drawn visitors in their hundreds of thousands since

St Austell Brewery Visitor Centre. Traditional brewers for 140 years. Guided tours and beer sampling at 11am and 2:30pm. Licensed shop. Open M-F 9.30-4.30. (A8) www.staustellbrewery.co.uk

Tregrehan Gardens. Woodland garden created in the C19 by the Carlyon family. Nursery. Camellias. Open mid-Mar to end-May W-Su & BH Ms 10.30-5. (B7) 01726 814389 www.tregrehan.org

Where to Stay...

Anchorage House B&B, Nettles Corner. Tregrehan Mill. A warm welcome, enormous beds and superb bathrooms await you plus an indoor pool, hot tub, spa and gym. New disabled facility. Evening meals by arrangement. Their crazy interior designs match their humour. No children (u 16). (B8) 01726 814071 www.anchoragehouse.co.uk

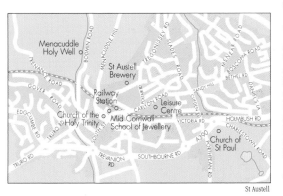

St Austell

ST AUSTELL

A major route centre which has seen much recent development and prosperity since the opening of first, Heligan Gardens and then, the Eden Project. Brewing centre and formerly an old tin mining village whose prosperity later relied very much on the china clay industry. The hinterland is made up of white mountainous pyramids, man-made lakes, and palm trees. There is a fine C15 perpendicular church, the Holy Trinity, an C18 coaching inn, The White Hart Hotel and a Georgian Quaker meeting house built in 1829. Below are listed four luxurious places to stay, all on the east side of St Austell and all within a short distance of Eden. (A8) www.staustelltown.co.uk

Special Places to Visit...

Bens Playworld. Mega-slides, giant tubes, assault course... fun for kids. Cafe. Open daily 10-7. (A8) www.bensplayworld.co.uk

Church of the Holy Trinity. The exterior is more interesting than the restored interior. The tower has sculptures set in the niches and the

Eden Project ac

opening in Spring 2000. Open daily from 10. (B7) www.edenproject.com

Kids Kingdom, Albert Road. Indoor play centre for family fun. Open daily East-Sept, winter Tu-Su (& M in school hols), 10-6. (A8)

Mid Cornwall School of Jewellery, 19 High Cross St. Holds a wide range of courses. You can even make your own wedding ring! Open by appoint. 01726 73319. (A8) www.mcsj.co.uk

Boscundle Manor, Tregreham Mill. Small, C18 country house hotel, restaurant and spa. Luxuriously furnished in contemporary designs, perhaps boutique style. Impressive wine list. 5 acres of private grounds. (B8) 01726 813557 www.boscundlemanor.co.uk

The Noah Carving, St Winnow Church

Nanscawen Manor House.
Spacious house set in five glorious acres of rhododendrons and camellias. 4-poster beds. Swimming pool. No children (u 12). (B6) 01726 814488 www.nanscawen.co.uk

Wisteria Lodge, Boscundle, Tregrehan.
Small, luxurious hotel with five bedrooms, all with their own whirlpool baths and lounges. Light suppers. Self-catering apartments. Available for private functions; weddings, parties etc. (B8) 01726 810800 www.wisterialodgehotel.co.uk

Where to Eat, Drink & Be Merry...

Austell's, 10 Beach Road, Carlyon Bay.
Brett Camborne-Paynter has a fine pedigree having cooked at The Ivy, The Waldorf and The Four Seasons. Modern British cuisine is his recipe for a succulent meal. Open Tu-Su 7-10 pm Easter-Christmas, and W-Su Jan-Easter. (B8) 01726 813888 www.austells.net

Special Places to Visit...

Carnglaze Slate Caverns.
Famous subterranean lake with crystal clear blue-green water in huge underground chamber. Open all year M-Sa 10-5. (H1) www.carnglaze.com

Cornish Orchards.
Handmade apple juices, ciders and honeys from West Country orchards. Farm shop open Good F-Oct from 10. (L5) www.cornishorchards.co.uk

Dobwalls - Southern Gallery.
Features wildlife artists Carl Brenders (Wolves, Big Cats and North American Birds) and Stephen Townsend (Dogs). Some originals, mainly limited editions for sale. New iconic Culture Centre with fifteen Eco-Lodges opening in 2009. Gallery open daily 10.30-4.30 (K2) 01579 320325 www.dobwalls.com

Haye Farm Cider, St Veep.
Real, traditional, local farm scrumpy cider matured in wooden barrels. Open daily. (F7) 01208 872250

Herodsfoot Forest.
Deer park, walks and cabins for self catering holidays. (J4)

Lanreath Church

Paul Corin's Magnificent Music Machines.
The Marquis of Campden's 1912 Aeolian Pipe Organ, orchestrions and the Mighty Wurlitzer Theatre Organ. Open daily Good F-Oct 10.30-5. (M4)

Porfell Animal Land.
Designed for all ages to enjoy domestic and exotic wild animals, play area and walks in lovely countryside. Open daily Apr-Oct 10-6. (H5) www.porfellanimalland.co.uk

Rum Store, Carnglaze Caverns.
Classical and pop concerts put on in underground 400-seat auditorium. Superb acoustics. (H1) 01579 320251

St Neot Pottery, The Old Chapel.
Pots made on premises from earthenware clay and decorated by hand. Open M-Sa. (H1) 01579 320216

Churches of Interest...

Lanreath Church.
Norman cruciform, medieval screens and carved figures, and colourful monuments of the Grylls family. (H6)

Lanteglos-By-Fowey.
Norman origins. C13 font. Brasses of the de Mohuns. C16 bench ends. (F8)

Liskeard Church.
Separated from the town by slim valley. It is Perpendicular and the second largest in the county. 13 consecration crosses - a unique feature, and undistinguished new tower. (M2)

St Martin-By-Looe Church.
Norman origins with C15 additions, and ceiled wagon roof. Parclose Screen and C17 monuments. (M7)

St Neot's Church.
Imposing building in scenic valley famous for the 15 medieval stained glass windows. Restored in 1830 by John Hedgeland. Perhaps only outshone in the West Country by those of Fairford in Gloucestershire. Wagon roof. Monuments of William Bere and family. The font is C13 and C15. (H1) www.stneot.org.uk

St Winnow.
In idyllic location overlooking the River Fowey. Superb bench ends; a ship with wood carver's mistake and a Cornishman drinking a flagon of cider. St Winnow settled here in 670 AD. Next door, a small agricultural museum serves teas. (E6)

The Rum Store, Carnglaze Caverns ss

Polkerris

Beaches and Surfing...

Charlestown. To west of harbour, sand and pebbles, strong currents. (A8)

Carlyon Bay. Spacious golden sandy beach with all amenities in adjacent leisure centre.

Polgaver Bay. Cornwall's first official naturist beach. Boat hire, water skiing etc P/WC/cafe/bars. No dogs. (B8)

Par Sands. Large extensive sandy bay. Very popular with children, seaside amusements, boating lake, easy access, private harbour, china clay works, effluent on west side. P/WC/cafe/huts. (C8)

Polkerris. Small sandy family beach sheltered by curving harbour wall. Safe bathing, S-B hire/P/WC/cafe/inn. Surfing - Popular. Big swell required. (D8)

Poldridmouth Cove. 15 mins walk fron P. Sheltered sandy cove. (D9)

Fowey - Readymoney Cove. 20 mins walk from town centre. Small sandy beach at LT. Good bathing, sheltered. WC/tea rooms. (E9)

Lantic Bay. 10 mins walk from NT P. Follow path across fields, and down a steep 400ft climb to a lovely beach at LT. (F9)

Lantivet Bay. 15 mins walk from Lansallos, secluded beach with pebbles and shingle. (G9)

Talland Bay. Access via a steep narrow lane, shingle, rocks and sand at LT flanked by cliffs. P/WC/cafe. (K9)

Portnadler Bay. Follow the coastal footpath for 1 1/4 mile from West Looe to a quiet sandy beach with rock pools. (L9)

West Looe - Hannifore. Rock pools and pebbles, sandy patches at LT. WC/cafe/kiosk. (M8)

East Looe - Banjo Pier. Suntrap behind pier, sands and pebbles, good bathing. (M8)

East Looe - Plaidy Beach. Access by foot from Banjo Pier. Rock pools and shale. WC/cafe. (M8)

Coastal Footpath...

Porthpean to Looe Approx 30 miles. It is worth exploring the port of Charlestown and seeking out a cup of coffee. You may be in luck and be able to admire a tall ship in the dry dock. The path is easy going across Carlyon Bay, the coast does become more built-up as you approach Par Sands, past the thriving china clay harbour of Par. Lovely walk through pretty Polkerris, then up to the impressive cliffs of Gribbin Head (224ft) and an 84ft landmark, erected by Trinity House in the 1820s. There are fine views across towards the Lizard and Rame Head. At Polridmouth, you will come across sub-tropical flora, and on following the path, you will soon spy fine views of Fowey and its busy Harbour. Soon to pass the remains of St Catherine's Castle. Follow road into Fowey where there is a regular ferry to Polruan. Then, six miles of magnificent, lonely, cliff-top walking to Polperro. Inland are grazed fields and gentler contours, but the coast path is often steep and hard going in places. Polperro must first be explored before setting out again along a well maintained path that follows the cliff edge to Looe.

Looe

CONTEMPORARY ARCHITECTURE

Jubilee Wharf, Penryn

The Library, St Ives

Knowledge Spa, Truro Hospital

Tremough Campus, Penryn

Tremough Campus, Penryn

Truro College

Truro College

RNLI Lifeboat Station, Trevose Head

Tate St Ives

National Maritime Museum, Falmouth

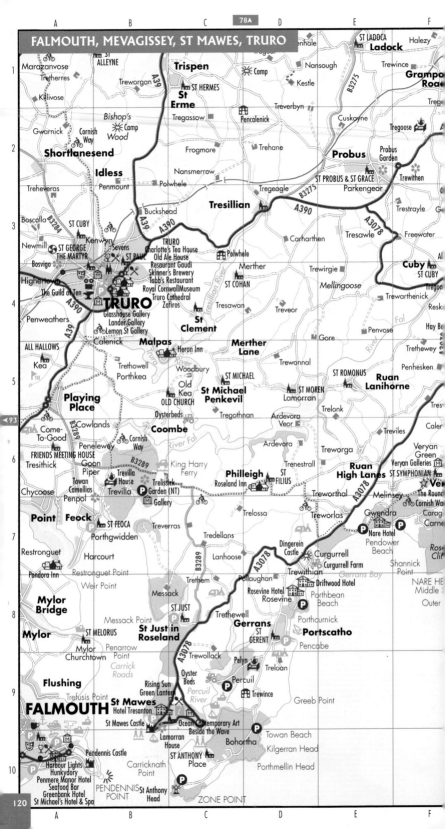

FALMOUTH, MEVAGISSEY, ST MAWES, TRURO

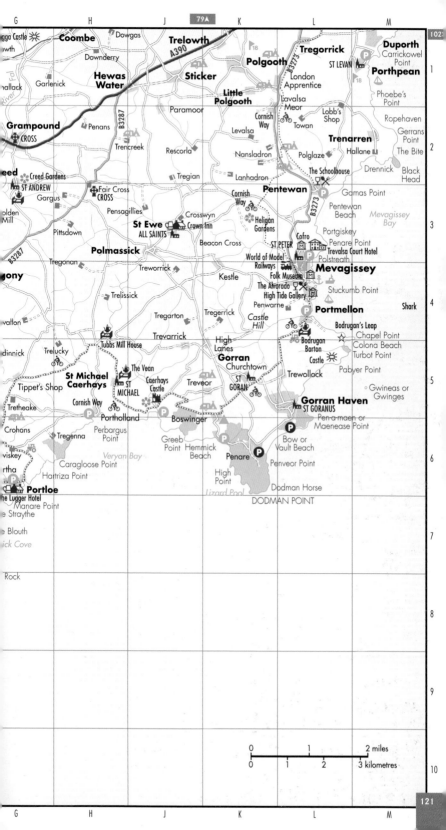

Map Labels

G **H** **J** **K** **L** **M**

gga Castle
owth
Coombe
Dowgas
Trelowth
A390
Tregorrick
Duporth
Carrickowel
Point

Downderry
Polgooth
ST LEVAN
Porthpean

allack
Garlenick
Hewas
Water
Sticker
London
Apprentice

1

Grampound
Penans
Little
Polgooth
Paramoor
Lavalsa
Meor
Cornish
Way
Towan
Lobb's
Shop
Ropehaven

CROSS
Trencreek
Rescorla
Levalsa
Trenarren
Gerrans
Point
The Bite

2

eed
Creed Gardens
Fair Cross
CROSS
Tregian
Nansladron
Lanhadron
Polglaze
Hallane
Drennick
Black
Head

ST ANDREW
Gargus
Pensagillies
Crosswyn
Pentewan
The Schoolhouse

olden
Mill
Pittsdown
St Ewe
ALL SAINTS
Crown Inn
Heligan
Gardens
Gamas Point
Pentewan
Beach
Mevagissey
Bay

3

ony
Tregonan
Polmassick
Beacon Cross
Cornish
Way
Cofro
ST PETER
Portgiskey
Penare Point
Trevalsa Court Hotel

Treworrick
Kestle
World of Model
Railways
Polstreath

vatton
Trelissick
Tregarton
Tregerrick
Folk Museum
Mevagissey

The Alvorado
High Tide Gallery
Stuckumb Point

4

dinnick
Trelucky
Tubbs Mill House
Trevarrick
Castle
Hill
Penwarne
Portmellon
Shark

Tippet's Shop
St Michael
Caerhays
The Vean
High
Lanes
Bodrugan's Leap
Chapel Point

Tretheake
Cornish Way
ST
MICHAEL
Caerhays
Castle
Gorran
Churchtown
Bodrugan
Barton
Colona Beach
Turbot Point

5

Crohans
Portholland
Treveor
ST
GORAN
Castle
Trewollock
Pabyer Point

viskey
Tregenna
Perbargus
Point
Boswinger
Gorran Haven
ST GORANUS
Gwineas or
Gwinges

rtha
Caragloose Point
Veryan Bay
Greeb
Point
Hemmick
Beach
Penare
Bow or
Vault Beach
Pen-a-maen or
Maenease Point

Portloe
Penveor Point

6

he Lugger Hotel
Manare Point
Hartriza Point
High
Point
Dodman Horse

e Straythe
Lizard Pool
DODMAN POINT

e Blouth

7

ick Cove

Rock

8

9

| 0 | 1 | 2 miles |
| 0 | 1 | 2 | 3 kilometres |

10

G **H** **J** **K** **L** **M**

Falmouth

FALMOUTH

Overlooks a superb natural harbour. The Phoenicians and Romans came here in search of tin. In the late C16, Sir Walter Raleigh persuaded the Killigrew family to develop the harbour's potential, and for 200 years Falmouth became the centre of the Mail Packet Trade, smuggling and piracy. Falmouth is a busy and likeable town with many places in which to sink a pint or fill an empty stomach. The town has seen much new architectural development, notably the National Maritime Museum with its adjacent area of shops and cafes. Outside the town the new Tremough Campus (Art College) at Penryn. Popular yachting centre. Cinema and 3 beaches. Regatta week - mid Aug. E/C W. (A10)
www.falmouth.co.uk
www.falmouth.tv (webcam)
www.falmouth.ac.uk (Art College)

Galleries & Museums to Visit and Things to See & Do...

Beside The Wave, 10 Arwenack St.
Established in 1989 to provide an outlet for Cornwall's leading contemporary artists and craftsmen. Open M-Sa 9.30-5. (A10) www.beside-the-wave.co.uk

Fal River Links, The Quay.
Travel by ferry or take a cruise up river to Trelissick or Truro. Cross to St Mawes. (A10) Details: www.falriverlinks.co.uk

Falmouth Art Gallery, The Moor. Maritime pictures and quality temporary exhibitions. Work by J W Waterhouse and Henry Scott Tuke. Open all year M-Sa 9-5.30 (A10) www.falmouthartgallery.com

Falmouth Arts Centre, 24 Church St. 200 seat theatre (cinema) holds music, theatre and dance. Four galleries put on changing exhibitions. Open daily. (A10) www.thepoly.org

Falmouth School of Sailing, The Dinghy Park, Grove Place.
Courses range from dinghy to keelboat to powerboats, taking you to varying levels of seamanship. (A10) 01326 211311 www.falmouthschoolofsailing.co.uk

Great Atlantic Falmouth Gallery, 48 Arwenack Street.
A leading Cornish gallery with a wealth of talent to hand. Regular exhibitions of paintings, sculpture and jewellery. (A10) 01326 318452 www.greatatlantic.co.uk

National Maritime Museum.
With breathtaking views from the 29m tower, one of only three natural underwater viewing locations in the world. Hands-on inter-actives, audio-visual immersive experiences,

talks, special exhibitions and the opportunity to get out onto the water. This new generation of museum has something for everyone. Open daily. (A10) 01326 313388 www.nmmc.co.uk.

Ocean Contemporary, 29 Church St.

Wide range of paintings and crafts in light, airy gallery. Open M-Sa 10-5.30. (A10) www.ocean-contemporary.co.uk

Where to Eat, Drink & Be Merry...

Hunkydory, 46 Arwenack St.

If art, the young and beautiful, chic decor, and sumptuous food (especially fish) feed your desires, this is it. Dinner 6-10. (A10) 01326 212997 www.hunkydoryfalmouth.co.uk

Seafood Bar, Lower Quay St.

Underground bar (Madrid-like) serves up enormous dishes of crustacea and locally caught fish. Followed by fulsome desserts with toppings of clotted cream. Dinner 7-10.30. (A10) 01326 315129

Three Mackerel, Swanpool.

Location, location cries the Estate Agent, and by gad, he got it right here. Popular, award-winning restaurant produces imaginative dishes of fish (mussels, scallops, mackerel) and meats. Lunch 12-2.30, Dinner 6-9.30. (A10) 01326 311886 www.thethreemackerel.com

National Maritime Museum ss

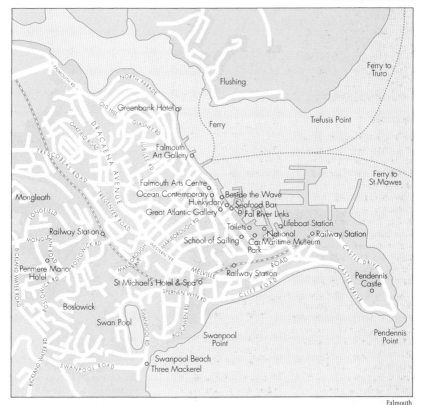

Falmouth

Mevagissey

And Sleep...

The Greenbank Hotel, Harbourside. Falmouth's oldest and recently refurbished hotel has sweeping views of the harbour. Ancient stone-flagged floors, leather sofas and polished wood provide an aura of permanence and comfort. Fine restaurant. (A10) 01326 312440 www.greenbank-hotel.co.uk

Penmere Manor Hotel, Mongleath Rd.
Georgian country house set in a 5 acre tropical garden. Large beds and all the facilities of a Best Western. Bolitho Restaurant. Fountains Leisure Club. Beauty/Therapy Room. Not everyone's cup of tea - too corporate for some of us.
(A10) 01326 211411
www.penmeremanorhotel.co.uk

St Michael's Hotel & Spa.
This hotel has undergone a complete makeover to appease those seeking a hedonistic lifestyle. It's all contemporary décor, Flying Fish restaurant (very child-friendly) amidst sub-tropical gardens.
(A10) 01326 312707
www.stmichaelshotel.co.uk

The Nare Hotel. A haven of tranquility with stunning sea views. The Nare enjoys a reputation for delicious food; seafood a speciality, and a comprehensive wine cellar. The over crowded décor may not suit everyone. No minimalism or contemporary design in evidence. (E7) 01872 50111 www.thenare.com

And Special Inns to Visit...

Heron Inn. In fine situation overlooking the tidal River Fal. Modern, light decor provides a nautical ambience. Children welcome. Best visited on a warm summer's evening. (C5)

Pandora Inn. C13 thatched pub beside the estuary has a bagatelle of flagstone floors, cosy alcoves and low ceilings. Al fresco pontoon over the river. Children and dogs welcome. (A7) 01326 372678 www.pandorainn.co.uk

FLUSHING

Tall elegant C18 houses line the waterfront of this former steam packet centre. Claims to have the mildest climate in Cornwall. It invites the retired and somnambulist, so don't be surprised to see copies of the Daily Telegraph covering bald, red faces above starch-fronted gentlemen dressed in blazer and slacks. Only kidding. (A9)

MEVAGISSEY

One of Cornwall's most picturesque and unspoilt fishing villages. The fine inner, and more recent outer harbour has been at the centre of the town's history for hundreds of years. A famous shark fishing centre, World of Model Railways, Folk Museum and ferry to Fowey. Nearby, Heligan Gardens. Feast Week - late June. (L4) www.mevagissey-cornwall.co.uk

Special Places to Visit...

Bodrugan's Leap. Sir Harry Trelowth of Bodrugan rode his horse over the cliff to be picked up by a passing fishing boat after fleeing the Battle of Bosworth in 1485. (L4)

Cofro, 14 Fore St.
Affordable works of art by 30+ Cornish artists: jewellery, glass, sculptures, paintings. Open Su-F 10.30-5. (L4) www.cofro.co.uk

Mevagissey Folk Museum, East Quay. Exhibits of local origin; fishing, agriculture and domestic life in an old 1745 building where luggers (fishing boats) were built. Open East-Oct 11-6. (L4)

World Of Model Railways, Meadow St. Over 2,000 models, 50 trains controlled in sequence. Model shop. Open daily Mar-Oct (Nov-Feb W & Su only). (L4) www.model-railway.co.uk

Where to Eat, Drink & Be Merry...

The Alvorada, 2 Polkirt Hill.
Family-run, Portugese restaurant with a lively atmosphere. Dinner 6.30-12. (L4) 01726 842055

The Schoolhouse, Pentewan.
Good value cooking in large Victorian schoolroom. Dinner Tu-Sa. (L4) 01726 842474

Pandora Inn

TRURO

Cornwall's Cathedral city and administrative centre is spacious and has some elegant and beautiful buildings of the Georgian and Regency period. In Lemon Street the Assembly Rooms of 1772, and the Mansion House and Prince's House in Princes Street, and the Cathedral, 1880-1910. The city has seen much development of late; there are multiple stores and offices and flats overlooking the river, and a wealth of contemporary architecture as in Truro College and the new hospital buildings. Always a busy town, it has the finest shops in the county. Educational centre. Cinema. (B4) www.truro.gov.uk

Special Places to Visit...

Glass House Gallery, Kenwyn St. Well established gallery showing contemporary art and ceramics on two floors. Extensive jewellery display. Open M-Sa 10-5.15. (B4) www.glasshousegallery.co.uk

Guild Of Ten, 19 Old Bridge Street. Co-operative of craftsmen and women living in Cornwall. They seek to produce workmanship of the highest quality: knitwear, designer clothing, glass blowing, ceramics etc. Open M-Sa 9.30-5.30. (B4) www.guildof10.co.uk

Lander Gallery, Lemon Street Market. Spacious open gallery displays - C19 and C20 Cornish masters to contemporary fine art and crafts. Coffee shop. Open M-Sa 9-6. (B4) www.landergallery.co.uk

Truro Cathedral

1720   Samuel Foote, Comedian and Playwright, is born in Truro

1720   Thomas Newcomen erects an Atmospheric Engine at Wheal Fortune, Ludgvan

Truro

Lemon Street Gallery, Lemon St.
Quality gallery whose aim is to introduce the British Art Scene to Cornwall. Modern and Contemporary art, sculpture and ceramics. Open M-Sa 10.30-5.30. (B4)
www.lemonstreetgallery.co.uk

Royal Cornwall Museum, River Street. World-famous collection of minerals, archaeology, ceramics, paintings and old master drawings. Open M-Sa 10-5 (except BH's). (B4)
www.royalcornwallmuseum.org

Truro Cathedral. The first English Cathedral to be built after St Paul's. An imposing building designed by John Pearson, in the Gothic style, 1880-1910. Three soaring spires, and an unrivalled collection of stained glass windows. Refectory for light meals, 10-4. Open daily 8-6, shop and Chapter House from 10. (B4)
www.trurocathedral.org.uk
www.trurochoralsociety.co.uk

Where to Eat, Drink & Be Merry...

Charlotte's Tea House, Colnage Hall, 1 Boscawen Street.
Step back in time into a sanctuary of Victoriana. Full range of teas, coffees, sandwiches, scones, cakes and a formal, waitress service. Open M-Sa 9.45-4.45. (B4)
01872 263706

Old Ale House, Quay Street.
A great atmosphere pervades this busy town pub. Food produced in full view and it's good, too. Wide range of local and East Anglian ales. Recommended. (B4)

Restaurant Gaudi, 8 Edward St.
Open for breakfast and brunch, also great value for lunch and dinner with main courses under £15. Vegetables freshly dug up from the restaurant's own allotment.
01872 227380 www.gaudis.co.uk

Skinner's Brewery, Newham Rd. Visit a working brewery and sample their fine ales. Guided tours & tastings (11 & 2.30), visitor centre and shop. Open M-F. (F4) 01872 271885
www.skinnersbrewery.com

Tabb's Restaurant, 85 Kenwyn St.
Formerly in Portreath as a Chocolatier. Their new venture is gaining a loyal following. Lilac covered walls. Formal dining. Adventurous menu. Open Tu-Sa, Lunch 12-2, Dinner 6.30-9.pm. (F4)
01872 262110
www.tabbs.co.uk

Zafiros, 3 New Bridge Street.
Trendy new coffee house and restaurant. Breakfast, lunch and light suppers. Funky evening bar with live music every month. (F4) 01872 223163

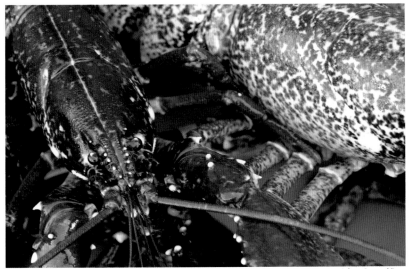

Lobster, Curgurrel Farm

THE ROSELAND PENINSULA

In Cornwall the landscape can, in the main, be hard and unforgiving. One thinks of the rugged North Coast and the interior of the county, not known for its aesthetic qualities. But, every now and again, you will come across a gentle, pastoral landscape that is magical. This peninsula is just such a place. From the country lanes switching back and forth from the Fal and Tresillian Rivers taking you through woodland to the little ports of Portloe and Portscatho. It is a place to travel slowly and to succour the isolated churches and views across the brooding creeks. The road from Truro to St Mawes seems to take an age for the traveller in a hurry. More fool him who follows a sat-nav (and misses everything). October Music Festival www.roselandfestival.co.uk

PORTLOE

Little fishing village with a narrow and rocky harbour. A wonderful view can be had from the coastal path to the north. (G6)

The Lugger Hotel.

C17 smugglers' inn has been turned into a chic, trendy restaurant. The local boats supply the fish. Accommodation. Lunch 12-2, Dinner 7-9. (G6) 01872 501322 www.luggerhotel.co.uk

PORTSCATHO

Old harbour on the Roseland shore with narrow streets running down to a tiny pier. Popular pub. Art gallery. (D8)

Curgurrel Farm.

The farmer is Portscatho's Harbour Master who owns a bevy of lobster and crab pots. You can drop in and buy freshly caught crustacea, and fish caught off the line - bass, plaice etc. Open M-Sa 10-12, 5-7. Self-catering accommodation. (E7) 01872 580243

Where to Stay, nearby...

Driftwood Hotel. Nothing washed up here except chic, contemporary design. Many of the furnishings are sculpted pieces of driftwood: mirrors, table lamps etc. A relaxed ambience pervades and the sea views are stunning. You can relax in the garden or follow the path down to the private beach. Impressive restaurant. Family-friendly. No dogs. (D8) 01872 580644 www.driftwoodhotel.co.uk

Rosevine Hotel. A new style of hotel designed for families and groups. Separate independent units offer self-catering but have the added bonus of a top-notch restaurant and hotel facilities to hand. All set within gardens overlooking the sea. (D8) 01872 580206 www.rosevine.co.uk

Roseland Inn.

Friendly, crowded pub with log fires and low ceilings. Cornish produce makes up the menu. Daily specials. Booking advised. Dogs and children welcome. (D6) 01872 580254 www.roselandinn.co.uk

Roseland Country Lane

Sailing at the Hotel Tresanton ss

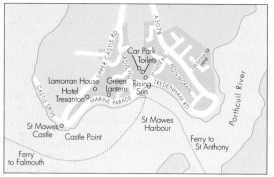

St Mawes

ST MAWES

Attractive, sunny haven popular with yachtsmen and second home-owners on a tributary of the Fal Estuary. The main centre for the Roseland Peninsula with easy, ferry access to Falmouth. Castle, boat/fishing trips, Percuil Regatta - Aug. (B9)
www.stmawes.info
www.stmawessailing.co.uk
www.stmawes-ferry.co.uk

Where to Eat, Sleep & Be Merry...

Hotel Tresanton. This hotel has raised the bar by which all are judged in Cornwall. It's a chic, family-friendly hotel owned by the interior designer Olga Polizzi (of the Forte family) and her husband, the political commentator William Shawcross. The bedrooms are bright and colourful, and finely tuned with a blend of contemporary and antique furnishings. Note the mosaics in the bathrooms. All have sea views. Sculptures and fine art is everywhere. The service is discreet. The highly acclaimed restaurant is noted for seafood. (B9) 01326 270055
www.tresanton.com

The Rising Sun.
This friendly inn provides imaginative cuisine and comfortable seating areas outside, or in the lounge or bar. Food is available from the restaurant or bar. Dogs and children welcome. B&B in brightly coloured rooms with all the mod cons. (B9) 01326 270233
www.risingsunstmawes.co.uk

Green Lantern, Marine Parade.
With fine views over the harbour this little, unpretentious restaurant adds a fusion of flavours to the raw materials provided locally. Dinner 7-9. (B9) 01326 270878

St Mawes at Dawn

1743   John Wesley makes the first of his forty trips to Cornwall

1747   Admiral Boscawen (Cornish hero) engages the French fleet almost single-handedly off the coast of Finisterre

Caerhays Castle & Gardens ss

Castles, Houses & Gardens to Visit...

Bosvigo. A plantsman's garden, best seen in summer (June-Aug); series of enclosed and walled gardens with herbaceous borders. Nursery. Open Mar-Sept Th F. 11-6. (A3) www.bosvigo.com

Caerhays Castle & Gardens. 60 acres of informal woodland gardens created by J C Williams who sponsored plant hunting expeditions to China. Noted for camellias, magnolias and rhododendrons. Garden open daily mid-Feb to end May, 10-5.00. Castle from mid-Mar 12-3 M-F. (J5) 01872 501310 www.caerhays.co.uk

Creed Gardens. 5 acre Georgian Rectory garden. Tree collection, rhododendrons, sunken alpine and walled herbaceous gardens, trickle stream and ponds. Open daily Mar-Sept 10-5.30. (G2)

Heligan Gardens. Explore 200 acres of Cornish countryside, including award-winning productive garden restoration, atmospheric pleasure grounds, sub-tropical 'Jungle', valley and estate land incorporating a pioneering wildlife conservation project. Open daily, all year from 10. (K3) 01726 845100 www.heligan.com

Lamorran House Gardens. 4 acre Mediterranean garden overlooking the sea. Water, palms and sub-tropical features. Open Apr-Sept W, F (& first Sa of every month) 10.30-5. (B9) 01326 270800

Probus Gardens. A unique garden demonstrating a wide variety of methods, and 'water-wise gardening' practices. Ideas for planting displays, hanging baskets, greenhouses. Advice centre. Guided tours. Plant Centre. Cafe. Open daily Mar-Dec 9.30-5, Jan-Mar M-F 9.30-4. (E2)

Trelissick Garden (NT). Extensive park, farmland and woods. Large garden, lovely in all seasons with beautiful views over Fal Estuary and Falmouth Harbour. Woodland Walks beside River Fal. Open daily 1 Feb- 2 Nov 10.30-5.30. Nov-Feb 11-4. Woodland walk open all year. (B6) 01872 862090 www.nationaltrust.org.uk

Heligan Gardens ss

St Mawes Castle

Trewithen Gardens.
30 acre garden renowned for its magnificent collection of camellias, rhododendrons, magnolias and many rare trees and shrubs, surrounded by traditional parkland landscaped in the C18. New sculpture fountain. Gardens open Mar-Sept M-Sa 10-4.30. Su Apr-May only. House open M & Tu Apr-July, & Aug BH M 2-4. (F2) 01726 883647 www.trewithengardens.co.u

Pendennis Castle (EH). Built
1544-46 in the age of the Cannon and gunpowder as one of a chain of castles Henry VIII erected from 1538 to deter French Invasion. Circular keep with drawbridge, portcullis, spy holes and spiral staircase. Superb viewpoint. To the south-east is the blockhouse built on the rocks. Open as English Heritage times. (A10)

St Mawes Castle (EH). Built in
1540-43 as a link in Henry VIII's chain of coastal defences. A fortress of striking symmetry; trefoil shaped with gun emplacements, drawbridge and heraldic decorations, and set in sub-tropical gardens. Superb viewpoint. Great place for a wedding. Open as English Heritage times. (B10)

Ancient Cornwall...

Castle Dore. Prehistoric earthwork with inner ramparts. Deserted in AD 100, occupied in C5. Legendary setting for the love story of Tristan and Iseult. (D7)

Hay Barton, Tregony.
Just the perfect accommodation for groups of four. The house is split into two, so the B&B area of two (light and airy) bedrooms is separate from the main house. All the fabrics are Cath Kidston and Colefax & Fowler, the beds are zip-link doubles, the breakfasts of yoghurt, grenola and farm eggs are made on the premises. Tennis Court. Wi-Fi Internet access. (F4) 01872 530288 www.haybarton.com

Pelyn B&B, Gerrans.
The location is an ornithologist's or naturalist's delight. Isolated across a field, the house overlooks the beautiful Pelyn Creek and is decorated with oil paintings and antiques. The two bedrooms have luxurious bathrooms. Your host is a Bon Viveur, and enthusiast for wine

and all crustacea. Bon Appetit! Self-catering cottage. (D8) 01872 580837 www.pelyncreek.com

The Vean, Caerhays.
The recently restored Georgian rectory on the Caerhays Estate has been transformed into a sumptuously decorated country house (for house parties) with all things Cornish thus helping reduce their carbon footprint. (J5) 01872 501310 www.thevean.co.uk

Tregoose B&B, Grampound.
This private house exudes old style country house living. Generations of family portraits line the walls, the furnishing are antique and tasteful. The bedrooms are comfortable. Evening meals, an option. Set on farmland belonging to the Trewithen Estate. WL. (F2) 01726 882460 www.tregoose.co.uk

Trevalsa Court Hotel, School Hill Road, Mevagissey.
New owners plan to turn this into a small, luxurious, boutique-style hotel. Fabulous sea views. (L3) 01726 842468 www.trevalsa-hotel.co.uk

Trevilla House, Feock.
The perfect location for garden lovers as it's close to Trelissick. Jonti, your charming hostess, will treat you as a house guest and will become invaluable to you as a mine of local knowledge. Family portraits and photographs adorn the walls, the beds are high with custom-made mattresses, breakfast is taken in the conservatory overlooking Carrick Roads. (B6) 01872 862369 www.trevilla.com

Fal Estuary from Trelissick Garden

St Michael Penkevil Church

Tubbs Mill House, Nr Caerhays.
If you can find it, and manage to
arrive without a scrape, bravo. A
welcome refuge from our politically
correct world. Your funny hostess
calls a spade a spade, and her
catholic taste in interior design is
hers alone. From contemporary
minimalist furnishings, to Victorian
erotica, to African art. The bathrooms
are top-notch. Evening meals.
(H4) 01872 530715
www.tubbsmillhouse.com

Churches to Visit...

Creed. Lavish windows in south
aisle. C13 trefoil arch. (G3)

**Falmouth, St Charles The
Martyr Church.** Classical C17
with oblong tower. Sir Peter Lely
portrait of Charles I. C15 pulpit
embellished with vine carvings.
Memorials reflect Falmouth's role as
a Royal Mail Packet Station. (A10)

Fowey. A mighty church that was
sadly sacked by French pirates in the
C15, Jacobean pulpit made from a
Spanish galleon. Tall tower. C12 font,
Rashleigh monuments are
exceptional. (E8)

Golant. Beautifully situated
C15 with fine wagon roofs, small,
intricate bench ends and C15 glass.
Holy well. (E7)

Mylor. Celtic cross with Norman
doorway and superb setting above the
creek overlooking hundreds of
yachts at anchor. (A8)

Probus. C16 tower, tallest in county
of Somerset design (striking and
intricate tower) similar to North
Petherton, C16 brasses. (E2)

St Clement.
C13-14. Above the Tresillian River.
Well restored in 1868. (C4)

Drawing Room, Tregoose ss

1769   Bodmin to Launceston turnpike road in operation   1777   Dolly Pentraeth dies. The last true speaker of the Cornish
                                                                        vernacular (language)

133

St Just In Roseland. In a quite gorgeous situation overlooking the creek within a tropical garden. Fascinating tombstones. Best visited at high tide so you can see the reflections. (C8)

St Michael Penkevil. Large, statuesque building of late C13-14 in feudal village with C17 & C19 monuments, and later restoration which has covered earlier work of great interest. (C5)

Special Places to See & Visit...

Carrick Roads. 4-mile long valley fed by 5 tributaries. Boat trips from Falmouth to Truro and St Mawes from Prince of Wales Pier. At Custom House Quay, trips to Helford Passage and Roseland in summer season. Popular with yachtsmen. (B6) www.falmouthport.co.uk

Floe Creek. Haven for wildfowl and herons. Start of 6 1/2 mile walk around peninsula:- to Towan Beach, coast path to Zone Point, Carricknath Point, St Anthony and back. Shorter 3 1/2 mile walk:- Westwards direct to Porthmellin Head and St Anthony. (C10)

Loe Beach, Feock. Watersports and the kids club will keep your children amused for hours and days. (B7)

The Round Houses, Veryan

Mylor Churchtown (Harbour). Flourishing yachting centre complete with chandlers and three eateries: or Mylor Harbour Café, open all year, fish restaurant and bistro. Car park. (A8) www.harbourviewfalmouth.co.uk

The Square Gallery, The Arcade, St Mawes. A wonderful mixture of paintings, jewellery, ceramics and sculptures. (B9) 01326 270720 www.thesquaregallery.co.uk

Trelissick Gallery. Set within the National Trust's garden, it is run in partnership with Cornwall Crafts to show off the best of Cornwall's arts and crafts. Open Feb-Dec M-Sa 10.30-5.30. (B6) www.cornwallcrafts.co.uk

Veryan - The Round Houses. Five circular thatched houses built during the days of superstition. Designed with conical roofs, pointed doorways and window arches, so that 'the devil could find no niche in which to hide'. (F6)

Mylor Harbour

1778 James Watt installs the first Pumping Engine in the county at Wheal Busy, Chacewater

1789 Bread riots in Truro

Portscatho

Beaches and Surfing...

Falmouth - Swanpool Beach.
Sandy cove, safe bathing, boating adjacent. P/WC/cafe. (A10)

Falmouth - Gyllynvase Beach.
Popular family beach with spacious sands, access P/WC/cafe. (A10)

Falmouth - Castle Beach. Safe bathing, rockpools and sands. All facilities. (A10)

Towan Beach. Sand dunes, shingle, rock pools and unspoilt. P. (D10)

Porthcurnick Beach.
Sandy patches, facilities in Portscatho. P. (D8)

Pendower / Carne Beach. Lovely sands extend for 1 mile. Fine bathing and rocks. P/WC. (E7)

Kiberick Cove. Secluded and tricky access, sand exposed at LT. (F7)

Portloe. Good bathing with grey shingle at LT. P/WC/inn. (G6)

East & West Portholland.
Shingle with sand at LT. HZ cliffs to sides P/WC. (H6)

Porthluney Beach. Popular sheltered family beach with extended sands. P/WC/kiosk. (J6)

Hemmick Beach. Steep 1 in 5 descent to small sandy beach. (K6)

Bow Or Vault Beach. Steep tricky path down to spacious sands and shingle. (L6)

Gorran Haven. Family resort with fine bathing and spacious sands. P/WC/boats for hire. (L5)

Portmellon. Good bathing off small sandy beach, rocks at both sides. P/WC/inn/cafe. (L4)

Pentewan. Spacious sands, HZ bathing; strong currents, avoid channel. P. Surfing - Sheltered spot. Waves only occur after an enormous swell, rarely in summer. Hollow beach break. (L3)

Porthpean. Popular family beach with safe bathing, rock pools and old fish cellars. P/WC/cafe. (M1)

Coastal Footpath...

Falmouth To Porthpean.
Approx. 40 miles. Two ferry journeys are required to continue along the path. The first, a regular ferry trip to St Mawes sails all year, the second in summer only, across the Percuil Estuary from St Mawes to St Anthony-in-Roseland. At other times, it's usually possible to make arrangements with local boatmen. From St Anthony Head and Zone Point, there are superb views south overlooking Carrick Roads, or looking north east towards the coast up to Portscatho. The route is easier along Pendower Beach and up to Nare Head (331ft), slate cliffs and hedgerows of foxgloves and red campion in summer with a lovely descent to Portloe. From this juncture you will come upon sandy beaches, smugglers' coves and evidence of the china clay industry. East past delightful Portholland and remote farmland meeting the sea, then the steep climb to Dodman Point where there is a granite cross erected in 1896 as a mark for fishermen. Offshore are some notorious currents and the scene of many shipwrecks. The path carries on down to Gorran Haven past the long sweep of Vault Beach. Beyond Chapel Point and Bodrugan's Leap, the path becomes easy going, the landscape has softened. The harsh cliffs and thunderous roar of the north coast, Penwith and Lizard are far behind. Beyond Mevagissey, you are in holiday country as you cross Pentewan Sands, but soon the path is lonely and remote again towards Black Head as it sweeps into St Austell Bay.

Flushing Tender

For Contemporary Art, Dramatic Cliffs, Fabulous Beaches, Mediterranean Light, Stone Circles, Sub-Tropical Gardens and Wild Flowers

A magical spirit embraces these two peninsulas as the elements have shaped the landscape and its hardy people.

From the tall cliffs of Land's End, to the great granite boulders of Nanjizal, to the brilliant white sands of Porthcurno, the interior is a patchwork of treeless fields separated by drystone walls. Yet, on the south east corner are the sheltered harbours, Newlyn and Mousehole, and the valleys, Lamorna and Penberth.

Early Man settled here leaving stone circles and ancient burial mounds. The Early Celts came too, and their ancient crosses remain. For a brief period tin and copper mining brought affluence, and the haunting Engine Houses can be seen at Pendeen and Botallack.

In the C19 and C20 the brilliant Mediterranean light beckoned artists and their followers. The names of Patrick Heron, Barbara Hepworth and Bernard Leach became synonymous with the St Ives movement in the C20. The number of artists increased into the C21, and the towns of Penzance, St Ives and St Just are today thriving centres of art and craftsmanship.

The Lizard is the most southerly point of Britain, and off Lizard Point lie the graveyards of many fine ships. This peninsula shares many characteristics with its neighbour Penwith; a warm, equable climate is rarely touched by frost or snow. The Lizard is a National Nature Reserve of over 4,000 acres, and is a wonderland for botanists, geologists, ornithologists, and the amateur nature lover.

It is also a place of many contrasts, from the thrashing waves of Porthleven Sands to the peace and calm of the Helford River (a mere six miles to the east) overlooked by the sub-tropical gardens of Trebah and Glendurgan,

Not to be forgotten, the fabulous family beaches (Kynance Cove and Kennack Sands) and little harbours (St Anthony and Helford). Whether you choose to beach it, or muck about in boats, you'll be hard pressed to find a safer or better destination for your summer holiday.

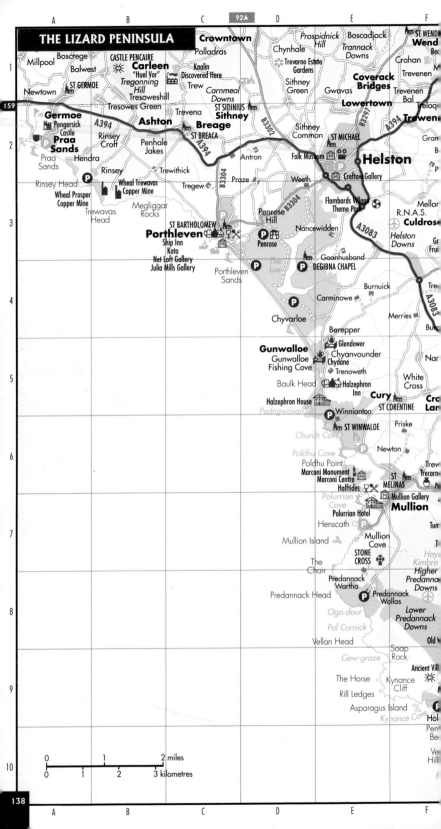

THE LIZARD PENINSULA

Crowntown

Millpool
Boscrege
Balwest
ST GERMOE
Newtown
Germoe
Pengersick
Castle
Praa
Sands
Praa Sands
Hendra
Rinsey Head
Wheal Prosper
Copper Mine
Trewavas
Head

CASTLE PENCAIRE
Carleen
"Huel Vor"
Tregonning
Hill
Tresoweshill
Tresowes Green
Ashton
Rinsey
Croft
Penhale
Jakes
Rinsey
Wheal Trewavas
Copper Mine
Megliggar
Rocks

Polladras
Kaolin
Discovered Here
Trew
Trevena
ST SIDINIUS
Breage
ST BREACA
Trewithick
Tregew
Praze

Prospidnick
Hill
Chynhale
Trevarno Estate
Gardens
Sithney
Green
Gwavas
Sithney
Common
ST MICHAEL
Folk Museum
Antron
Weeth
Penrose
Hill
Nancewidden

Boscadjack
Trannack
Downs
Coverack
Bridges
Lowertown
Helston
Crefftow Gallery
Flambards Village
Theme Park

ST WENDRON
Wendron
Crahan
Trevenen
Trevenen
Bal
Trelog
Trewennack
Gram
Mellor
R.N.A.S.
Culdrose
Helston
Downs

ST BARTHOLOMEW
Porthleven
Ship Inn
Kota
Net Loft Gallery
Julia Mills Gallery
Porthleven
Sands

Penrose
Goonhusband
DEGIBNA CHAPEL
The
Loe
Carminowe
Chyvarloe

Burnuick
Merries
Berepper
Glendower
Gunwalloe
Gunwalloe
Fishing Cove
Chyanvounder
Chydane
Trenoweth
Baulk Head
Halzephron
Inn
Halzephron House
Pedngwinian
Church Cove
Winnianton
ST WINWALOE
Poldhu Cove
Poldhu Point
Marconi Monument
Marconi Centre
Halftides

Burn
Nar
White
Cross
Cury
ST CORENTINE
Priske
Newton
ST
MELINAS
Cross
Lane
Trev
Trecarne

Polurrian
Cove
Polurrian Hotel
Henscath
Mullion Island
The
Chair
Predannack Head
Vellan Head
Ogo-dour
Pol Cornick
Gew-graze
The Horse
Rill Ledges
Asparagus Island
Kynance Cove

Mullion Gallery
Mullion
Mullion
Cove
STONE
CROSS
Predannack
Wartha
Predannack
Wollas
Lower
Predannack
Downs
Soap
Rock
Ancient Vill
Kynance
Cliff
Hol
Pen
Be
Ve
Hill

Tur
Hay
Kimbro
Higher
Predann
Downs
Old

0   1   2 miles
0   1   2   3 kilometres

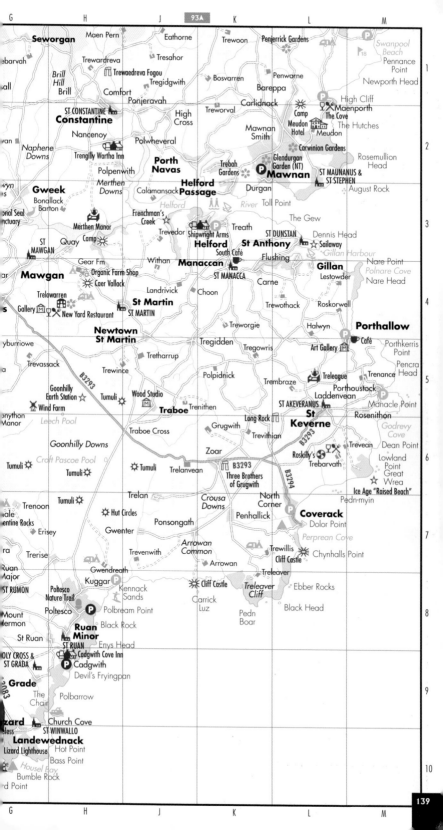

HELSTON

Market town for the Lizard Peninsula and venue for the Floral Dance (around 8 May). Elegantly dressed couples dance through the streets to welcome the coming of Spring, and locals take this opportunity to sample too much of the Spingo brew in the Blue Anchor. It is possibly the only day in the Cornish Year when you will see such sartorial formality, and a perfect coiffeur, a rare sight indeed - the prevailing winds put paid to this. It is worth exploring Church and Coineagehall Streets, location for fine, sophisticated architecture. Birthplace of Henry Trengrouse, inventor of the rocket lifesaving signals. Boating lake, Folk Museum, Flambards Experience. Harvest Fair - Sept (Ist week). (E2) www.helstone-online.co.uk

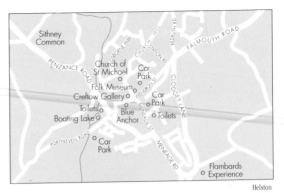

Helston

Where to Go, What to See in and around Helston...

Creftow Gallery, Church St.
Artists co-operative. Open M-Sa 10-5. (E2) 01326 572848

Folk Museum. Church St.
Exhibits of rural life, crafts and industries which flourished in the C19 and C20. Open daily M-Sa 10-1 (-4 holidays), all year. (E2) www.kerrier.gov.uk.

Flambards Experience. All weather attraction: Victorian Village and Britain in the Blitz experiences, Space Quest, live entertainment, Science Centre, Wildlife Experience, best thrill rides in Cornwall.

The Blue Anchor

Open most days early Apr to end Oct 10.30-5. (E3) 01326 573404 www.flambards.co.uk

Huel Vor. Cornish for 'Great Work'. A disused mine with 30 foot wide seams worked at depths of 2,500 ft. (C1)

Loe Pool. The largest natural lake in the West Country inhabited by wildfowl and surrounded by rhododendrons and wild flowers. In evidence since the C14, the River Cober was blocked by silt and the Loe Bar developed to form a bank of flint shingle. (D3) www.nationaltrust.org.uk

Pengersick Castle. Fortified Tudor manor c. 1500 with evidence of apothocarian garden in C14, to be renovated. This place of legend and mystery welcomes visitors by appointment on 01736 762579. (A2) www.ghosthunting.org.uk

Where to Eat, Drink & Be Merry in Helston...

The Blue Anchor, Coineagehall St. Brewers of Spingo Beer, a strong ale. Beware on leaving, the gutters beside the pavement can be overlooked and a tumble, or mishap, should be avoided. (E2) 01326 562821 www.spingoales.com

CADGWITH

Thatched cottages of darkly mottled serpentine rocks, and boats beached on the shingle cove create a picturesque yet workaday scene. Haunt of artists. Superb coastal scenery. Café & Inn. Fresh fish for sale. Gallery. Suggest you park at top of village and walk down, otherwise you may well get stuck in the bottleneck. (H9) www.cadgwith.com

COVERACK

Charming old fishing village and former smuggling centre. Small protected harbour. Fish (& chip) restaurant in the old lifeboat station. (L7)

The Blitz Experience, Flambards ss

1793 James Rush, a Cornishman is deported on the first Australian convict ship   1800 Birth of William Lovett in Newlyn, Chartist and pamphleteer

Grey Seal

GWEEK

Attractive village with shop and pub was formerly the port to Helston and the surrounding mining areas until the C19. It lies at the head of the Helford Estuary where you will see the old quays, a busy boatyard and entrance to the Seal Sanctuary. (G3)

Helford River

What to visit...

National Seal Sanctuary.
The UK's leading Grey seal rescue centre. Home to permanent resident seals and sea lions. Feeds and talks throughout the day, real working seal hospital, Cornish coast rock pool, otter creek trail, café & gift shop. Open daily from 10. (G3) www.sealsanctuary.co.uk

HELFORD RIVER

Beautiful tree-lined (hollies and oaks) tidal river with romantic creeks (Frenchman's Creek, immortalised by Daphne du Maurier's novel) and inlets. Picturesque villages of Durgan, Helford (passenger ferry) and St Anthony (SailAway organise dinghy hire 01326 231357) popular with 'muck abouters' in boats. www.stanthony.co.uk Oyster farm at Porth Navas. On the north shore, a profusion of wonderful gardens, see below for details. (J3)

Gweek

1801   Richard Trevithick operates the first road-going locomotive

1802   Richard Trevithick invents the High Pressure Steam Dredge

St Christopher: Breage

Glendurgan Garden mw/nt

Gardens to Visit...

Carwinion Gardens. Valley garden with camellias, rhododenrons, azaleas, wild flowers and 100 species of bamboo. Incorporating Towan Camellia and Hydrangea Nursery. Also B & B. Open daily 10-5.30. (L2) 01326 250258 www.carwinion.co.uk

Glendurgan Gardens (NT). Valley garden of great beauty. Fine trees and shrubs, a maze, a giant's stride, a wooded valley of primulas and bluebells runs down to Helford River. Garden open 8 Feb-1 Nov Tu-Sa & BH M's (M in Aug) 10.30-5.30. (L2) 01326 250906 www.nationaltrust.org.uk

Trebah Gardens. Magical sub-tropical ravine gardens running down to private beach on Helford River, a canvas of everchanging colour from Spring to Autumn. A garden for the plantsman, artist, family, and a paradise for children. Art Gallery holds the Hunting Art Prizes in Spring. Open daily all year 10.30-5 (or dusk if earlier). (K2) 01326 250448 www.trebah-garden.co.uk

Churches to Visit...

Breage Church. C15 granite building with fine C15 wall painting of St Christopher. (C2)

Gunwalloe Church. C14 unusual detached tower with remains of C15 rood screen illustrated with paintings of the apostles. It lies in dunes beside the beach, and is a popular local venue for weddings. (E6)

Wallpainting, Breage Church

Landewednack (Church Cove) Church. Tower and Norman doorway of serpentine stone. (H9)

Mawgan In Meneage Church. C13-C15 wagon roof and brasses in lovely setting. (G3)

St Keverne Church. Spacious interior, C14, with tall spire. Resting place for many drowned sailors. (L5)

Ancient Cornwall...

Halliggye Fogou. The largest underground store chamber in Cornwall 9ft x 6ft. (H4)

Trebah Gardens ss

THE LIZARD

The most southerly village in England. Popular walking centre. Gift shops galore, many selling ornaments made from the purplish Serpentine Rock, unique to the Lizard. There are haunting photographs of shipwrecks in the local pubs. At Church Cove, pretty cottages and converted lifeboat station. Walks to Lizard Point and Kynance Cove, both have cafes. (G10) www.lizard-peninsula.co.uk

Church Cove

Special Places to Visit on The Lizard Peninsula...

Goonhilly Downs.

High central plateau on Lizard Peninsula. One of the oldest nature conservancy reserves in the country. Thus, of great interest to botanists, geologists and archaeologists. Profusion of wild flowers, the summer air is acute with scent. Buzzards soar up high. Green serpentine rock forms. Croft Pascoe Nature Reserve. (H6)

Goonhilly Satellite Earth Station. Transmitting millions of phone calls, TV pictures & computer data via the famous massive satellite dishes. Tours, exhibits, films, shop, cafe and more. 0800 679 593. (H5) www.goonhilly.bt.com

Grange Fruit Farm.

PYO fruit (strawberries). Farm shop. Cream teas and light lunches. Open daily May-Oct. (F4) www.thegrangecornwall.com

Lizard Lighthouse. Large and famous building completed in 1752, with alterations in 1903. Stands amid the treacherous coast haunted by many shipwrecks. Open daily East-Oct, weather permitting. (G10)

Poltesco Nature Trail. Three miles of wooded valley caves and cliffs. (H8)

Porthallow Arts. Gallery and workshop promotes local artists' work, and runs day courses. Open East-Oct M-Th & Sa 10-6, Su 12-4. (M4)

RNAS Culdrose. The largest helicopter base in Europe. Much is underground. Viewing enclosure with café and shop. Open Day in August; see local adverts for details. (F3) www.forcesculdrose.2day.ws

Trelowarren Gallery.

Original home of the Cornwall Crafts Association; with fellow gallery at Trelissick holds members and touring exhibitions. Education Projects. Open daily 10.30-5.30 Mar-Nov. (G4) 01326 221567 www.cornwallcrafts.co.uk

Trelowarren. Home of the Vyvyan family since 1427. Acres of woodland and farmland surround the house. Chateau camping, eco-buildings for sale and rent, and woodland walks. House open East-Sept, Ws & BHMs 2.30-4.30 (45" tour). (G4) www.trelowarren.co.uk

Wood Studio, Rosuick Farm.

Sculptural woodturning by Samvado. The wonder of wood, turned into amazing shapes: bowls, spheres, obelisks. Open most days 11-6. (J5) 01326 231783

Goonhilly Earth Station ss

MULLION

A busy village, and centre for much of the Lizard Peninsula. It has a splendid church, some popular pubs, an active cricket club and a successful school. The One-Way system will draw you in and lead you out. A visit to the Cove is a must. The beaches close to, Poldhu and Polurrian, are popular with the locals and will often be empty of visitors. (E6) www.mullioncornwall.com

Mullion Gallery ss

Old Inn, Mulllion

What to See & Visit...

Marconi Monument. The first transatlantic morse code messages were transmitted from this spot on 12 December 1901, and picked up by Gugliemo Marconi in St John's, Newfoundland. (E6)

Mullion Cove. Dramatic cove at foot of tall cliffs, with harbour built in 1895. Lifeboat until 1901. Offshore, a bird sanctuary on Mullion Island. Fishing trips. (E7)

Mullion Church. Late medieval with fascinating bench ends. (F6)

Mullion Gallery, Nansmellyon Rd. Work of over 80 artists living on the Lizard Peninsula: paintings, ceramics, sculptures, wood carvings. Open M-Sa summer, W-Sa winter, 10-1, 3-5. (E7) 01326 241170 www.mulliongallery.supanet.com

Trecarne Pottery, Meaver Road. Michael Roux creates colourful and functional stoneware with a touch of gallic humour, inspired by the sea and elements. (F6) 01326 241294 www.trecarnepottery.co.uk

Where to Stay in Mullion...

Halftides, Laflouder Lane, Mullion. B&B. If you seek peace and solitude, sea views across a verdant landscape, your own private footpath to a sandy beach and a vivacious hostess who can paint colourful works of art, this is it. Ideal for families, or those seeking refuge from our mad, crazy world. Also a self-catering cottage. (E6) 01326 241935 www.halftides.co.uk

Polurrian Hotel. Overlooks Polurrian beach guaranteeing stunning views. Restaurants. Pools. Gym. Tennis. Creche. Games Room. Terraces. Gardens. The High Point Restaurant provides fish and local produce at reasonable prices. (E7) 01326 240421 www.polurrianhotel.com

Mullion Church

Porthleven Harbour

PORTHLEVEN

Attractive large harbour with ship building yard, C19 Harbour House and imposing Wesleyan chapel c.1890. The vulnerable harbour faces south-west and was built for the mining industry in 1811. A south-westerly gale in 1824 washed it away, later to be rebuilt in 1855, with lock gates. Surf break for the hardy. (C3)

Where to East, Drink & Be Merry...

Kota, Harbourside.
Foodies love this place. Always something new to look forward to. Fish is the speciality in all its delicate forms with a twist of the Polynesian (Maori). Dinner 6.30-9. Rooms available. (C3) 01326 562407 www.kotarestaurant.co.uk

Ship Inn. Fine pub with loads of character offers down to earth food cooked to order, at reasonable prices. Built in the C18, it is one of the harbour's oldest buildings. Free house. Recommended. (C3) 01326 564204

Galleries to Visit...

Julia Mills Gallery. A beach-hut style gallery incorporating the workshop of glass-designer, Julia Mills. A perfect setting for the sea-inspired work on show. All her work depicts some aspect of the Cornish environment. Open M-F 10-5, Sa 11-5. (C3) 01326 569340 www.juliamillsgsllery.co.uk

Net Loft Gallery, The Harbour.
Range of seascapes and landscapes paintings, ceramics, bronzes and jewellery. Open daily Apr-Oct & Xmas. (C3) 01326 569365

Where to Stay on the Lizard Peninsula...

Chydane B&B, Gunwalloe.
In a quite spectacular location overlooking Loe Sands and Mounts Bay, and decorated with exquisite Dutch taste. Conveniently located within spitting distance of the local hostelry. (D5) 01326 241232 www.chydane.co.uk

Glendower B&B, Gunwalloe.
Bright and cheerful Cornish cottage rooms decorated with Farrow and Ball paintwork, designer fabrics and cosy rugs. Spanking new Wet Rooms with all mod cons. (E5) 01326 561282 www.glendower-gunwalloe.co.uk

Halzephron House, Gunwalloe.
Described in the Press as "The most stylish holiday home in Britain".

Sleeps up to 12. Set in 3-acres of headland with staggering views over Mounts Bay. Conservatory and walled garden for parties and barbecues. Visiting chef, yoga and treatments available. (E5) 07899 925816 www.halzephronhouse.co.uk

Landewednack House. Intimate and luxurious small hotel decorated with considerable care and finesse provides superb food and wines. All set within a protected walled garden. Heated pool. (G10) 01326 290877 www.landewednackhouse.com

Julia Mills Gallery

Halzephron House

Pentraeth Cove

Merthen Manor.
The Vyvyans have lived in this fortified manor for 300 years. Set in 100 acres of woodland overlooking the Helford River. B&B is country house style. Child friendly. Barns to let. Tennis Court. (H3) 01326 340664 www.merthenmanor.co.uk

Treleague B&B, St Keverne.
C17 converted barns afford fine views over Falmouth Bay. Comfy beds and gleaming new bathrooms. Close to the family beaches of Kennack and Coverack. Self-catering cottage. (L5) 01326 281500 www.treleague.co.uk

Meudon Hotel.
Family-run Country House Hotel with sub-tropical valley gardens leading to private beach. Old-fashioned style of décor popular with the retired and middle aged. (L2) 01326 250541 www.meudon.co.uk

Where to Eat, Drink & Be Merry...

Cadgwith Cove Inn.
This could well be a fine start off point for cliff top walks. Park at the top end of village. Snug bars with parquet floors. Photos and log fire provide the cosy ambience. Sit outside on warm summer evenings. Good value food and real ales to plunder. (H9)

The Cove, Maenporth Beach.
Relaxed and well-priced restaurant offers a tasty selection of fish and meat dishes. Tapas. Opens 10.30, Lunch 12-3, Dinner 6-9.30. (L2) 01326 251136

Trengilly Wartha Inn.
Popular inn known for its expansive wine list, infinite Malts and restaurant. Beer mats cover the ancient beams. Children and dogs welcome. B&B. (H2) 01326 340332 www.trengilly.co.uk

Halzephron Inn.
This C16 award-winning pub is cosy, friendly and the daily specials provide a rewarding treat, especially if you have been battling the coast path. Serves delicious Doom Bar. Bright artworks line the walls. Family room. B&B. (E5) 01326 240406 www.halzephron-inn.co.uk

New Yard Restaurant, Trelowarren.
Al fresco dining within an enchanting C14 estate. Simple lunches, more adventurous dinners. Open daily Tu-Su. (G4) 01326 221595

Roskilly's.
Working organic farm sells its own ice cream, fudge, clotted cream, preserves etc. Fabulous pasties. Art & Crafts gallery (furniture, a speciality). Restaurant. Open daily 10-dusk (W/Es in winter). Footpaths to woods, meadows and ponds. (L6) www.roskillys.co.uk

South Café, Manaccan.
Martyn Warner's café mirrors his world-wide travels and interest in local art and suppliers. Child friendly. Opens 10.30 for coffee, lunch and dinner. (K4) 01326 231331 www.south-cafe.co.uk

Roskilly's

Kynance Cove

Beaches and Surfing...

Praa Sands. Mile of firm golden sands. Good family beach but HZ to bathe at LT. P/WC/LG/café. Surfing - Bigger swell than Perranathnoe. Hence a popular beach. N end protected from W winds and may produce a fast R break. E end can create HZ rips in a big swell. (A2)

Porthleven Sands. 4 miles of sands. A steep, shelving beach with undertow. For strong swimmers only. Scene of many shipwrecks. P. Surfing - On W side of harbour channel. A much discussed reef break, produced by a big swell. LT is hollow and dangerous. HT is affected by the backwash. Strong rips when big. For the experienced only and not for the squeamish! (C4)

Church Cove. Pebbles and sand sided by low cliffs. Dunes cover St Winwalloe church. NT P/LG/WC/shop. (E6)

Polurrian Cove. Access via 3/4 mile path from Mullion church to sandy beach edged by high cliffs. Strong tidal currents. Bathing HZ at LT. (E7)

Poldhu Cove. Popular family beach. Bathing HZ one hour either side of LT. P/WC/LG/Café. (E6)

Mullion Cove.
Tiny beach at LT. Beautiful harbour walls. P/WC/café. (E7)

Kynance Cove. Large P area. 10 minute walk to steps. Good bathing. White sand at LT. Very popular in summer. Wild-shaped serpentine rocks. At HT the roaring noise of the blow holes. (F9)

Pentraeth Beach.
Access down slippery path to beach of grey sand and rocks. (F10)

Polpeor Cove. Steep walk down to rocky shore; the most southerly point in Britain. Old lifeboat station. P/WC/café. (G10)

Hounsel Bay. For the agile only down a steep path to the small sandy beach. Overlooked by hotel. (G10)

Carleon Cove. Peaceful cove, 10 min walk from Poltesco. (H8)

Hounsel Bay

Kennack Sands.
Popular bucket and spade family beach with rock pools. Fine bathing. S-B hire/P/WC/cafe. Surfing - Good waves only created after big swells. (J8)

Coverack. Tiny beach, shingle at LT. P/cafe. (L7)

Lowland Point. Ice age 'Raised Beach" on which the passenger liner Paris was shipwrecked in 1899. Access from St Keverne via Trevean or Trebarvath Farms. (M6)

Porthoustock. Pebbled shelving beach, quarries to either side. P. (M5)

Porthallow. Small pebbled beach, rocks to sides. P/inn. (M4)

Men-Aver Beach. 20 min coastal walk from Gillan. Isolated with sandy patches and rock pools. (M4)

Gillan Harbour. Shingle and sand, rocky promontory. (L3)

Flushing. Isolated shingle beach with sand at LT. (L3)

Helford Village. Sand and shale visible at LT. P/WC. (K3)

Helford Passage. Small stony beach in front of Ferry Boat Inn. Sand at LT. P. (J3)

Durgan Beach. Small stony beach down steep hill. P. (K3)

Porthallack Beach.
Shingle beach along coastal path from Durgan. (K3)

1825   Treffry Viaduct under construction.   1827   Liskeard and Looe Canal opens.

151

Loe Bar at Dusk

Bream Cove. Isolated sandy beach and rock pools popular with skin-divers. (L2)

Maenporth. Popular family beach with sheltered and spacious sands. Surfing, P/WC/LG/cafe. (L1)

Coastal Footpath...

Praa Sands to Lizard.

Approx 18 miles. Interesting coastal path: craggy cliffs and splendid sandy beaches. Start with a stiffish climb up to Trewavas Head, then a cliffside walk to Porthleven. Path follows cliff edge to Loe Bar, Gunwalloe and Church Cove, apparently buried treasure is hidden here. On to the caves, arches and black rocks of Mullion Cove. Fine walking on cliff tops around Vellan Head and past breath-taking precipices to Pigeon Ogo, a vast amphitheatre of rock. The crowning glory is Kynance Cove, a spectacle of swirling currents (at HT), whooshing blow holes and wild shaped serpentine rocks, great bathing at LT and a cafe. Well-trodden path to Britain's most southerly point, Lizard Point. Caves and caverns about Polpeor Cove. East is the Lion's Den, a large collapsed sea-cave, a sudden vast hole in the cliff turf.

Lizard to Falmouth.

Approx 26 miles. The east side of the peninsula is less rugged, the slopes are gentler, the landscape becomes more hospitable as one travels northward. First you pass pretty Church Cove, and along cliff top to the Devil's Frying Pan, a larger version of the Lion's Den, its blow hole roars when the easterlies blow. Through thatched Cadgwith to Kennack Sands where the path is easy going, hugging the cliff edge, and almost at sea level from Coverack to Lowland Point, scene of an Ice Age 'Raised Beach'. Offshore, at low tide 'The Manacles' are visible, a treacherous reef that has caused the death of more than 400 sailors, many are buried in St Keverne's churchyard. The 60ft spire of the church serves as a daymark for sailors and fishermen. At Godrevy Cove, the path turns inland to Rosenithon and Porthoustock to avoid quarries, returning to the coast at Porthallow. A peaceful stretch to Gillan Harbour, possible to wade the creek at low tide, or continue to bridge crossing the head of the creek at Carne. Through tangled woods to Helford village and ferry across Helford estuary, which runs from Easter to end of October, to either Helford Passage or the beach at Durgan. From here the path passes Mawnan Church and along the cliff tops to Swanpool Beach (Falmouth).

Trebah Beach ss

Ogo-dour, Predannack

Sennen Cove

Crab Pattern, Portreath

Porth Nanven

Kynance Cove

Sandy Mouth

Cawsand

Duckpool

Early Morning Jog, Porthmeor, St Ives

Rock Slide, Bedruthan Steps

Duckpool

Sennen Cove

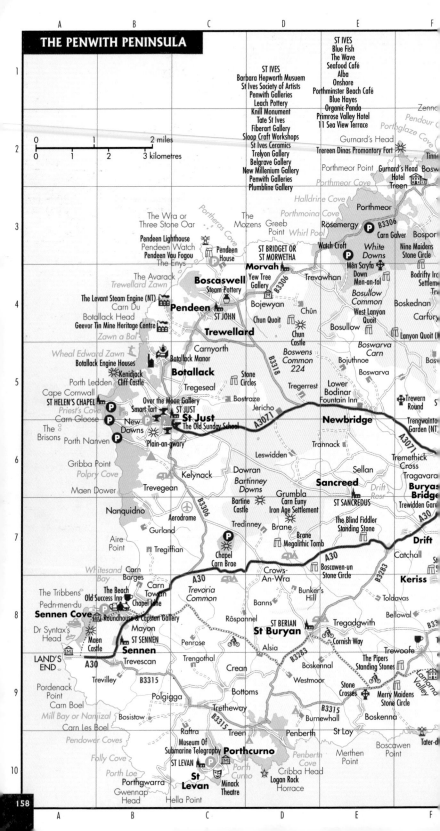

THE PENWITH PENINSULA

Penzance Harbour

PENZANCE

A lively and busy town tempered by a gentle climate; sub-tropical flowers grow in the Morrab Gardens and at nearby Trengwainton. The town trail takes you to Chapel Street and the Egyptian House and on to the exquisite shops and restaurants of Market Jew Street, dominated by the Ionic columns of Market House, and the Statue of Sir Humphrey Davy, inventor of the miners' Davy lamp. Floating Harbour, Ship and Helicopter ferries to the Isles of Scilly, shark and deep sea fishing trips, swimming pools (in & outdoor), West Cornwall Spring Show - late March. (H6) www.penzance.co.uk

Madron Church.

Mother-Church of Penzance; granite, and a good size with fine wagon roof. Jacobean Tower Screen, bench ends and C17 brass. (G5)

Where to Stay...

Abbey Hotel, Abbey St.

A sweet gem dating from the C17 stands hidden behind a walled garden and courtyard. Luxuriously decorated with fabulous fabrics, awash with colour. Call it shabby chic, or an antique emporium, whatever, it has style, panache and will leave you with sweet memories. (H5) 01736 366906 www.theabbeyonline.co.uk

Penzance Arts Club, Chapel St.

A touch of bohemia in colourful surroundings (decor and conversation). Restaurant. Poetry readings, jazz nights...art on view. Cricket Club. (H5) 01736 363761 www.penzanceartsclub.co.uk

Abbey Hotel ss

Summer House, Cornwall Terrace. An enthusiasm for life pervades this small hotel. Be it art, design or food with a Mediterranean edge, it all goes to amplify this hostelry's unique qualities. They describe themselves as a boutique B&B with 5 double-rooms. (H5) 01736 363744 www.summerhouse-cornwall.com

Where to Eat, Drink & Be Merry...

Abbey Restaurant, Abbey St. Award-winning cuisine combined with a classical and modern technique, to great effect. Proudly uses local suppliers. Dinner times are seasonal and vary from 7-9.30, Lunch F-Su 12-1.30. Three courses for £25.00. (H5) 01736 330680 www.theabbeyonline.com

Chapel St Bistro. Set in the basement of the Penzance Arts Club surrounded by sculptures and artworks, the atmosphere is

Penzance Docks

Penzance

Simon Stooks, Cornwall Contemporary ss

congenial, the food is local produce, and excellent. Dinner 6.30-9.30. Tu-Th & Sa. (H5) 01736 332555

Harris's, 46 New St.
Well organised establishment with a loyal clientele provides uncommonly good food. Interesting French house wines. Lunch 12-2, Dinner 7-10. M-Sa. (H5) 01736 364408
www.harrissrestaurant.co.uk

Chapel Street Pubs...

The Turks Head.
C13 inn, claimed to be the oldest in Penzance. Selection of real ales and serves fresh fish, steaks and veggie meals. (H6) 01736 363093
www.turksheadpenzance.co.uk

The Admiral Bembo.
A pub of great character. The décor in unique and resembles the Lower Deck of a galleon. Lots of artefacts to admire if conversation is muted. Good beers. (H6)

Galleries to Visit in Penzance...

Belerion Gallery, Bread St.
Eclectic mix offering a fresh look at the Cornish art scene: pottery, sculpture and paintings. Open Tu-Sa from 10.30. (H6) 01736 351249

Cornwall Contemporary, 1 Parade Street.
One of the leading galleries in the South-West managed by Sara Brittain who has had a long and active interest in the Cornish art scene. Make sure you keep abreast of their ever-changing exhibitions. Open M-Sa 10-5. 01736 874749
www.cornwallcontemporary.com

The Exchange, Princes Street.
A major new art space developed in conjunction with the Newlyn Art Gallery. This showcase for national and international art holds regular educational programmes. Open M-Sa 10-5, Su 11-4 (closed M/Tu in winter). 01736 363715
www.newlynartgallery.co.uk

Lighthouse Gallery, 25 Causeway Head.
Light, fresh and friendly gallery featuring a fine selection of artists. Open M-Sa 10-5. (H6) 01736 350555
www.lighthouse-gallery.com

Summer House ss

1840   Mass emigration of miners to Real del Monte, Mexico, Lake Hurn, Canada and Wisconsin, USA

1850   Mass emigration of miners to South African copper mines

Penlee House Gallery & Museum, Morrab Road.
An elegant gallery and museum set within a Victorian house and park. Changing exhibitions mainly feature famous 'Newlyn School' artists (1880-1930). There is an excellent cafe and well-stocked shop open daily M-Sa East-Sept 10-5, Oct-East 10.30-4.30. (H6) 01736 363625
www.penleehouse.org.uk

Shears Fine Art, 58 Chapel St.
The Early "Newlyn" and "St Ives" schools are featured here. Open M-Sa 10-5. (H6) 01736 350501

Stoneman Graphics Gallery, Orchard Flower Farm, Madron Hill. Run by Linda Stoneman whose late husband, Hugh Stoneman, the master printer, used a variety of techniques: etching, drypoint, woodcut and linocut to print works by Terry Frost and

Penlee House Gallery ss

many masters of their art. Open Th & F 10-5, Sa 10-1, or by appointment. (G5) 01736 351363
www.stonemangraphics.co.uk

The Goldfish Bowl, 56 Chapel St. New, quirky or original look at figurative art, with paintings, ceramics and sculpture. Open M-Sa 10-5. (H6) 01736 360573
www.the-goldfish-bowl.co.uk

Trengwainton Gardens (NT). Large shrub garden with a vast collection of rhododendrons. Colourful in spring/early summer. Views over Mounts Bay. Open 10 Feb-2 Nov Su-Th 10.30-5. (F6) 01736 363148

Trereife Park. Queen Anne manor house and home to the Le Grice family whose descendant, Valentine Le Grice, was a poet and friend to the

Romantics, Wordsworth and Coleridge. Fine plasterwork and wood panelling. The garden is classically Cornish with parterres and terraces. Christina's Café. Open Su-F, early May to early Sept, 2-5. 01736 362750
www.trereife.co.uk

Tresco Abbey Gardens, Scilly Isles. A sub-tropical garden with palms, proteas, South African succulents. Garden open daily all year round, 10-4. Shop open Feb-Nov. Day trip by Helicopters from Penzance Mar-Oct.

Trewidden Gardens.
Originally planted in the C19 by T B Bolitho, the garden comprises ten acres of paths and dells with a fine collection of camellias and magnolias. Open daily mid-Feb to 30 Sept 10.30-4.30. (F7) 01736 366800

The Abbey Restaurant ss

Trengwainton ab/nt

Ben Catt, Lighthouse Gallery ss

Linda Styles, Over The Moon Gallery, St Just.

MARAZION

Reputed to be the oldest town in Cornwall. Lies opposite St Michael's Mount, where the ancient harbour used to trade in tin from galleries. Popular location for windsurfing and kitesurfing. A fine place to stay if Penzance is not to your fancy. (K6) www.marazion.net

Where to Stay...

Ednovean Farm B&B, Perranuthnoe.
This is luxury B&B. Three gorgeous bedrooms decorated in designer fabrics. Immaculate bathrooms. Italian garden. A visit to their website will seduce you and lure you to Ednovean. (L6) 01736 711883 www.ednoveanfarm.co.uk

Ednovean B&B ss

Ennys B&B, St Hilary.
A perfectly proportioned Cornish farmhouse laid down with flagstone floors, large square rooms and high ceilings. All tastefully and luxuriantly decorated with comfy sofas, book-lined walls and contrasting styles of art, from Indian wall hangings to Cornish abstracts. The bedrooms have all the latest fixtures and fittings, the beds are enormous. Self-catering cottages, too. (M5) 01736 740262 www.ennys.co.uk

Mount Haven Hotel, Turnpike Road. A friendly and relaxed ambience pervades this hotel whose bedrooms have been completely refurbished in contemporary designs. The owner's

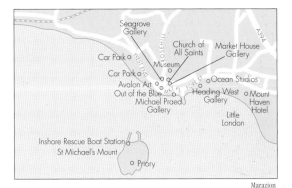

Marazion

travels to the Far East and her interest in Buddhism are mirrored by the eclectic range of paintings and sculptures on view. The views from the terrace across to St Michael's Mount are quite superb. The restaurant boasts fresh fish caught just off the Newlyn Quay. (K6) 01736 710249 www.mounthaven.co.uk

Ocean Studios, Mounts Bay House, Turnpike Hill.
Quality, self-catering, contemporarily designed accommodation. Therapies on hand to help you unwind. (K6) 01736 711040 www.mountsbayhouse.com

Galleries in Marazion...

Avalon Art, West End.
Well established gallery with a mix of naive and abstract paintings: landscapes and seascapes. Open daily 10.30-5.30. (K6) 01736 710161

Heading West Gallery, Fore Street. Specialises in black and white photography and jewellery.

Worth a visit to see images in this often neglected form. (K6) 01736 711770 www.headingwest.co.uk

Market House Gallery, The Square. Large gallery with a wide range of paintings, ceramics and glass. Open daily. (K6) 01736 719019

Michael Praed Gallery, Market Place. Contemporary art by Michael Praed and large display of ceramics and sculpture. Open as advertised. (K6) 01736 711400

Out Of The Blue, The Square.
Full mix of crafts: driftwood, copper, stained glass, jewellery and paintings by resident Cornishmen. Open daily. (K6) 01736 719019 www.out-of-the-blue-gallery.co.uk

Seagrove Gallery, The Square.
Wide range of textiles, jewellery, paintings, pottery and paintings. Courtyard for al fresco coffee and cakes. Self-catering. Open daily summer, winter Th-M. (K6) 01736 710732

Seagrove Gallery, Marazion

St Michael's Mount

St Michael's Mount   rr/nt

St Michael's Mount (NT). A legendary place of romance and pilgrimage and a child's dream of a fairy castle. Originally the site of a Benedictine chapel established by Edward the Confessor. In the C14, the spectacular castle was added. Later to be used as a nunnery and military fortress before the St Aubyn family purchased it in 1659, living here ever since. Church dates from 1275. Exquisite Blue Drawing Room with Chippendale furniture. Pictures by Gainsborough and the Cornish artist, John Opie. Harbour, railway. Open 16 Mar-2 Nov M-F & Su 10.30-5, last admission 4.15. Guided tours Nov-Mar if weather and tides permit. Mar-May Tu for pre-arranged educational visits. Church opens on Sunday at 10.30 for 11am Service. Restaurant and shop open daily Apr-Oct. Special family ticket available. Please Note: access on foot over the causeway at low tide, or during summer months only, by ferry at high tide (return ferry tickets should not be taken). Make sure the Mount is open before crossing on the ferry! (J6) 01736 710507 www.nationaltrust.org.uk

Blue Drawing Room, St Michael's Mount   nt

Lamorna Cove

Lamorna Cove

MOUSEHOLE

Pronounced 'Mowzle'. Arguably the most attractive of Cornish fishing villages. The stone cottages huddle around the harbour, facing east, sheltered from the prevailing winds. Originally called Port Enys, it was sacked and burnt by Spanish invaders in 1595. It is worth exploring the hidden alleyways where you will come across art galleries and exceptional restaurants, or if you are in need of rest, sit on the harbour wall and watch a time capsule of fishing boats, and children at play. Famed for Christmas Lights and Tom Bawcock's Eve, and children's story, The Mousehole Cat. (G8)

LAMORNA

A straggling village that became popular with artists in the early C20. The heavily wooded valley ends at the small harbour overlooking a bay of great granite boulders, many embellished with green seaweed. Summer craft exhibitions are held here. A café overlooks the cove. (F9)

Where to Eat, Drink & Be Merry...

The Cove Restaurant. In quite exceptional location overlooking the valley, and sea beyond. The restaurant has large windows providing sea views. Fish dishes: red mullet, turbot and scallops...rich, yummy puddings. Luxurious self-catering. (F9) 01736 731411 www.thecovecornwall.com

Lamorna Wink Inn. In the same family for many, many years, and it tells, for all their bric-a-brac that most of us would hide away in cupboards is hanging from the ceiling. A place of character, serves pub grub. Seating area outside. (F9)

Lamorna Wink Inn

Mousehole

Where to Stay, Eat, Drink & Be Merry...

Old Coastguard Hotel & Restaurant, The Parade.
Panoramic views from this light and airy restaurant. Fish (from Newlyn Market) a speciality. Steak and Vegetarian menus too. Stylish modern accommodation. Lunch and dinner. (G8) 01736 731222
www.oldcoastguardhotel.co.uk

The Cornish Range, 6 Chapel St. Established specialist fish restaurant exploits the local Newlyn market. Dinner only. Three stylish double-rooms available for B&B. (G8) 01736 731488
www.cornishrange.co.uk

Ship Inn, Harbourside.
Popular, busy pub decorated with beams and panelling. Open fires and memorabilia. Bar food and local fish dishes a speciality. St Austell ales. (G8)

2 ForeStreet. A new friendly venture specialising in yes, fresh fish and fish dishes galore. The design is modern and clean, and self-catering accommodation is available. Open daily in High Season, Nov, Jan-Feb only five days. Closed between lunch and dinner. (G8) 01736 731164
www.2forestreet.co.uk

Galleries in Mousehole...

Essex Tyler Gallery, 3 Brook St. Ornamental Raku pottery based on old Japanese methods. Also paintings, jewellery and mixed media. Open daily Mar-Dec 10-6. (G8) 01736 731109
www.tylergallery.co.uk

Millpool Gallery, Mill Lane.
Claims to be refreshingly different, with off-beat, idiosyncratic and naive art from the West Country. Open daily East-Oct 11-5. (G8) 01736 731115
www.millpoolgallerymousehole.co.uk

Nigel Hallard Studios, 6-8 Keigwin Place.
Nigel has crafted his art in Mousehole for 40 years, painting canvases in all styles and form, from his own Cubist style to more realistic methods. Originals and Limited Editions for sale. Open daily Su-F 11-5.30. (G8) 01736 731095
www.nigelhallard.com

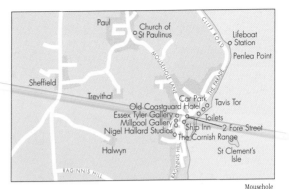

Mousehole

Nigel Hallard Studios, Mousehole

Red Gurnards, J H Turner & Co., Fish Merchants, Newlyn

NEWLYN

Home of Cornwall's largest fishing fleet and the busiest fish market with cannery for pilchards and mackerel. The medieval quay is a delight. Like St Ives, a favourite haunt for artists - Edwardian painters formed the 'Newlyn School' artists' colony. Much of their work is on show at the Penlee House Gallery in Penzance. The Newlyn Art Gallery continues the tradition of pioneering artists. Similarly, neighbouring Mousehole, and much of old Newlyn, was destroyed by Spanish Raiders in 1595. Art galleries. Fresh fish and shellfish merchants aplenty. Fish Festival Aug BH M. (G7) www.newlyn.info

Skate , Newlyn Fish Market

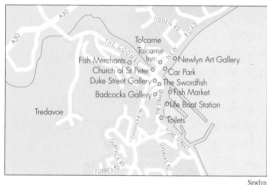
Newlyn

Galleries in Newlyn...

Badcocks Gallery, The Strand.
Changing exhibitions every three weeks Mar-Dec. Leading Cornish artists, sculptors, jewellers and craftsmen. Open M-F 10.30-5.30, Sa 11-5.30. (G7) 01736 366159 www.badcocksgallery.co.uk

Duke Street Gallery & Coffee Shop.
Combines painting and ceramics with sculpture, photography and crafts by local artists. Open daily. (G7) 01736 331188

Newlyn Art Gallery, New Road.
Leading contemporary art venue with changing exhibitions of painting, sculpture, drawing and photography. Gallery shop and cafe. Open daily M-Sa & BHs 10-5. (G7) 01736 363715 www.newlynartgallery.co.uk

Where to East, Drink & Be Merry...

Tolcarne Inn, Tolcarne Place.
C18 oak beamed pub is the traditional venue after many "Newlyn Openings". Exhibits local artists and photographers. Jazz on Su. Home-cooked meals and "Specials". Open daily. (G7)

The Swordfish. Pub beloved by the local trawler-men who when just back from a long trip may be a touch bellicose and unruly. So beware. Open all day. (G7)

Sea Bass, Newlyn Fish Market

Newlyn

PORTHCURNO

Small village leads down to one of the great beaches of Cornwall (or anywhere) with its effervescent, turquoise sea and white sands. Best viewed from the western side of the coastal footpath, or the steps below the Minack Theatre. Café. (C10)

Logan's Rock.

A huge naturally balanced rock weighing 66 tons. It was dislodged in the early C19 by a young naval officer, a nephew of Oliver Goldsmith, and such was the outcry that he was forced to return it almost bankrupting himself. (D10)

Minack Theatre.

Open Air Theatre cut out of the cliff side affords stupendous views. Season of plays, musicals, operas in unique 750 seat theatre. Season; End of May to mid-Sept. Exhibition Centre tells the story of Rowena Cade who built the theatre, open all year

mid-Mar to Oct 9.30-5.30, Nov to mid-Mar 10-4 (closed 24/25 Dec). (C10) 01736 810181 www.minack.com

Porthcurno Museum.

Secret wartime communication centre built in tunnels. Cable ships and cable laying. Open East-Oct Su-F & BH Sa 10-5, & winter M 10-4. (C10) www.porthcurno.org.uk

ST IVES

A labyrinth of narrow streets, whitewashed cottages, brightly coloured boats, sandy beaches and light, so bright, piercing and clear that you could be forgiven for thinking you were in a Mediterranean village. It was the light that drew the early artists in the C19 and C20s. The town's charm remains unaltered by the thousands who flock here. It is a special place and worth intense exploration around the many side streets.

Perhaps, a course in painting may take your fancy. St Ives is a centre for art galleries and seafood. The beaches are almost white, and the sea shimmers in the sunlight. Music & Arts Festival - Sept. (K1) www.stives-cornwall.co.uk www.stives.co.uk

Where to Eat, Drink & Be Merry...a selection

Alba, Wharf Road.

Great views over the harbour from this old Lifeboat Station through wide glass windows. Modern European cuisine. (K1) 01736 797222 www.thealbarestaurant.com

Blue Fish, Norway Lane.

Spanish style fish restaurant overlooks the rooftops and harbour. Choose your meal from the Blue Fish tank. Lunch and Dinner. (K1) 01736 794204 www.bluefishrestaurant.co.uk

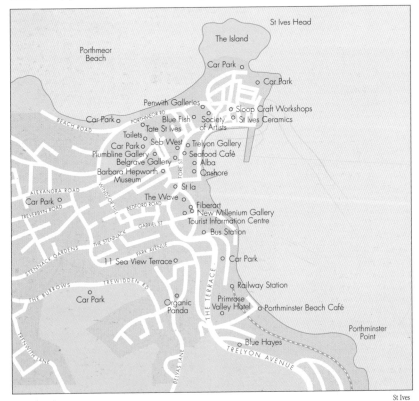

St Ives

Onshore, The Wharf.
Great pizzas and fresh fish but it's the position that counts which overlooks the harbour. Child friendly. (K1) 01736 796000

Porthminster Beach Cafe.
This great blend of café and serious restaurant overlooks magical white sands. It is child friendly, and considered by many to be The Place to eat in the South West. Open daily Mar to mid-Oct from 10. Lunch 12-4. Dinner 6-10. (K1) 01736 795352 Also, has a new café overlooking Porthgwidden Beach.
www.porthminstercafe.co.uk

Seafood Cafe, 45 Fore St.
Choose your meal from the food counter: fish, meat or fowl, and a sauce to suit you. Super fresh food, and a pleasant place to relax and dine with your cherished other half.
(K1) 01736 794004
www.seafoodcafe.co.uk

The Wave, St Andrews Street.
An intimate atmosphere breaks over this little restaurant where the food is everything. So Bon Appetit.
(K1) 01736 796661
www.wave-restaurant.co.uk

Where to Stay in St Ives...

Blue Hayes Private Hotel, Trelyon Avenue.
Small and informal, luxurious rooms and décor to a minimum, yet ever so relaxing and a five minute stroll to the beach. No wonder this hotel enjoys such success. With superb views across the bay and a cocktail in your hand you won't want to be anywhere else. (K1)
01736 797129
www.bluehayes.co.uk

Organic Panda B&B & Gallery, 1 Pednolver Terrace.
A fervent passion for recycling, sustainable living and organic produce drives this little business. The sheets are organic, the towels bamboo, the bedsteads reclaimed timbers in fantastic shapes. Rustic, laid-back, and a venue for their own art. Rooms are comfy too.
(K1) 01736 793890
www.organicpanda.co.uk

Minack Open Air Theatre ss

Organic Panda B&B ss

Sea Bass, Seafood Cafe

Primrose Valley Hotel ss

Primrose Valley Hotel, Primrose Valley, Porthminster Beach.

Another business passionate about sustainable living and protecting the environment. The luxurious rooms are decorated with bespoke furnishings and the latest sound systems. An eclectic wine cellar greets all devotees of the grape. Restaurant. (K1) 01736 794939 www.primroseonline.co.uk

11 Sea View Terrace.

Neat, luxurious and immaculately turned out little B&B. Your host has a passion for art and it shows. The walls are festooned with bright, colourful paintings only matched by the fabulous view you get of St Ives from here. Self-catering apartment nearby. (K1) 01736 798440 www.11stives.co.uk

Just Outside St Ives...

Boskerris Hotel, Boskerris Road, Carbis Bay.

Small, family-run hotel decorated in a contemporary style. The bedrooms are bright and minimalist with up-to-the-minute bathrooms. The terrace affords superb views across the bay. (K2) 01736 795295 www.boskerrishotel.co.uk

Jamies B&B, Wheal Whidden, Carbis Bay. Hospitality from a different age greets you. Former hoteliers of some note, your host Jamie and his artist wife have created a home of great comfort and elegance awash with books and artworks, and a seemingly endless view of sea and sand. Magnificent. (K2) 01736 794718 www.jamiesstives.co.uk

Arts, Crafts & Galleries to Visit in St Ives...

Barbara Hepworth Museum & Sculpture Garden, Barnoon Hill. The house, studio, sculpture garden and workshop of the late sculptress. 40 sculptures, paintings and photographs. Open all year Tu-Su 10-4.30 and daily Mar-Oct 10-5.30. (K1) 01736 796226 www.tate.org.uk/stives/hepworth

Belgrave Gallery, 22 Fore St.

Specialises in the Modern Movement which centred around St Ives, 1940 - 1960s, plus contemporary British artists. Open M-Sa 10-1, 2-6. (K1) 01736 79488 www.belgravegallery.com

Fiberart Gallery, 5 Street-an-Pol.

Showcase for artists using fibrous materials. Displaying wall hangings, sculptural forms, wearable pieces and interior design. Open Mar-Oct M-Sa 10.30-5. (K1) 01736 799077 www.fiberartgallery.com

Leach Pottery, Upper Stennack.

Founded by Bernard Leach in 1920. Ceramics by Janet Leach, Trevor Corser and Joanna Wason. Open daily: summer M-Sa, winter M-F, 10-5. (K1) 01736 796398 www.leachpottery.com

New Millennium Gallery, Street-an-Pol. Leading gallery with contemporary paintings and ceramics in three-storey building. Open Mar-Oct M-Sa 10.30-4.30. (K1) 01736 793121 www.newmillenniumgallery.co.uk

Penwith Galleries, Back Rd West. Continuous exhibitions of paintings, sculpture and ceramics. Open Tu-Sa 10-1, 2.30-5. (K1) 01736 795579

Plumbline Gallery, 2 Barnoon Hill. Specialises in glass forms and ceramics of exceptional individuality. Open daily. (K1) 01736 797771

St Ives Ceramics, Lower Fish St.

Collections of high quality ceramics. Work by John Bedding, Clive Bowen, Bernard Leach and Japanese artists from Mashiko. Open daily 10-5 except Su Jan-Feb. (K1) www.st-ives-ceramics.co.uk

Barbara Hepworth Museum ss

Fiberart Gallery

1935 The Cornish writer, Silas K Hocking, is the first living author to sell in excess of 1,000,000 copies of his work

1951 Formation of the society, Mebyon Kernow, The Sons of Cornwall

Plumbline Gallery

HAYLE

Formerly a small port and industrial centre. The foundries once made all the castings for every Cornish mine, and at nearby Copperhouse there were tin and copper smelting works. The Saltings is a reserve for migratory birds. 3 miles of superb sands. (A7) www.hayle.co.uk

Special Places to Visit...

Carnsew Gallery, 42-43 Penpol Terrace. Original work by resident artists and craftsmen from Cornwall. A blend of mixed media-through-ceramics. Open May to mid-Oct M-Sa 10-4.30. (A7)

The Salt Gallery, 57 Fore St. Great enthusiasm drives this little gallery punctuated with monthly exhibitions for paintings and ceramics and separate installation space. Open Tu-Sa 10-5.30 or by appoint. (A7) 01736 753356 www.thesaltgallery.co.uk

Paradise Park. Wildlife conservation sanctuary with 400 birds and animals in 100 aviaries in a 7 acre garden. Australian Aviary. Eagles of Paradise flying displays. Open daily summer 10-5, winter 10-4. (A7) www.paradisepark.org.uk

Xtreme Air Co, Castle Gate. Learn to Speedsail, Blo-kart, FlyBoard, Speedkite action-packed adventures. And more. Tuition on hand. B&B. (H4) 01736 332648 www.speedsailuk.copm

Lelant Attractions...

Adrian Brough Pottery, 5 Tyringham Place. Beautifully decorated pots of marine life using ceramic styles from Portugal and Korea. Open M-F 9-5, W/Es by appoint. (L3)

Galerie Pelar, The Old Cottage, Church Road. Sculpture garden with paintings and murano glass. Open weekends 12-5 or by appointment. (L3) 01736 758211 www.wingett.com

Cheney Mill Farm Park. 12 acres to roam and see farm and wild animals. Adventure Park. Birds of Prey. Picnics. Battery Bikes. Open daily East-Oct 10-5. (M4) www.cheneymillfarmpark.co.uk

St Ives Society Of Artists, Norway Square.

Founded in 1927, the Society is a well-established artists' group and holds regular exhibitions. Open mid-Mar to Nov M-Sa 10-4.30. (K1) 01736 795582 www.stivessocietyofartists.com

Tate St Ives, Porthmeor Beach.

Displays of contemporary work in a variety of media. Open all year Tu-Su 10.30-5.30 and M in July/Aug. (K1) 01736 796226 www.tate.org.uk/stives

The Sloop Craft Workshops, Fish St.

Twelve crafts people work here: from patchworks to driftwood furniture. Open daily 10-5. (K1) 01736 796051

Trelyon Gallery, Fore St. Work of over thirty contemporary leading British jewellers. Open daily 10-5 (-10 summer). (K1) 01736 797955

Seb West Studio, Slipway. Born in St Ives, Seb paints relief landscapes, abstracts of the Cornish sea and countryside. Open most days. (K1) 01736 794828 www.sebwestgallery.co.uk

Adrian Brough Pottery

ST JUST-IN-PENWITH

A handsome little town, formerly a
hectic mining centre. Imposing
Doric facaded Methodist church. The
area is rich in prehistoric antiquities.
Home to a thriving Arts and Crafts
community, hence the multitude
of galleries. By Bank Square, the
amphitheatre 'Plain-an-Gwary',
where medieval Cornish miracle
plays were performed. Water
sports festival, Priest's Cove - July.
(C5) www.stjust.org
www.west-penwith.org.uk/just

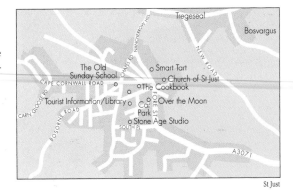

St Just

What To See, Where To Go...In and Around St Just

Botallack Engine Houses.
Remains of famous tin mine
operational from 1720-1914 which
employed 500 people. Tunnels and
galleries were projected beneath the
sea. The roaring Atlantic clearly
audible above the miners' heads. In
1893 the roof collapsed drowning 29
men, 500 feet down and never
recovered. NB Please keep to paths.
(B5) www.trevithic-society.org.uk

Geevor Tin Mine.
Mining history centre set in
magnificent coastal scenery.
Underground tours, museum, cafe
& shop. Open daily except Sa. Last
admission 4pm in summer; 3pm
in winter. (B7) 01736 788662
www.geevor.com

Levant Mine & Beam Engine
(NT), The oldest steam-powered
engine in Cornwall, restored after 60
years. Open all year F 10-5 (winter
not steaming) plus East & Spring
BHs, Su June-Sept, W mid Apr to
Oct 11-5. (B7) 01736 786156
www.nationaltrust.org.uk

Land's End Aerodrome, St Just.
Pleasure Flights and Trial Flying
Lessons over the stunning Cornish
coastline. Scheduled services to the
Isles of Scilly. Small cafe. Free
parking for Pleasure Flights. Open
daily 9-6. (C7) 01736 785227
www.landsendairport.co.uk

Pendeen Lighthouse. Built in
1900 to protect vessels from Wra
Rocks. Visible for 20 miles. Open
daily Apr-Oct, 10-1 hour before
sunset Su-Sa. Closed in fog. (C3)
www.trinityhouse.co.uk

Steam Pottery. Distinctive work
by Patrick Lester, also featuring
work of other ceramicists. Open
daily 10-5. (C7)

Art Galleries & Craft Studios in St Just...

**Boscean Pottery, Boswedden
Rd.** Apprenticed to the Leach Pottery,
Scott Marshall uses ash glazes on
his 'oven-to-table' ware. Ceramics
on sale. Open daily from 10. (B5)
01736 787093 www.studiopottery.com

**Great Atlantic Gallery,
5 Bank Square.** Specialises in
work of over 60 West Cornwall
artists. Open M-Sa 10-5, Su 2-5.
(B5) 01736 788911
www.greatatlantic.co.uk

**Nancherrow Studio, 34
Nancherrow Terrace.**
Two floors of local landscape
paintings and sculptures in bronze
and stainless steel. Ceramics.
Open 10-5. (B5) 01736 788552
www.theartangle.co.uk

Geevor Tin Mine ss

1966 Memorial erected in St Keverne to Thomas Flamank
leader of the 1497 Cornish Rebellion

1967 The freighter Torrey Canyon pollutes the south coast
with 119,328 tones of crude oil

Land's End

The Cookbook, 4 Cape Cornwall St. Home-made soup, cakes, coffee and cream teas. Supports local artists and writers. Specialist cookery bookshop. Open Tu-Su 10-5. (C6) 01736 787266

The Old Sunday School, Cape Cornwall St. C18 chapel home and studio of D Meehan and N Pickard; landscape paintings and wacky post punk jewellery. Open Tu-Su. (B5) 01736 788444 www.nancypickard.co.uk

Yew Tree Gallery, Morvah. Spacious gallery and sculpture gardens in the grounds of Keigwin Farmhouse, with contemporary fine & applied art by well-known artists within and beyond Cornwall. Open May-Nov Tu-Sa 10.30-5.30. (D7) 01736 786425 www.yewtreegallery.com

Plus...The One & Only...

Land's End. The natural landscape (a mass of incredible rock falls and dramatic cliffs) is a sight to behold. The purist's way to reach and see these cliffs is via the coastal path but if you choose to arrive by car there is a parking charge and you will have to pass by the various attractions including the Return to the Last Labyrinth, the Air Sea Rescue, the End-to-End Story and the Doctor Who Extravaganza. Open all year 10-dusk. (A9) 0870 4 580044 www.landsend-landmark.co.uk

Over The Moon Gallery, 41 Fore St. Wide range of paintings, sculpture and crafts - simplistic, vivid imaginations at work. Promotes new artists. (B5) 01872 552251 www.overthemoongallery.co.uk

Smart Tart, Blackbird Barn, Bank Square. Karen Arthur makes functional, quirky bags in colourful, hand dyed fabrics. Open Tu-Sa 10-5, (Summer Su 2-5). (B5) 01736 787091 www.smarttart.co.uk

Stone Age Studio, 8 South Place. Sculptures inspired by the Penwith landscape in Fantastic Realism and Floral Cubism. Open most days from 1pm. Call first. (B5) 01736 787872

Heather Duncan, Over The Moon Gallery

Round House & Capstan Gallery

SENNEN COVE

This most westerly village in England has developed into a centre for surfing and family beach holidays. The turquoise sea is a sight to behold. The Lifeboat Station was established in 1853, the stone pier in 1905. Whitewashed cottages and the Round House Gallery line the front. Fishing trips. Cafes. Amazing surf shop (www.sennenbeach.com) in the car park with Celtic cross. (A8) www.sennen-cove.com

Round House & Capstan Gallery. Built in 1876. Houses a huge, man-powered capstan as well as work from Cornwall's finest artists and craftspeople. Open daily from 10 in summer, winter varies: 01736 871859. (B8) www.round-house.co.uk

Where to Eat, Drink & Be Merry...

The Beach Restaurant. A view to die for. Décor of wood and glass with black slate floors. Freshly prepared local produce. Breakfast until 11.30, light lunches and supper 7-10. (B8) 01736 871191 www.thebeachrestaurant.com

The Old Success Inn. A popular inn with surfers and coastal walkers, and those seeking an inn for its location, rather than style. The ambience is relaxed and unpretentious. You get what you see. The rooms are simple and comfortable. The restaurant serves locally caught fish. Location, location - surely that will do? (B8) 01736 871232 www.oldsuccess.com

ZENNOR

Small village noted for the legendary 'Mermaid of Zennor' carved into an old bench end in the C15 church. A blow-hole roars below Zennor Head. Tregerthen Cottage was for a short time the home of DH Lawrence and his German wife, Frieda von Richthofen. (F2)

Wayside Folk Museum. Oldest privately owned museum in Cornwall. Over 5,000 items in 16 rooms. Cornish crafts, bookshop and riverside garden. Open Apr-Oct Su-F (Sa School & BHs). (F2)

The Mermaid of Zennor

Where to Stay, Eat, Drink & Be Merry...

Gurnard's Head Hotel. A welcome refuge if you've battled against a sou'westerly head wind on the coast path. Rich, wholesome fare will appease a mighty appetite. Family room. Dogs in bar only. Recently refurbished rooms for B&B. (F2) 01736 796928 www.gurnardshead.co.uk

Tinners Arms, Zennor. An ancient and friendly pub with its own brew, Tinners Ales. Simple décor of settles and benches. Serves tasty food. Close to bracing cliff-top walks. (G2)

Zennor Backpackers & Café. Dormitory accommodation for those seeking the camaraderie of the Open Road, and a good deal. Laid back ambience. Evening meals. Communal spirit. Camping available. (G2) 01736 798307 www.backpackers.co.uk/zennor

Fisherman, Sennen Cove

Ancient Cornwall...

Boscawen-Un Stone Circle (Nine Maiden). Bronze Age circle of 19 stones. Sometimes site of Cornish Gorsedd. (D7)

Carn Euny Ancient Village. Iron Age village discovered in C19. Well preserved 65ft long fogue. (D7)

Castle An Dinas. Good viewpoint with three circular defensive walls. Two barrows. 1920 excavations unearthed arms and water supply. (H4)

Chun Castle. Impressive fort with two concentric stone ramparts of 300ft diameter. (D7)

Chun Quoit. Mushroom shaped neolithic tomb with massive capstone, 8ft square. (D7)

Chysauster Ancient Village (EH). The best-preserved Iron Age village in Cornwall. Eight-circular houses. Occupied during Roman Conquest. Access via half-mile path from road. Small shop. (H4)

Lanyon Quoit

Merry Maidens Stone Circle

Gurnards Head. Cut off by ramparts and ditches. Circular stone huts. (F2)

The Giants House. 13 ft long chamber within barrow 26ft in diameter. (F3)

Lanyon Quoit (NT). Stone Age dolmen; three upright and capstone re-erected c.1824. Hidden entrance over stile beside road. (F7)

Maen Cliff. Iron Age fort with ramparts and ditches. (A8)

Men-An-Tol. A large circular slab with a hole pierced through centre set between 2 upright slabs. Famous for its legendary magical healing powers - children were passed through to cure them of rickets. Fifteen minute walk from parking area. Teas at Lanyon Farm, from Apr-Oct Tu-Su 2-5. (A7)

Merry Maidens Stone Circle. 19 stones form this perfect circle. The Legend relates that nineteen virgins were turned to stone for dancing on a Sunday. You have been warned! (E9)

Nine Maidens Stone Circle. 2 circles of standing stones, 50ft and 60ft in diameter. (F3)

Pendeen Vau Fogou. Lengthy passage, stone faced and roofed with lintels. In yard of Pendeen Manor Farm. (C3)

Plain-An-Gwarry. Circular embankment (cattle pen) where old Cornish miracle plays were performed. (B6)

Trencrom Hill (NT). Well preserved fort with stone walls. (K3)

Treryn Dinas. Well fortified with five lines of ramparts and ditches. Overlooks fluorescent sea. Site of Logan Rock. (D10)

Zennor Quoit. One of England's largest dolmens. A double-chambered tomb with a massive slab. Pieces of Neolithic pottery discovered here. (G2)

Men An Tol

Porthmeor Beach

Beaches and Surfing...

Hayle, The Towans.

A vast expanse of firm golden sands ideal for families who want to spread out. Swift currents to be avoided at mouth of estuary, surfing with S-B hire/WC/LG. (M2)

Lelant - Porth Kidney Sands.

Massive expanse of sand, ideal for beach games, HZ bathing; avoid estuary. LG. (L2)

Carbis Bay.
Popular family beach with firm sands and rocks. WC/cafe. P is a problem. (K2)

St Ives - Porthminster Beach.

Sheltered, good for children. Access from road, all facilities. (K1)

St Ives - Towan Beach (Harbour).
Sand at LT, easy access and all facilities. (K1)

St Ives - Porthgwidden Beach.

Sheltered, good bathing, popular with children. East of St Ives Head, all facilities. (K1)

St Ives - Porthmeor Beach.

Heavy surf, strong currents, spacious at LT, most popular St Ives beach. S-B hire/LG/all facilities. Surfing - popular with locals. Fine peaks from S-SW winds. (J1)

Portheras Cove.

Isolated, sandy cove reached by foot from P at Pendeen Lighthouse. (C3)

Porth Nanven

Pendeen Beach.
Sandy cove at LT. Rock fishing below lighthouse. (C3)

Cape Cornwall.
Tiny, visible at LT, strong currents around headland. WC/cafe. (B5)

Porth Nanven (Cot Valley).
Sand at LT. Boulders like sculpture or pieces of ceramic. (B6)

Gwenvor (Aire Point).
Surfing - Guaranteed a swell in most weather. Works well at 3-6 feet. Has shifting peaks and strong rips. (B7)

Porthminster Beach

1988   Camelford poisoned due to the pollution of the local waterworks

1989   Martin Potter of Newquay is crowned World Surfing Champion

Sennen Cove

Whitesand Bay, Sennen Cove. Superb rolling surf and turquoise sea, bathing safest at HT. P/WC/LG/cafe. Surfing - Crowded in summer. Constant swell with shifting peaks and strong rips. (B7)

Porthgwarra. Tiny beach with WC/cafe. (B10)

Porth Chapel. Isolated sandy cove below St Leven church, steep descent from coast path. (C10)

Porthcurno. Superb white shell-sand beach and turquoise sea, surrounded by high granite cliffs. Good bathing, P/WC/LG/shop. Surfing - Fine waves after a big SW swell. (C10)

Lamorna Cove. Patches of sand and huge granite boulders, harbour P/WC/cafe. (F9)

Newlyn. Pebbled beach, sand at LT, access P. (G7)

Penzance. Wide expanse of shingly sand stretches from Eastern Green Beach to Marazion. Entrance under railway line at Eastern Green. Two other access points at Longrock. WC/cafe at east end. (H6)

Marazion. Popular and safe family beach, firm, spacious sands. Causeway to St Michael's Mount at LT. WC/cafe. (J6)

Perran Sands (Parranuthnoe). Surfing, spacious sands. P/WC. Surfing - Novices beach. Good RH breaks close to rocks at NW end of beach. (L7)

Prussia Cove. No real sandy/pebbly beach, but there are rocks to lie on. Accessed via rough, private track from parking area. (M7)

Old Harbour, Newlyn

Porthcurno

Botallack Engine Houses

Coastal Footpath...

St Ives to Land's End. Approx 22 miles. Considered by some to be the finest stretch of all: wild, rugged and besieged relentlessly by the elements. The path is lonely and remote, up and down and at times, very hard going following the cliff edge and cliff top. Seals laze on the Carracks. A blow hole roars below Zennor Head. It's worth a detour to Zennor for refreshments and to meet the mermaid in the church. On to Gurnard's Head (good pub), sphinx-like with great views, and then you are entering the heart of tin mining country, so beware of unprotected mine shafts. The cliffs between St Ives and Pendeen sometimes glitter with minerals. Hereabouts, paths criss-cross in all directions and there's much to interest the industrial archaeologist, especially at Geevor, Levant and Botallack. Following the cliff tops, Cape Cornwall appears, marked by a lonely stack, remains of mine abandoned in 1870s. The cliff drops to Aire Point, and ahead the thunderous breakers, and the dedicated surfers of Whitesand Bay. And now, the well worn path to Land's End.

Cliffs, Land's End

Logan Rock (Treryn Dinas)

1992 Prince Charles opens the Tate Modern in St Ives

1998 The closure of South Croft Mine brings an end to 4,000 years of mining metals

Mine Shafts, Botallack

Land's End to Hoe Point. Approx 27 miles. Another superb stretch of coastline: precipitous cliffs, great blocks of granite, sandy coves and minute valleys with sub-tropical vegetation. Spectacular rock formations to Gwennap Head, equally as wild a headland as Land's End. Here are great gnarled granite boulders, cracked and sculpted by the elements - a popular place for climbers, and below a haunt for seals. There are two paths: the first follows every cranny and contour, the second cuts off along the headlands for a wonderfully invigorating walk. Down into tiny Porthgwarra, and on up to St Levan's Well above the little cove of Porthchapel. Then along to Porthcurno passing the famous open-air Minack Theatre; beyond an improbably turquoise sea and the outline of Logan's Rock. On around the dramatic granite columns of Treen Cliff and then Cribba Head, to the tiny fishing cove of Penberth. Along clifftops to Lamorna Cove, a favourite spot for artists. The path continues along the clifftop until Mousehole. The path resumes east of

Cape Cornwall from Sennen Cove

Penzance at Eastern Green where it crosses the railway line to follow the line of the beach to Marazion, with spectacular views of St Michael's Mount just offshore. Then inland to Perranuthnoe. The going is fairly easy to Hoe Point (Praa Sands).

Mousehole Reflections

Morley Contemporary Art, Polbathic

Saratwo, Salt Gallery, Hayle

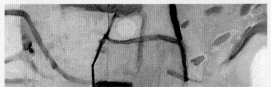

Salt Gallery, Hayle

Lighthouse Gallery, Penzance

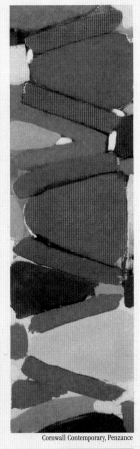

Cornwall Contemporary, Penzance

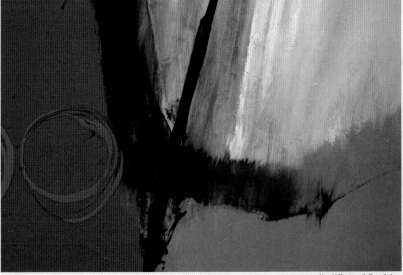

New Millenium Gallery, St Ives

THE MODERNIST ARTISTS OF ST IVES

Alfred Wallis, Tate St Ives

A mere seven miles separates the two communities of St Ives and Newlyn. Visited by JMW Turner in 1811, to be followed by Whistler, Brangwyn and the English Impressionist, Walter Sickert in 1895, other famous artists to St Ives included Alfred Munnings and Augustus John but they did not settle here. An active, if migratory artist's community, based on marine and 'plein air' painting began in the late 1870s with the advent of the railway, coinciding with the downturn in the local fishing industry. Bernard Leach set up his pottery in 1920 and the writers DH Lawrence and Virginia Woolf visited, and wrote about the area.

With the arrival of Ben Nicholson and Barbara Hepworth at the outbreak of WWII, St Ives became an outpost of the abstract avant-garde movement. But its real heyday was in the 50s and 60s following the War. A new generation of artists arrived to flee the cities of dark, satanic mills and to bathe in the brilliant, Mediterranean light. The light shone on these artists who revelled in their new freedoms. Gone were the shackles of realism. A New Age was dawning. It was to become the Age of the Beatles and the Pill.

Leading Figures (in order of birth)

Alfred Wallis, 1855-1942

Artist, Fisherman, Marine Scrap Merchant. Born in Davenport. He took up painting at the age of 70 following the death of his wife, 'for company' according to Ben Nicholson and Christopher 'Kit' Wood who discovered him on a walk through the back streets of St Ives. He was illiterate and inarticulate; his style is Primitive, simple paintings of ships, harbours, seascapes and St Ives. Despite recognition and admiration from artistic circles, Wallis's work did not capture the public's imagination during his lifetime and he died in poverty in Madron Workhouse unaware of what his work would fetch at auction in later years.

Julius Olsson, ARA, RA, 1864-1942

Seascape Painter. Born in London. A self trained artist who exhibited at the Royal Academy in 1890, the same year he settled in St Ives (for 20 years) and founded the School of Painting in 1895. He was an energetic man of great enthusiasm. He painted Cornish coastal scenes and seascapes and during WWI he was a Lieutenant in the Royal Naval Voluntary Reserve.

Borlasse Smart 1881-1947

Painter. An enthusiastic supporter of the more experimental work of Barnes-Graham, Ben Nicholson and Barbara Hepworth.

Bernard Leach, 1887-1979

Potter. Born in the Far East where his father was a Hong Kong Judge, and his maternal grandparents missionaries in Japan. Educated at the Slade School of Art and the London School of Art. He returned to Japan in 1909, learnt the craft of Raku from Kenzan VI, the great ceramicist and heir to a ceramics dynasty. Built a lasting friendship with the great Japanese potter Shoji Hamada, an inspiration for many studio potters. He returned to

England in 1920 and settled in St Ives. Later, in 1927, the Elmhirsts invited him to set up a rural arts and crafts centre at Dartington, before setting up his own pottery in 1932. A struggling potter until his first book was published after WWII, he gained instant recognition with The Potter's Book, his third of thirteen books. He started a Leach dynasty of potters with his descendants, potting from Hartland to Muchelney, and beyond.

Ben Nicholson OM, 1894-1982

Painter. Born in Denham, Buckinghamshire and educated at Greshams School and the Slade School of Art. The son of artists Sir William Nicholson and Mabel Pryde, his early work was influenced by his father, post-Impressionism, synthetic Cubism and early English Art. As a young man he travelled widely through France, Italy and Spain (1912-14) and the United States (1917-19). His first marriage to artist Winifred Nicholson 1920-31 was followed by his second, to the sculptor Barbara Hepworth, 1933-51. With her he met and was influenced by Brancusi, Braque, Mondrian, Moore and Picasso. He moved to Cornwall in 1939 to and resumed painting landscapes and abstracts but added more colour. He had retrospectives at the Venice Biennale, 1954 and the Tate Gallery, 1955. In 1958 he moved to Switzerland with his third wife Felicitas Vogler. He is among the most celebrated and internationally-recognised painters of the C20, his work represents the embodiment of British Modernism.

Barbara Hepworth DBE, 1903-1975

Artist & Sculptress or. Born in Wakefield, she was educated at Wakefield Girls High School, and won scholarships to Leeds School of Art and the Royal College of Art. Travelled to Italy with her first husband, sculptor John Skeaping and received a thorough training in carving. Her early work was quasi-naturalistic with detail submerged in simple forms. By the early 30s she was working closely with Moore and Nicholson (whom she married) and developing an abstract style. She moved to St Ives in 1939

staying there until she tragically died in a studio fire. She worked both in wood and stone exploring mass and space and the relationship between the inside and the outside of her sculptures. Her understanding of the materials she used was immense. By the 1950s she was one of the most internationally famous of sculptors and received the commission for a memorial outside the United Nations in New York. Her Trewyn Studio is now the Barbara Hepworth Museum and Sculpture Garden.

Wilhelmina Barns-Graham, CBE, RSA, 1912-2004

Painter, Teacher. Born in St Andrews, Fife and educated at the Edinburgh College of Art. She moved to St Ives in 1940 and became a member of the Penwith Society of Artists living all her life in Cornwall but for two short-term teaching jobs in Leeds and London. From 1960 she spent her summers in Cornwall and winters in Scotland. One of our foremost abstract painters with an exceptional sense of colour, her images derive from acute observations of natural forms and sense of place. Exhibited at the Tate, V&A and the British Museum.

Sir Terry Frost RA, 1915-2003

Abstract Painter, Prisoner of War, Teacher. Born in Leamington Spa, he began painting during his time as a Prisoner of War after the fall of Crete. He received an Ex-Serviceman's grant and moved to St Ives in 1946, before enrolling at the Camberwell School of Art in 1947. In 1950 he became a member of the Penwith Society of Arts and assistant to Barbara Hepworth. Encouraged by Ben Nicholson towards abstraction. Later as an established painter he taught at the Bath Academy of Art. An abstract painter after beginning in the realist tradition, his canvases were inspired by the Cornish light, boats and reflections and often of geometric shapes - crescents, balls, spots, hearts, or curves in bright, joyous colours.

Peter Lanyon, 1918-1964

Painter, Sculptor, Teacher. Born in St Ives. Educated at Clifton College, Penzance School of Art and the Euston Road School. Took private tuition with Ben Nicholson. Served with the RAF in the Western Desert during WWII. Founder member of the Penwith Society of Artists and a leading figure in the St Ives group of artists. Taught at the Bath Academy of Art, Corsham. Specialised in abstract landscapes, constructions and sculpture. Very taken with Rothko's work on visit to New York in 1957. Sadly died in a gliding accident, a devastating loss for the St Ives community.

Patrick Heron, 1920-1999

Painter, Art Critic, Designer, Teacher, Writer. Born in Headingley, Leeds, where his father, a businessman and founder of Cresta Silks, worked. Aged 13 he was overwhelmed by Paul Cezanne's paintings at the National Gallery, and as a part-time student aged 17 he enrolled at the Slade School of Art. As a Conscientious Objector during WWII he worked as a farm labourer, then as assistant at the Leach Pottery until 1945. He travelled widely in 1953 and his early influences were Braques, Bonnard and Matisse. From 1953 – 56 he taught at the Central School of Arts & Crafts. His later influences were the American Abstract Expressionists, Pollack, Rothko and de Kooning. They prompted new themes such as more vibrant colour, and an analysis of space and form, stripes and organic shapes using oils and gouaches. He also designed textiles and the window for Tate St Ives. He lived at Eagle's Nest, Zennor from 1956 until his death in 1999.

A list of other artists associated with St Ives

Sven Berlin, Naum Gabo, Paul Feller, Leonard Fuller, Roger Hilton, Denis Mitchell, Adrian Stokes, Karl Weschke, John Wells and Bryan Winter.

Newlyn Harbour

Penlee House Gallery ss

Groups and individual artists descended on Newlyn and its environs, Penzance and Lamorna, in the late C19 and early C20. The opening of the Great Western Railway in 1877 made travel easier and Cornwall more accessible. The artists were drawn to Newlyn by the brilliant light, the beauty of the coastline, the drama of the sea and the cheap living. There was much to draw and paint - scenes from rural life and a fascination with the community of fishermen and their wives and children, and nature in its purest form.

The colony of artists drew much of their inspiration from the clear, natural light and can be compared to the Barbizon School in France. The leading figure, Stanhope Forbes, was greatly impressed and influenced by the Plein Air movement, or outdoor painting, as opposed to painting in the studio. Forbes wished to follow in the role undertaken by the French artist, Jules Bretton, who undertook to mirror society in a realistic style. Forbes, along with his great friend Lamorna Birch, encouraged all who came to live and paint in Newlyn. He set up a School of Painting to teach the Plein Air method and to study the weather in all its changing moods. Strong colours attracted them. Paint would be used straight out of the tube rather than a mixed concoction. Forbes wrote to his mother following a trip to Brittany: "Newlyn is a sort of English Concarneau, and is the haunt of many artists." Forbes was an inspiring teacher. His encouragement and genial temperament provided a warm haven of creativity for the many who had pulled up their roots and perhaps taken a risky decision to follow their creative instincts and move west to Cornwall, and the unknown.

Leading Figures (in order of birth)

Stanhope Forbes RA, ARA, 1857-1947

Born in Dublin. Irish Realist Painter. Studied at the Lambeth School of Art, and in Paris under Leon Bonnat. Moved to Newlyn in 1884 and Father of the Newlyn School, influential member and great encourager to his fellow artists. Passionate about the Plein Air Movement (painting outdoors) after a visit to Brittany in 1881. He founded the Newlyn School of Painting in 1899.

Henry Scott Tuke, 1858-1929

Marine Painter of controversy. Cornish born. He studied at the Slade School of Art, in Florence and Paris. His paintings depict the Cornish coast and homoerotic scenes of naked boys. This caused much controversy amongst Victorian society when exhibited. He lived in Newlyn and Falmouth having bought an old brig, the Julie of Nantes, and anchored it in Falmouth Harbour using it as a floating studio.

Lamorna Birch RA, 1869-1955

Born in Cheshire. A self-taught artist who worked in oils and watercolours. He settled in the Lamorna Valley where he could follow his passion for nature and fishing. Very much regarded as a leading figure of the "Newlyn School", he had over 200 works exhibited at the Royal Academy. Taken under the wing of Stanhope Forbes, the father figure of the Newlyn ensemble.

Herewith a list of other artists associated with Newlyn

Albert Chevalier Taylor, Fred Hall, Thomas Cooper Gotch, Norman Garstin, Elizabeth Forbes, Walter Langley, Laura Knight, Harold Knight, Fred Bramley, Fred Millard, Ralph Todd, Ernest Procter.

The Sunny South, Penlee House Gallery ss

These Celebrities are listed by order of birth. They have been selected because they have achieved greatness or notoriety in their chosen fields, sometimes posthumously, and have an attachment to Cornwall either by birth or by choosing to live in Cornwall.

St Piran (Sen Piln)

Patron Saint of Tin Miners, and the National Saint of Cornwall. His origins are steeped in mystery but he is thought to have been born in the C6 in Ireland. He studied scripture in Rome and returned to monastic life in County Ossary later to export his missionary zeal to Cornwall landing on Perrran Beach where he built a tiny oratory (chapel). St Piran's flag is the white cross on a black background, and St Piran's Day is the 5th March. Thousands flock to the dunes dressed in black, white and gold carrying the Cornish flag.

St Petroc

The Patron Saint of Cornwall. A Welsh nobleman educated in an Irish monastery in the C6 or C7. With a band of followers he landed on the Camel Estuary and set up a monastery at Lanwethnic, all according to the Domesday Survey. Built churches at Padstow (Petroc's-Stow), Little Petherick and Bodmin which was to become a religious centre in the Middle Ages. In 1177 his bodily remains were carried off to the Abbey of St Meen in Brittany but such was the outcry that the Prior of Bodmin set forth to recover his relics. In 1994 his casket was stolen from St Petroc's Bodmin, later to be found in Yorkshire.

Thomas Flamank and Michael an Gof (Michael Joseph)

Co-Leaders of the Cornish Rebellion of 1497. Two patriotic Cornishmen, one a lawyer, the other a village blacksmith, they shared passionate dreams for their beloved county. Henry VII was fighting a war against the Scots and required funds. He raised taxes and these two men believed, along with 15,000 rebels, that Cornwall and her poverty-stricken citizens could ill afford such sufferage. The rebels reached Blackheath Common but poorly armed with bows, arrow, scythes and pitchforks were no match for the King's mercenaries. These two were found guilty of high treason. Their punishment to be dragged on hurdles from the Tower to Tyburn, then hung, drawn and quartered, and their heads displayed on pike staffs on London Bridge. In 1997 a statue was unveiled in St Keverne to commemorate the 500th Anniversary of these fine Cornishmen: "a name perpetual, and a fame permanent and immortal".

Sir Humphrey Arundell, 1513-1550

Conservative Catholic, Landowner, Proud Cornishman, Soldier. Born in Helland near Bodmin. Commanded a small garrison at St Michael's Mount. Took military charge of the rebels (to hold back their excesses) during the Prayer Book Rebellion against Edward VI. Found guilty of high treason and was subsequently hung, drawn and quartered at Tyburn. His estates were thus distributed to Sir Gawen Carew.

Sir Richard Grenville, 1542-1591

Explorer, Privateer, Soldier. He was born at Buckland Abbey in Devon. Educated at Cambridge and the Inner Temple. Immortalised in Tennyson's poem "The Revenge". His voyages to Virginia, the Azores and Roanoke Island were the stuff of legend. Later became Sheriff of Cornwall in 1577. Turned Bideford into a major trading centre. Fought with Raleigh to defend Cornwall and Devon against the Spanish Armada.

Sir Bevil Grenville, 1596-1643

Civil War Commander, Cornish Hero, Cornish Landowner, MP, Royalist. Born near Withiel, educated at Exeter College, Oxford. Knighted in 1639 having served in the King's bodyguard. He raised an army in Cornwall to fight for the King. Won battles at Braddock Down, Stratton Hill (Bude) and Lansdown outside Bath where he was mortally wounded. Buried in Kilkhampton Church. Monument erected in a field above Bath to commemorate his heroism and those of his Cornish Pikemen.

Jonathan Trelawney, 1650-1721

Bishop, Catholic Zealot, Royalist, Scholar. Born in Pelynt. Educated at Westminster School and Christ

St Piran

Sir Richard Grenville, Kilkhampton Church

age of seven. Accompanied Captain James Cook in Resolution on his third, fatal voyage to the Pacific where he learned much of his navigational skill. Appointed Commander of the Bounty in 1787, a merchant vessel sent to Tahiti to collect breadfruit trees for cultivation in the Caribbean slave trade. The Mutiny on the Bounty, 28 April 1789, saw him and eighteen of his loyal crew placed in a 23-foot launch. They sailed an incredible 3,619 nautical miles in 47 days before reaching Timor, an unheard of piece of navigation. One crewman lost his life in the ordeal. He was acquitted at his Court Martial. All records show him to be a just man not given to ruthless punishment. He believed in exercise, regular bathing, clean laundry and a healthy diet learnt in the company of Captain Cook. In Australia, he experienced the Rum Rebellion in 1810.

Henry Bone RA, 1755-1834
Enamel Painter. Born in Truro. He became the enamel painter to George III and painted portraits on watches, brooches and fans.

William Gregor, 1761-1817
Chemist, Geologist, Inventor, Rector. Born at Trewarthenick near Tregony. Educated at Bristol Grammar School and St John's College, Cambridge where he excelled in Classics and Mathematics. Known as the "Scientific Parson" of Creed and through his interests in minerals and the discovery of black powder on the Lizard, he was to discover "menachite", later to be called Titanium.

John Carter, 1770-1807
Fisherman, Pirate, Rogue, Smuggler. Born in Breage near Helston, Carter became known as the "King of Prussia" for his admiration of Frederick the Great and because his smuggling activities centred around Piskey's Cove, Prussia Cove and Bessies Cove. Always at odds with the Customs, his running of contraband around the English and French coasts was the stuff of legend. Despite

Church, Oxford. He became Bishop of Bristol, Exeter and finally, Winchester. Famous as one of the seven bishops who took umbrage at James II for his "Declaration of Indulgence" in 1682 which declared religious freedom in England. The bishops were temporarily committed to the Tower. This invited the ballad "The Song of the Western Man" by Stephen Hawker, "And shall Trelawney die" etc.

Admiral Edward Boscawen, 1711-1761
Sailor, MP, Privy Councillor. Joined the Navy at twelve, appointed midshipman at fourteen. Known as "Old Dreadnought" or "Wry-necked Dick" due to his courage and resilience. Reputation grew during the War of the Austrian Succession, 1740-48. Appointed Admiral in 1758 and led expedition to Cape Breton. Later, in 1759, his greatest victory over the French in the Battle of Lagos prevented their invasion plans. Died of a fever and is buried at St Michaels Penkivel.

Samuel Wallis, 1728-1795
Naval Officer, Navigator, Pacific Explorer. Born in Lanteglos-By-Camelford, he rose through the ranks under the patronage of Admiral Boscawen. In 1766 he was given command of HMS Dolphin to explore the Southern Hemisphere. He discovered Tahiti, Easter Island and Wallis Island in 1767, to eventually reach Batavia (Jakarta) where most of his crew perished from dysentery.

John Arnold, 1736-1779
Inventor, Watchmaker. The son of a Bodmin watchmaker who learnt much of his trade in Holland. Returning to London he set up a chronometer factory in Essex. His most innovative design was to solve the problems of friction in a balance spring and to use a bi-metallic strip to aid temperature compensation. His watches were used by King George III and his chronometers by Captain James Cook on his South Sea voyages. The great quest of the day was to calculate Longitude aboard ships. His travails were documented in Dava Sobel's book, Longitude.

Captain William Bligh, 1754-1817
Cartographer, Naval Officer, Navigator, Governor of New South Wales. Born in Plymouth to Cornish parents. Joined the Royal Navy at the

this he was known as an upright, honest and god-fearing man who forbade drink on Sundays. He disappeared off the coast of Cornwall in 1807, never to be heard of again.

John Opie, FRA, 1770-1807

Portrait Painter. Born near St Agnes. Apprenticed as a carpenter then discovered by Dr John Walcot who recognised his enormous potential and so taught him mathematics and science. Walcot introduced him to Sir Joshua Reynolds, President of the Royal Academy. Opie's style was considered similar to Rembrandt's and for twenty years he was London Society's most sort after portrait painter. He was appointed Professor of Painting at the Royal Academy. He died, sadly very young, and lies buried in St Paul's Cathedral. The Newlyn Gallery was founded in 1895, in his honour.

Richard Trevithick, 1771-1833

Cornish Giant, Inventor, Mining Engineer, Pioneer. Born at Tregajorran near Camborne where his father was a mine 'Captain'. His early life was spent tinkering with the machinery. He became one of the leading figures and a pioneer of the Industrial Revolution. A man of vision, ahead of his times, who lacked business acumen, and who sadly failed to capitalise on his success as an inventor. His inventions included the High Pressure Steam Engine, Floating Docks, London Steam Carriage, Ship's Propeller, Iron Tanks, Water-Jet Propulsion, Thames Dredger, Portable Stoves, Threshing Machine and Railway Locomotives, and whilst in Peru, he built a gun for the Rebels. He died of pneumonia in Dartford, in extreme poverty.

Henry Trengrouse, 1772-1854

Cabinet Maker, Cornish Hero, Inventor, Saver of Lives. Born and educated in Helston. He invented the rocket line apparatus which fired a rope to stricken ships. This invention went on to save at least 20,000 lives. The idea originated in having witnessed the shipwrecked HMS Anson off Loe Bar with her loss of

Sir Bevil Grenville, Hartland Abbey

120 drowned sailors, and a firework display honouring George III's birthday The government bought a dozen off him then manufactured their own giving him £50 in compensation. The Czar of Russia awarded him a diamond ring in recognition of lives saved in the Baltic. The Life Jacket was another of his inventions. He died a pauper.

William Bickford, 1774-1834

Currier, Leather-maker, Inventor of the Safety Fuse. Born in Ashburton, Devon, he was to move to Truro, then Tuckingmill where he was to establish a factory making safety fuses. This was prompted by his early days working in the mining industry where loss of life from explosions inspired his invention. Prompted after visiting a friend who owned a rope factory. He never saw the fruits of his labours having suffered a

stroke but in its first year his factory made 45 miles of fuse, and one hundred years later had made 104,545 miles of fuse. The general design has changed little having saved hundreds of lives.

Sir Humphry Davy, 1778-1829

Chemist, Inventor, Lecturer, Physicist, Surgeon. Born in Penzance, he was apprenticed to an apothecary-surgeon. He moved up to London, became a Professor of Chemistry in 1801 and became a popular and entertaining lecturer of chemical experiments at the Royal Institution, often experimenting with gases by inhaling them and causing himself near fatal injuries. His most famous invention, the Miner's Safety (Davy) Lamp, saved thousands of lives. Electrolysis was another favourite subject. He was appointed President of the Royal Society, and gave

Sir Humphry Davy, Penzance

considered one of the leading scientific minds of his day. Buried in Launcells churchyard.

Richard Lander, 1804-1834

Adventurer, Explorer, Mariner, Servant. Born in Truro at the Fighting Cock Inn (now Dolphin). Aged 9 he walked to London, aged 11 he sailed to the West Indies on a merchant ship and later joined explorations to West Africa seeking the course of the Niger River. He was awarded the first Gold Medal of the Royal Geographical Society in 1832. On his third trip to West Africa he was attacked by natives and died of his wounds. A statue celebrates his life at the top of Lemon Street in Truro.

Neville Northey Burnard, 1818-1978

Sculptor. Born in Alarnun, the son of a stonemason. He became a celebrated society sculptor and exhibited at the Royal Academy. His sculpture of Richard Lander stands at the top of Lemon Street, Truro. The death of his daughter turned him to drink. Thrown out of house and home he took to the road and lived as a tramp to eventually die in a Redruth Workhouse.

Sir Arthur Quiller-Couch, 1863-1944

Editor, Journalist, Lecturer, Novelist, Professor, Yachtsman. Born in Bodmin, educated at Clifton College and Trinity College, Oxford. A prolific writer of Cornish tales under the pseudonym "Q", many of his stories tackled the supernatural. He became a Professor of Literature at Cambridge and edited The Oxford Books of English Verse and English Prose. He also edited anthologies of ghost stories. His novels often featured Troy (or Fowey) where he lived from 1892. Commodore of the Royal Fowey Yacht Club and Gorseth Bard.

Selina Cooper, 1864-1946

Anti-Fascist, Pacifist, Suffragette, Trade Unionist. Born in Callington but moved to Lancashire as a child. Started work in a textile mill aged 12. Became a trade unionist activist

employment to Michael Faraday who was to eclipse all his deeds.

Joseph Austen (Thomas) Treffry, 1782-1850

Engineer, Mining Industrialist, Landowner. Born in Plymouth, later to inherit the family estate in Fowey. As a partner in various mines he instigated the construction of harbours at Fowey and Par, as well as canals, railways, trams and the Treffry Viaduct.

Edward John Trelawney, 1792-1881

Adventurer, Biographer, Novelist, Pirate, Romantic, Sailor, Soldier. A friend of Byron and Shelley, he was at Livorno (Leghorn) when Shelley was drowned in 1822 (he plucked Shelley's heart from the funeral pyre on the beach) and later served with Byron in the Greek War of Independence. His biographical accounts of the lives of Byron

and Shelley are considered a little rich and fanciful. He was buried beside Shelley in Rome's Protestant Cemetery.

Sir Goldsworthy Gurney, 1793-1875

Architect, Builder, Chemist, Inventor, Pianist, Scientist, Surgeon. Born near Padstow and educated at Truro Grammar School, he was apprenticed to a Doctor of Medicine where he became a GP in Wadebridge. He later moved to London, and in 1832 devised the Oxy-Hydrogen Blowpipe. His other inventions included the Steam Carriage in 1825, or Horseless Carriage known as the 'Gurney Drag', and the Gurney Stove, used in various abbeys and cathedrals. The Bude Light was another invention designed for lighthouses. He built The Castle in Bude as his home causing much controversy. Not justly recognised in his own lifetime, he is today seeking equal rights. Chosen by her local NUWSS to represent Nelson as an independent Parliamentary candidate but was turned down by the male dominated Labour Party.

Anne Treneer, 1891-1966

Author, Biographer, Poet, Schoolteacher. Born in Gorran, the daughter of the local schoolmaster. She is best known for her autobiographical trilogy of a Cornish childhood, Schoolhouse in the Wind, recently brought back into print, and her biography of Humphrey Davy.

Rowena Cade, 1893-1983

Founder of the Minack Theatre. Born in Derbyshire and brought up in Cheltenham. During the First World War she broke in horses for use on the Front Line. Then moved to Lamorna with her mother, bought the Minack (a rocky place) for £100 and built a house on it with granite from St Levan Quarry. Her interest in theatrical productions grew out of her experience as a wardrobe mistress for local productions. She started cutting out the rock in the winter of 1931-32, and continued to work well into her eighties. Many of today's stars began their careers here - Michael York, Sarah Brightman, John Nettles, Charlotte Church, to name a few.

Sir John Betjaman, 1906-1984

Essayist, Poet, Satirist, Travel Writer. Born in Highgate, North London the son of a Cabinet Maker who owned many properties in North Cornwall around the Trebetherick/Polzeath area. Family holidays were spent here and his love of Cornwall developed from an early age. Educated at Marlborough and Magdalen College, Oxford. He had a life-long passion for architecture and English churches. His poetry reflected the vicissitudes and enigmas of the Home Counties. He is buried at St Enodoc near Rock.

Daphe du Maurier (Lady Browning), DBE, 1907-1989

Biographer, Novelist, Playwright. Born in London where her father was the actor-manager Sir Gerald du Maurier. Most of her life was spent living at Menabilly, west of Fowey.

She married Lieutenant-General Sir Frederick "Boy" Browning and bore him three children. Commander of the 1st Airborne Division, he was the chief architect of the disastrous Operation Market Garden filmed as "A Bridge Too Far" which incensed du Maurier and led here to write letters to the press decrying the film producers unforgivable treatment of her husband's memory. Her novels have sold millions of copies in many languages and have been filmed many times. Who can forget Rebecca, Jamaica Inn, The Birds, or Frenchman's Creek, an unforgettable blend of romanticism, suspense and escapism?

Winston Graham, 1910-2003

Coastguard, Novelist, Writer. Born in Manchester, he settled in Perranporth aged 17 where he was to write the first four Poldark novels between 1945 and 1953. These had a cult following, as did the TV series starring Robin Ellis and Angharad Rees. The bungalow overlooking the beach has disappeared but a plaque has been planned. His book, Marnie, was filmed by Alfred Hitchcock and starred the relatively unknown Sean Connery. A private and modest man, he lived to write 40 novels living to the grand age of 93. Fellow of the Royal Society of Literature.

Sir William Golding, 1911-1993

Essayist, Nobel Laureate (1983), Novelist, Pianist, Playwright, Poet, Seaman, Teacher. Born in Newquay, he was educated at Marlborough Grammar School where his father Alec was the Science Master, later Brasenose College, Oxford. He saw active service aboard HMS Galatea in the North Atlantic, later to take part in the D-Day landings and the

Sculpture of Thomas Flamank and Michael an Gof, St Keverne

invasion of Walcheren. Taught at the Bishop Wordworth's School, Salisbury. Lord of the Flies accepted for publication by Faber and Faber in 1953. Became full-time writer in 1962. Knighted in 1988. He was awarded the Booker Prize in 1980 for Rites of Passage; in all he wrote twelve novels.

George Lloyd, 1913-1998

Composer, Market Gardener, Naval Gunner, Romantic. Heralded as a musical genius at an early age. His first symphony was premiered by the Bournemouth Symphony Orchestra whilst he was only 19 years old. His second symphony was performed in Eastbourne in 1935. He expressed his music through the C19 traditions of melody and harmony. Inspired by the Late Romantics and the Italian Operatic Masters Verdi, Puccini, Donizetti, Bellini, and our own Elgar. His development as a musician was halted by his traumatic experiences in the arctic convoys. His ship was torpedoed by a German U-Boat and his fellow gunners were drowned in oil. His creativity dried up for twenty years. He enjoyed an Indian Summer to his career when the BBC eventually agreed to play his work in 1969 and at the 1981 Proms.

Charles Causley, 1917-2003

Cornish Poet, Naval Coder, Playwright, Primary School Teacher. Born in Launceston, he lived much of his life in Cornwall. His verse was simple and straightforward and much admired by Larkin and Betjamin. Ted Hughes was his closest friend who said of him, "One of our best loved and most needed poets". Very much influenced by William Blake and John Clare, his poems grew out of folk songs, hymns and ballads. Awarded the Queen's Gold Medal for Poetry in 1967.

John Le Carre.

Born Poole 1931. Novelist, Political Commentator, Schoolteacher, Spy. Resident of St Buryan for 40 years. Educated at Sherborne School, University of Berne and Lincoln College Oxford. Taught at Eton for two years, five years in the British Foreign Service, then recruited into MI6. Cover blown by Kim Philby. Took to writing spy novels. His later work has involved more social and political comment; see The Constant Gardener and The Mission Song, as opposed to his earlier work such as The Spy Who Came In From The Cold, The Russia House, Tinker Sailor, Soldier Spy etc., many of which have been turned into films. More recently he has written critiques of the Iraq War and the NHS. Turned down a knighthood.

Benjamin Luxon, CBE.

Born 1937, Redruth Baritone, Concert, Lieder & Opera Singer. He studied with Walter Grunner at the Guildhall School of Music and has performed major roles in Eugene Onegin (1972), Owen Wingrave (1971), Don Giovanni, Papageno, Wolfran and Eisenstein.

John Nettles

Born 1943, St Austell. Actor, Historian, Philosopher. Adopted at birth, he never knew his father. His mother was an Irish nurse. Studied history and philosophy at Southampton University. Starred in 87 episodes of Bergerac, and numerous Midsomer Murders. Member of the Royal Shakespeare Company for five seasons.

Sir Tim Rice

Born 1944, Amersham. Cricket Fanatic, Lyricist. Cornish resident who has won countless awards (Tony, Grammy, Academy) for his lyrics to world-famous musicals. Best known for his collaboration with Andrew Lloyd Webber on Joseph, Jesus Christ Superstar, Evita, Chess, and with Elton John in The Lion King and Aida. Past President of the MCC, and stalwart of the Heartaches Cricket Club.

Mick Fleetwood

Born Redruth 1947. Actor, Drummer, Musician. Brought up by an RAF father in Egypt and Norway. The drummer with the rock band, Fleetwood Mac, the name combined with John Mcvie, and led by Peter Green. In 1974 he invited Stevie Nicks and Lindsey Buckingham to join. They went on to produce the LP, Rumours, selling in excess of 30,000,000 copies. Now resident in Los Angeles, California where he has a second career as an actor.

Jethro.

Born St Buryan 1948. Carpenter, Comic, Timberman, Tin Miner. A born entertainer who has appeared in over 170 theatres. A keen bass singer, horseman and golfer, he is an active charity fundraiser. Lives at Lewdown on the Devon-Cornwall border.

Dawn French

Born 1957 Holyhead. Actress, Comedian. A resident of Fowey with her husband Lenny Henry. An English comedienne noted for her roles in French and Saunders, The Vicar of Dibley, Jam & Jerusalem, Wild West and winner of countless awards.

Lenny Henry.

Born 1958, Dudley. Actor, Comedian. A resident of Fowey with his wife Dawn French. Won the talent show New Face when he was 16 years old. A stalwart of Comic Relief and the BBC Red Nose Day, he has appeared in countless TV series such as Tiswas, Three of a Kind, Chef, The Lenny Henry Show. An avid supporter of West Bromwich Albion.

Tim Smit CBE

Born 1954 in Holland. Entrepreneur, Environmentalist, Gardener, Music Impresario. Educated at Cranbrook School and Durham University where he read Archaeology and Anthropology. Tiring of archaeology he moved into the music business for ten years and produced records for Barry Manilow and the Nolan Sisters. In 1987 he moved to Cornwall, met John Nelson and together they "discovered", then restored the Lost Gardens of Heligan, recently voted the Nation's Favourite Garden. With £40m of Lottery Money he had a vision to convert the massive clay dumps into what has become the Eden Project. Designed by Nicholas

Gimshaw Architects with assistance from the structural engineering firm of Anthony Hunt and Associates.

Kristin Scott-Thomas

Born Redruth 1960. Actress, Francophile. Educated at Cheltenham Ladies College and London's Central School of Speech and Drama. Her father was an RAF pilot killed in a flying accident. The same fate fell to her step-father six years later. Her sister, Serena, has appeared as a Bond girl opposite Piers Brosnam. She has collected numerous awards including BAFTA and the Legion d'honneur from the French government. Appeared in numerous films such as The English Patient, Four Weddings & A Funeral, Mission Impossible and Gosford Park, and on the London stage in Chekov's Three Sisters.

Patrick Gale

Born in 1962. Book Reviewer, British Writer, Pianist, Quirister (Cathedral Chorister). Educated at Winchester College and New College, Oxford. Resident of West Penwith and highly acclaimed contemporary novelist with 13 novels and numerous short stories in print. Father Prison Governor of Wandsworth and Camp Hill Prison, Isle of Wight. Latest book: Notes From An Exhibition.

Tori Amos

Born 1963 in North Carolina, USA. Award-Winning Singer-Songwriter. Now resident in Bude, North Cornwall and married to an English sound engineer. Her songs are emotionally intense, idiosyncratic and about love, sensuality and joy. Classically trained, she plays the piano, harpsichord and harmonium and has won numerous Grammy Awards having sold in excess of 12,000,000 discs.

The Eden Project ac

TOURIST INFORMATION CENTRES

Bodmin
Shire Hall, Mount Folly,
Bodmin PL31 2DQ
01208 76616
bodmintic@visit.org.uk
www.bodminlive.com

Boscastle
Boscastle Visitor Centre, Cobweb
Car Park, Boscastle PL35 OHE
01840 250010
boscastlevc@btconnect.com
www.visitboscastleandtintagel.com

Bude
The Crescent, Bude EX23 8LE
01288 354240
bude-tic@visitbude.info
www.budelive.com

Camelford
Apr - Oct
The Clease, Camelford PL32 9PL
01840 212954
manager@camelfordtic.eclipse.co.uk

Falmouth
11 Market Strand, Prince of
Wales Pier, Falmouth TR11 3DF
01326 312300

Fowey
Daphne Du Maurier Literary Centre,
5 South Street, Fowey PL23 1AR
01726 833616
info&fowey.co.uk
www.fowey.co.uk

Isles of Scilly
01720 422536

Launceston
Market House, The Arcade,
Launceston PL15 8EP
01566 772321
Launcestontica@btconnect.com
www.visitlaunceston.com

Padstow
Red Brick Building, North
Quay, Padstow PL28 8AF
01841 533449
padstowtic@visit.org.uk
www.padstowlive.com

Penzance
Station Road.
01736 362207
tourism@penwith.gov.uk

Perranporth
8 Tywarnhayle Square TR6 0ER
01872 575254
info@perranporthinfo.co.uk

St Ives
01736 796297
tourism@penwith.gov.uk

Tintagel
Tintagel Visitor Centre, Bossiney
Road, Tintagel PL34 0NJ
01840 779084
tintagelvc@btconnect.com
www.visitboscastleandtintagel.com

Truro
Municipal Building, Boscawen
Street, Truro TR1 2NE
01872 274555
truro@touristinfo.demon.co.uk
www.truro.gov.uk

Wadebridge, Rock & Polzeath
Rotunda Building, Eddystone
Road, Wadebridge PL27 7AL
0870 1223337
wadebridgetic@btconnect.com
www.visitwadebridge.com

St Neot's Church

For specific dates please contact the local
Tourist Information Centre

February
St Ives Hurling the Silver Ball

March
Cotehele Daffodils Festival
Eden Bulb Mania
Liskeard Annual Art Exhibition
Mount Edgcumbe Camellia Collection
St Piran's Day

April
Camborne Trevithick Day

May
Cornish International Male Voice Choir Festival
Padstow "Obby Oss" Celebrations
Falmouth Asparagus Festival
Fowey Daphne Du Maurier Festival of Arts & Literatre
Helston Furry/Floral Dance
Newquay Longboard Championships

June
Penzance, Golowan Festival
Kernow, Midsummer Bonfires
Liskeard Festival
Mevagissey Festival Week
Polperro Festival
Saltash Town Regatta
St Keverne, An Gov Day
Wadebridge, Royal Cornwall Show

July
Boconnoc Steam Fair
Bodmin Riding & Heritage Day
InterCeltic Watersports Festival
Liskeard & District Agricultural Show
Looe Lions Carnival Week
Pendeen Band Week
Perranporth Carnival
Porthleven Lifeboat Day
Ruan Minor Vintage Car Rally
St Endellion Music
St Germans, Port Eliot Lit Fest
St Mawes Regatta
Stithians Show
Tremough, Celtic Congress
Wadebridge Wheels

August
Bude Carnival
Bude Horticultural Show
Camel Sailing Week
Camelford Agricultural Show
Cornwall Folk Festival
Crying the Neck

May Day, Padstow

Delabole Wind Fair
Falmouth Week
Fowey Royal Regatta & Carnival Week
Hayle Festival
Henri-Lloyd Falmouth Week
Mount Edgcumbe Classic Car Rally & Fayre
Morval Vintage Steam Rally
Newlyn Fish Festival
Padstow Carnival
Padstow Lifeboat Day
Polruan Regatta
Morvah Pasty Day Festival
Newquay Rip Curl Boardmasters
St Agnes Festival
St Keverne Ox St Just Feast
Wadebridge Carnival

September
Bude Jazz Festival
Looe Valley Walking Festival
Penzance, Open Gorseth
St Ives Festival

October
Falmouth Oyster Festival
Perranporth, Lowender Peran

November
Falmouth & Penryn, Cornwall Film Festival
Looe Food Festival
Roseland Festival

December
Mousehole, Tom Bawcock's Eve

I would like to thank Mike Taffinder for reading my first and second drafts and for his impeccable proof reading skills, advice and enthusiasm. The same goes for Caroline, my dear wife, for her encouragement and great help in choosing the final images.

Thank you Mr and Mrs Roger Thorpe for their ever-lasting hospitality and for putting me up at Halzephron House time and again, often at a few minutes notice.

A big thank you to Arwen Fitch at Tate St Ives for checking my chapter on the Modernist Artists of St Ives and for her advice. The same goes to Alison Bevan at the Penlee House Gallery for her help.

Not to be forgotten, all the kind persons at the many attractions, places to stay and eat, for showing me around their establishments and for putting up with my endless questions.

Finally, I must thank Chris Dyer (Book Designer) and David Cox (Cartographer) for maintaining a passion for this project.

Photography

Until the introduction of digital photography most of my images were taken with a Nikon FE, a brilliantly robust and simple manual SLR, ably assisted by my trusty Manfrotto Tripod. I must have got through at least six bodies over a twenty-year period. I was a little hesitant, at first, to be fully sold into the use of digital machines but I have been truly bowled over by the flexibility and practicality of this medium for my type of work. I started using a Fuji S1 Pro because of its compatibility with my lenses and because of its wonderful range of colour. Its slowness was a complete bore. I now use a Nikon D300 and despite its 450-page manual I am just about coping with it. Its speed and quality of tone is awesome.

I am not a techno freak and have little knowledge of other cameras and their multitudinous effects. I am a firm believer in getting up early and staying out late. If you have the patience you never know what light will unfold. My maxim is: Understand the weather and tides, and swot up on your subjects; be they camellias in spring, or the autumn equinoxes. And, get closer to your subject.

William Fricker

Goldeneye would like to thank the following photographers for providing us with their images:

Ab Andrew Besley ac Al Churcher jh Jon Hicks nt National Trust's Cornwall Regional Library rr R Rowling ejs E J Spear

Loan of Images

Goldeneye would like to thank the following for allowing us to photograph their properties, or for providing us with an image to illustrate their properties: Mark Harold & Liz Luck of the National Trust (Cornwall Regional Office), Lady Stucley of Hartland Abbey, Cornwall Contemporary, Penzance, Restaurant Nathan Outlaw, Fowey, Primrose Valley Hotel, St Ives, Old Coastguard Hotel, Mousehole, Hotel Tresanton, St Mawes, Lugger Hotel, Portloe, Old Quay House Hotel, Fowey, The British Library, Morley Contemporary Art, Polbathic, The Rector, St Germans Church, Cotehele Gallery, Cotehele, Lakeside Gallery, Treburley,

North Cornwall Museum, Camelford, Wesley Cottage, Altarnum, Helland Bridge Pottery, Old Mill Herbary, Poughill Church, Morwenstow Church, Bush Inn, Morwenstow, Kilkhampton Church, The Castle Museum, Bude,

Curgurrel Farm, Portscatho, Outdoor Adventure, Bude, Launcells Church, Tamar Otter & Wildlife Centre, Prideaux Place, Padstow, Rick Stein, Padstow, St Kew Church, St Enodoc Bar, L'Estuaire Restaurant, Rock, RNLI Trevose Head, Fistral Blu, Newquay, Newquay Zoo, Lappa Valley Railway, Newquay, Dairyland Farmworld, Newquay, Extreme Academy, Watergate Bay, China Clay Country Park, The Beach Hut, Watergate Bay, Chapel Idne, Sennen Cove, Malcolm Sutcliffe, Penryn, Marine Villa Hotel, Fowey, Bodmin Railway, Cormorant Hotel, Golant, Pengellys Fishmongers, Looe, St Winnow Church, St Neot's Church, Lanreath Church, The Rum Store, St Neots, Tremough Campus, Penryn, The Library, St Ives, Truro College, Tate St Ives, National Maritime Museum, Falmouth,

Truro Cathedral, Heligan Gardens, Caerhays Castle, St Michael Penkevil Church, Tregoose B&B, The Harbour Master, Newlyn, Flambards, Helston, Breage Church, Trebah Gardens, Goonhilly Earth Station, Mullion Gallery, Mullion Church, Julia Mills Gallery, Halzephron House, Roskilly's, Abbey Hotel, Penzance, Summer House, Penzance, Penlee House Gallery, Penzance, Lighthouse Gallery, Penzance, Over The Moon Gallery, St Just, Ednovean, Marazion, Seagrove Gallery, Marazion, Nigel Hallard Studios, Mousehole, J H Turner, Newlyn, Minack Theatre, Organmic Panda, St Ives, Barbara Hepworth Museum, St Ives, Fiberart Gallery, St Ives, Plubline Gallery, St Ives, Adrian Brough Pottery, Hayle, Geevor Tin Mines, Round House Gallery, Sennen, New Millennium Gallery, St Ives, Salt Gallery, Hayle, Trereife Park.

INDEX

Index to the attractions, places to eat and stay
that have been described in this book

Abbey Hotel 160
Abbey Restaurant 161
Admiral Bembo 162
Admiral Edward Boscawen 194
Adrian Brough Pottery 177
Advent Church 42
Alba 174
Alfred Wallis 188
Altarnum 40
Alvorada, The 124
Anchorage House 113
Anne Treneer 197
Antony House 24
Antony Woodland Garden 24
Arthurian Centre 43
Austell's 116
Avalon Art 165

Badcocks Gallery 171
Banjo Pier 117
Barbara Hepworth 188
Barbara Hepworth Museum 176
Beach Restaurant 180
Beachmodern No 28 56
Bedruthan Steps 75
Bedruthan Steps Hotel 80
Belerion Gallery 162
Belgrave Gallery 176
Ben Nicholson 188
Benjamin Luxon 198
Bens Playworld 113
Bernard Leach 188
Beside The Wave 122
Big Blue Surf School 56
Blue Anchor 140
Blue Bar 98
Blue Fish 174
Blue Hayes Private Hotel 175
Blue Hills Tin Streams 89
Blue Peter Inn 112
Blue Reef Aquarium 80
Bodmin & Wenford Railway 104
Bodmin 104
Bodmin Moor 40
Bodmin Museum 105
Bodrugan's Leap 124
Booby's Bay 75
Borlasse Smart 188
Boscawen-Un-Stone Circle 181
Boscean Pottery 178
Boscundle Manor 113
Boskerris Hotel 176
Bossiney Haven 61
Bosvigo 131
Botallack Engine Houses 178
Bow or Vault Beach 135
Breage Church 144
British Cycling Museum 42
Bude 56
Burncoose Nurseries 95
Bush Inn 50
Buttervilla Farm 24

Cadgwith 140
Cadgwith Cove Inn 150

Caerhays Castle 131
Callestock Cider Farm 95
Calstock 37
Calstock Church 37
Calstock Viaduct 37
Camborne & Redruth 94
Camel Trail 105
Camel Trail 69
Camel Valley Vineyards 82
Camelford 42
Cape Cornwall Beach 182
Captain William Bligh 194
Carbis Bay 182
Cardinham Church 42
Carleon Cove 151
Carlyon Bay 117
Carn Brea 99
Carn Euny Ancient Village 181
Carnglaze Slate Caverns 116
Carnsew Gallery 177
Carrick Roads 134
Carwinion Gardens 144
Carwynen Quoit 99
Castle an Dinas 181
Castle an Dinas 83
Castle Beach 135
Castle Dore 132
Cawsand & Kingsand 24
Cawsand & Kingsand Beaches 29
Chapel Porth 99
Chapel St Bistro 161
Charles Causley 198
Charlestown 105
Charlestown Beach 117
Charlotte's Tea House 127
Chase Art Gallery 69
Cheney Mill Farm Park 177
China Clay Country Park 82
Chun Castle 181
Chun Quoit 181
Church Cove 151
Church of St Columba 82
Church of St John Baptist 50
Church of the Holy Trinity 113
Churchtown Arts 89
Chydane 149
Chysauster Ancient Village 181
Cliff House 24
Cofro 124
Colliford Lake Park 40
Collon Barton 111
Combe Valley Nature Trail 50
Constantine Bay 75
Cookbook 179
Cormorant Hotel 107
Cornish Birds of Prey Centre 81
Cornish Mines & Engines 94
Cornish Orchards 116
Cornish Owl Centre 27
Cornish Range 170
Cornish Tippi Holidays 69
Cornwall Contemporary 162
Cornwall Pearl 81
Cotehele 29
Cotehele Gallery 29
Cotehele House 29
Cotehele Quay 29
Cottage Restaurant 112
Cove Restaurant 169

Coverack 140
Coverack Beach 151
Crackington Haven 61
Crackington Haven Church 56
Crantock 90
Crantock Beach 90
Crantock Church 90
Crealy Adventure Park 81
Creed Church 133
Creed Gardens 131
Creftow Gallery 140
Crooklets Beach 60
Cubert Church 90
Curgurrel Farm 129

Dairyland Farmworld 82
Daphne Du Maurier 197
Daphne Du Maurier Literary Centre 105
Dawn French 198
Daymer Bay 75
Dolcoath Mine 94
Doniert's Stone 40
Downderry Beach 29
Dozmary Pool 40
Driftwood Hotel 129
Driftwood Spars Hotel 89
Duckpool 52
Duke of Cornwall's Light Infantry Museum 105
Duke Street Gallery 171
Durgan Beach 151

East & West Portholland 135
Ebenezer Gallery 112
Ed's 80
Eden Project 113
Ednovean 165
Edward John Trelawney 196
Eglos Pottery 69
Eleven 105
11 Sea View Terrace 176
Ennys 165
Essex Tyler Gallery 170
Extreme Academy 83
Fal River Links 122

Falmouth 122
Falmouth Art Gallery 122
Falmouth Arts Centre 122
Falmouth School of Sailing 122
Fernacre Stone Circle 40
Fiberart Gallery 176
Fifteen Cornwall 83
Finns Restaurant 80
Fistral Beach 85
Fistral Blu 80
Flambards Experience 140
Floe Creek 134
Flushing 124
Flushing Beach 151
Fowey 105
Fowey Aquarium 105
Fowey Church 133
Fowey Hall Hotel 107
Fowey River 107
Fowey River Expeditions 107
Fowey River Gallery 107
Fowey Town Museum 107
Fraddon Pottery 83
Freathy & Tregonhawke Beach 29

Freathy Colony of Huts 25

Galerie Pelar 177
Geevor Tin Mine 178
George Lloyd 198
Giants House 181
Gillan Harbour 151
Glass House Gallery 126
Glendower 149
Glendurgan Gardens 144
Globe Inn 111
Godolphin House 95
Godrevy Beach Café 99
Godrevy Towans 99
Golant Church 133
Goldfish Bowl 163
Golitha Falls 111
Goonhilly Downs 145
Goonhilly Satellite Earth Station 145
Gorran Haven Beach 135
Grange Fruit Farm 145
Great Atlantic Gallery 122
Great Atlantic Gallery 178
Great Western Beach 85
Green Lantern 130
Greenbank Hotel 124
Guild of Ten 126
Gunwalloe Church 144
Gurnard's Head Hotel 180
Gurnards Head 181
Gweek 142
Gwennap 95
Gwennap Pit 95
Gwenvor 182
Gwithian Towans 99
Gyllynvase Beach 135

Halftides 147
Halliggye Fogou 144
Halzephron House 149
Halzephron Inn 150
Hannifore Beach 117
Harbour Cove 75
Harlyn Bay 75
Harlyn Bay Ancient Burial Ground 70
Harris's 162
Hartswell Farm 111
Hay Barton 132
Haye Farm Cider 116
Hayle 177
Hayle Bay 75
Heading West Gallery 165
Helford Passage Beach 151
Helford River 142
Helford Village Beach 151
Heligan Gardens 131
Helland Bridge Pottery 43
Helston 140
Helston Folk Museum 140
Hemmick Beach 135
Henry Bone 194
Henry Scott Tuke 191
Henry Trengrouse 195
Heron Inn 124
Hidden Valley 36
Higher Lank Farm 43
Holywell Bay 90
Holywell Bay Fun Park 89
Hornacott 37

Hotel Tresanton 130
Hounsel Bay 151
Huel Vor 140
Humphry Davy 195
Hunkdory 123
Hurlers Stone Circle 40

Jamaica Inn 43
Jamies 176
Japanese Garden 70
Jethro 198
John Arnold 194
John Carter 194
John Le Carre 198
John Nettles 198
John Opie 195
Jonathan Trelawney 193
Joseph Austen Treffry 196
Jubilee Wharf 98
Julia Mills Gallery 149
Julius Olsson 188

Ken Caro Gardens 37
Kennack Sands 151
Kiberick Cove 135
Kids Kingdom 113
Kilkhampton Church 50
King Arthur's Great Hall 68
King Arthur's Hall 40
Kota 149
Kristin Scott-Thomas 199
Kynance Cove 151

L'Estuaire 71
Lakeside Gallery 37
Lamorna 169
Lamorna Birch 191
Lamorna Cove 183
Lamorna Wink Inn 169
Lamorran House Gardens 131
Land of Legend & Model Village 112
Land's End 179
Land's End Aerodrome 178
Lander Gallery 126
Landewednack Church 144
Landewednack House 149
Landulph Church 25
Laneast Church 42
Lanhydrock House 105
Lanreath Church 116
Lantallack Farm 24
Lanteglos-By-Camelford Church 43
Lanteglos-By-Fowey Church 116
Lantic Bay 117
Lantivet Bay 117
Lanyon Quoit 181
Lappa Valley Railway 82
Launcells Church 56
Launceston 36
Launceston Castle 36
Launceston Steam Railway 36
Laurelin Glass Gallery 40
Lavethan 43
Lawrence House Museum 36
Leach Pottery 176
Lemon Street Gallery 127
Lenny Henry 198
Levant Mine 178
Life's A Beach 56

Lighthouse Gallery 162
Linkinhorne Church 43
Liskeard 109
Liskeard Church 116
Little Petherick Church 70
Lizard Lighthouse 145
Loe Beach 134
Loe Pool 140
Logan's Rock 174
Longcross Hotel & Victorian Garden 69
Looe 110
Lostwithiel 111
Lostwithiel Church 111
Lowland Point 151
Lugger Hotel 129
Lusty Glaze 85
Luxulyan Valley 107

Madron Church 160
Maen Cliff 181
Makers Heights 25
Malcolm Sutcliffe Glass 98
Maltster Arms 71
Marazion 165
Marazion Beach 183
Marconi Monument 147
Marina Villa Hotel 107
Market House Gallery 165
Mary Newman's Cottage 27
Mawgan In Meneage Church 144
Mawgan Porth 85
Men-An-Tol 181
Men-Aver Beach 151
Merry Maidens Stone Circle 181
Merthen Manor 150
Mesmear 71
Meudon Hotel 150
Mevagissey 124
Mevagissey Folk Museum 124
Michael an Gof 193
Michael Praed Gallery 165
Michaelstow Church 43
Mick Fleetwood 198
Mid Cornwall School pf Jewellery 113
Middle Beach 61
Mill House Inn 69
Millendreath Beach 29
Millendreath Beach 29
Millook Haven 61
Millpool Gallery 170
Minack Theatre 174
Mineral Tramways Discovery Centre 94
Minions Heritage Centre 43
Minster Church 70
Molesworth Manor 71
Monkey Sanctuary 25
Morans Café 25
Morley Contemporary Art 25
Morwenstow 50
Mother Ivey's Bay 75
Mount Edgcumbe House 25
Mount Hawkes – Sk8 95
Mousehole 169
Mowhay Café 71
Mullion 147
Mullion Church 147
Mullion Cove 147
Mullion Cove Beach 151
Mullion Gallery 147

INDEX

Museum of Witchcraft 60
Mylor Church 133
Mylor Churchtown 134

Nancherrow Studio 178
Nanscawen Manor House
Napoleon Inn 60
Nare Hotel 124
National Lobster Hatchery 65
National Maritime Museum 122
National Seal Sanctuary 142
Neddi Donkey Sanctuary 70
Net Loft Gallery 149
Neville Northey Burnard 196
New Millennium Gallery 176
New Yard Restaurant 150
Newlyn 171
Newlyn Art Gallery 171
Newquay 80
Newquay Fun Factory 80
Newquay Zoo 80
Nigel Hallard Studios 170
Nine Maidens Stone Circle 181
No 6 Restaurant & Rooms 65
North Cornwall Museum 42
North Hill Church 37
Northcott Mouth 52

Ocean Contemporary 123
Ocean Studios 165
Odds The Restaurant 90
Old Ale House 127
Old Canal, Bude 56
Old Coastguard Hotel 170
Old Ferry Inn 109
Old Macdonalds Farm 70
Old Mill Herbary 43
Old Success Inn 180
Old Sunday School 179
Olde Plough House 109
Onshore 175
Organic Panda 175
Out Of The Blue 165
Outdoor Adventure 56
Over The Moon Gallery 179
Over The Moon Gallery 90

Padstow 64
Padstow Contemporary Art 65
Padstow Museum 65
Pandora Inn 124
Par Sands 117
Paradise Park 177
Patrick Gale 199
Patrick Heron 188
Paul Corin's Magnificent Music Machines 116
Pawton Quoit 70
Pelyn 132
Pencalenick House 109
Pencarrow House 43
Pendeen Beach 182
Pendeen Lighthouse 178
Pendeen Vau Fogou 181
Pendennis Castle 132
Pendower & Carne Beach 135
Pengersick Castle 140
Penhale & Perran Beach 90
Penjerrick Gardens 95
Penlee House Gallery 163

Penmere Manor Hotel 124
Penryn 98
Penryn Museum 98
Pentewan 135
Pentraeth Cove 151
Penwith Galleries 176
Penzance 160
Penzance Arts Club 160
Penzance Beach 183
Perran Sands 183
Perranporth 89
Pescadou 66
Peter Lanyon 188
Plaidy Beach 117
Plain-An-Gwarry 181
Plumbline Gallery 176
Plume of Feathers 83
Poldark Mine 94
Poldhu Cove 151
Polgaver Bay 117
Polkerris 112
Polkerris Beach 117
Polpeor Cove 151
Polperro 112
Polridmouth Cove 117
Polrode Mill Cottage 71
Polruan 113
Poltesco Nature Trail 145
Polurrian Cove 151
Polurrian Hotel 147
Porfell Animal Land 116
Port Isaac 66
Port Isaac Pottery 66
Port Quin 67
Porteath Barn 71
Porteath Bee Centre 70
Portgaverne 67
Porth Beach 85
Porth Chapel Beach 183
Porth Joke 90
Porth Kidney Sands 182
Porth Nanven 182
Porthallack Beach 151
Porthallow Arts 145
Porthallow Beach 151
Porthcothan 75
Porthcurnick Beach 135
Porthcurno 174
Porthcurno Beach 183
Porthcurno Museum 174
Portheras Cove 182
Porthgwarra 183
Porthgwidden Beach 182
Porthilly Cove 75
Porthleven 149
Porthleven Sands 151
Porthluney Beach 135
Porthmeor Beach 182
Porthminster Beach 182
Porthminster Beach Café 175
Porthoustock Beach 151
Porthpean 135
Porthtown 99
Portloe 129
Portloe Beach 135
Portmellon Beach 135
Portnadler Bay 117
Portreath 95
Portreath Beach 99

Portscatho 129
Portwrinkle Beach 29
Poughill Church 52
Praa Sands 151
Primrose Valley Hotel 176
Prindl Pottery 105
Probus Church 133
Probus Gardens 131
Prussia Cove 183
Prynns 66

Quad & Kart Centre 25

Rame Church 25
Raval's 42
Readymoney Cove 117
Rectory Tea Rooms 50
Restaurant Gaudi 127
Restaurant Nathan Outlaw 107
Restormel Castle 111
Richard Lander 196
Richard Trevithick 195
Rick Stein's Café 65
Rillaton Round Barrow 40
Rising Sun 130
Rising Sun Inn 40
Riverview Restaurant 107
RNAS Culdrose 145
Roche Rock 83
Rock 67
Rojano's 71
Roseland Inn 129
Roseland Peninsula 129
Rosevine Hotel 129
Roskear 71
Roskilly's 150
Round House & Capstan Gallery 180
Round Houses, Veryan 134
Rowena Cade 197
Royal Albert Bridge 27
Royal Cornwall Museum 127
Royal Oak 111
Rum Store 116
Rumps Point 70
Rusey Beach 61

Salt Gallery 177
Saltash 27
Saltwater 71
Samuel Wallis 194
Sands Resort Hotel 80
Sandsifter Bar 99
Sandy Mouth 52
School of Mines Geological Museum 94
Schoolhouse, The 124
Screech Owl Sanctuary 82
Seafood Bar 123
Seafood Café 175
Seagrove Gallery 165
Seaton Beach 29
Seb West Studio 177
Selina Cooper 196
Sennen Cove 180
Shears Fine Art 163
Sheviock Barton 24
Ship Inn 149
Ship Inn 170
Shipwreck & Heritage Centre 105
Shire Horse Farm 95

Sir Arthur Quiller-Couch 196
Sir Bevil Grenville 193
Sir Goldsworthy Gurney 196
Sir Humphrey Arundell 193
Sir John Betjaman 197
Sir Richard Grenville 193
Sir Terry Frost 188
Sir Tim Rice 198
Sir William Golding 197
Skinner's Brewery 127
Slate Quarry 69
Slaughter Bridge 43
Sloop Craft Workshops 177
Smart Tart 179
South Café 150
South Croft Mine 94
South East Cornwall Discovery Centre 110
Southern Gallery 116
Spirit of the West 82
Springfields fun Park 82
Square Gallery 134
St Agnes 89
St Agnes Museum 90
St Agnes Pottery 90
St Austell 113
St Austell Brewery Visitor Centre 113
St Charles The Martyr, Falmouth 133
St Clement Church 133
St Columb Major 83
St Endellion Church 70
St Enodoc Bar & Restaurant 71
St Enodoc Church 70
St Georges Cove 75
St Germans 27
St Ives 174
St Ives Ceramics 176
St Ives Society of Artists 177
St Just in Penwith 178
St Just in Roseland Church 134
St Keverne Church 144
St Kew Church 70
St Kew Inn 71
St Martin-By-Looe Church 116
St Mary Magdalene 36
St Mawes 130
St Mawes Castle 132
St Mawgan-in-Pydar Church 70
St Michael Penkevil Church 134
St Michael's Hotel & Spa 124
St Michael's Mount 167
St Moritz Hotel 71
St Neot Pottery 116
St Neot's Church 116
St Nonna Church 40
St Petroc 193
St Petroc's Church, Bodmin 105
St Petroc's Hotel 65
St Piran 193
St Piran's Oratory 90
St Piran's Round 89
St Protus & St Hyacinth 42
St Winnow 116
Stanbury Mouth 52
Stanhope Forbes 191
Stein's Fish & Chips 65
Stein's Seafood Deli 65
Stem Pottery 178
Sterts Arts Centre 37
Stone Age Studio 179

Stone Circle Sculpture Studio 68
Stoneman Graphics Gallery 163
Stratton 56
Summer House 161
Summerleaze Beach 60
Swanpool Beach 135
Swordfish 171

Tabb's Restaurant 127
Talland Bay 117
Tamar Lake Wildlife Refuge 52
Tamar Otter & Wildlife Centre 60
Tate St Ives 177
The Bay View Inn 56
The Beach Hut 83
The Castle Bude 56
The Cheesewring 40
The Cove 150
The Cribber 85
The Ebb 66
The Edge 66
The Exchange 162
The Hotel, Watergate Bay
The King of Prussia 109
The Kitchen 112
The Lizard 145
The Lugger 113
The Old Quay House Hotel 109
The Old School Hotel 66
The Old Vicarage, Morwenstow 50
The Seafood Restaurant 66
The Slipway Hotel 67
The Strangles 61
The Towans, Hayle 182
The Vean 132
The Waterfront 71
The Wave 175
Thomas Flamank 193
Three Mackerel 123
Tim Smit 198
Tinners Arms
Tintagel 68
Tintagel Castle 68
Tintagel Church 56
Tolcarne Inn 171
Tolcarne Sands 85
Tori Amos 199
Towan Beach 85
Towan Beach, Falmouth 135
Towan Beach, St Ives 182
Toy Museum 68
Trebah Gardens 144
Trecarne Pottery 147
Tregantle Beach 29
Tregantle Fort 25
Tregantle Longsands Beach 29
Tregeare Rounds 69
Treglisson 95
Tregoose 132
Tregrehan Gardens 113
Treleauque 150
Trelissick Gallery 134
Trelissick Garden 131
Trelowarren 145
Trelowarren Gallery 145
Trelyon Gallery 177
Trenance Leisure Park 81
Trencrom Hill 181
Trengilly Wartha Inn 150

Trengwainton Gardens 163
Trereife Park 163
Treryn Dinas 181
Tresco Abbey Gardens 163
Trethias, Pepper Cove & Fox Cove 75
Trethorne Leisure Farm 37
Trevadlock Manor 43
Trevalsa Court Hotel 132
Trevarno Estate Gardens 95
Trevaskis Farm 99
Trevathan Farm 66
Trevaunance Art & Design 90
Trevaunance Cove 90
Trevethy Quoit 40
Trevilla House 132
Trevithick's Cottage 94
Trevone Bay 75
Trewidden Gardens 163
Trewithen Gardens 132
Trewithen Restaurant 111
Treyarnon Bay 75
Tristan's Gallery 69
Truro 126
Truro Cathedral 127
Tubbs Mill House 133
Tunnels Through Time 81
Turks Head 162
2 Fore Street 170

Upton 61

View Restaurant 27

Wadebridge 69
Warmington House 42
Water Rail 110
Watergate Bay 83
Wave 7 Studio Gallery 69
Wayside Folk Museum 180
Welcombe Mouth 52
Wesley Cottage 42
Westcroft Gallery 27
Whitesand Bay 183
Whitsand Bay 29
Widemouth Sand 61
Wilhelmina Barns-Graham 188
William Bickford 195
William Cookworthy 82
William Gregor 194
Windswept Café 90
Winston Graham 197
Wisteria Lodge 116
Wood Design 69
Wood Studio 145
World in Miniature 89
World of Model Railways 124

Xtreme Air Co 177

Yew Tree Gallery 179

Yvonne Arlott Studio 69
Zafiros 127
Zennor 180
Zennor Backpackers 180
Zennor Quoit 181

MAP SYMBOLS EXPLAINED

♨	Abbey/Cathedral	♨	Pottery	⬱ Inshore Rescue Boat
✕	Battle Site	🍺	Pub/Inn	Leisure/Sports Centre
⚓	Bed & Breakfast Accomodation	🚂	Railway Interest	Lifeboat
☕	Café	✗✗	Restaurant	Ⓟ Parking
🏰	Castle	🏛	Standing Stone/Barrow	Picnic Site
⛪	Church/Chapel of Interest	♨	Theatre/Concert Hall	Tents & Caravans
☷	Cinema	ℹ	Tourist Information	Sailing
⚒	Craft Interest	☼	Tumulus/Tumuli	Surfing
✚	Cross	❀	Viewpoint	Tourist Information
🚲	Cycleway	✕	Windmill/Wind Farm	Windsurfing
🎡	Fun Park/Leisure Park	⊕	Airfield	Youth Hostel
✳	Hill Fort/Ancient Settlement	♪	Aquarium	Agricultural Interest
⊞	Historic Building	🚤	Boat Trips	Arboretum
🏨	Hotel	⛺	Camping Site (Tents)	Bird Reserve
🏭	Industrial Interest	⛺	Caravan Site	Garden of Interest
🏎	Karting	👥	Ferry (Pedestrians)	Vineyard
⚲	Lighthouse	⛴	Ferry (Vehicles)	Walks/Nature Trails
⚒	Mining Interest/Engine Houses	⚓	Fishing Trips	Wildlife Park
☆	Miscellaneous/Natural Attraction	⛳	9/18 Hole Golf Course	Zoo
🏛	Museum/Art Gallery	⚓	Harbour	Ⓟ National Trust Car Park

381m.	
305m.	
229m.	
152m	
76m.	

━━━━ A Road

▦▦▦▦ B Road

⋯⋯⋯ Minor Road

- - - - Other Road or Track
(not necessarily with public
or vehicular access)

●━━━ Railway

⋯⋯⋯⋯ Cycleway

Open Space owned
by the National Trust

Built-up Area

Scale 1:100,000

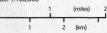

0   1   (miles)   2

0   1   2   (km)

St Christopher Wallpainting, Poughill Church